DEDICATION

To Raymond B. Walters, who asked me to do the
first edition of *Sports in Literature*

For suggestions about and help with this book,
I wish to thank the following:

Betty Bennett	*Karin Emra*	*Charles McGrath*
Bruce Brackett	*Dave Fisher*	*Nancy McGrath*
Billy Darrow	*Greg Lawrence*	*Pat Riccobene*
Mary DeBow	*Jerry Lowe*	*Rubee Scrivani*
Andy Dunn	*Kenny Margolin*	*Fred Smith*
Julie Emra		

And thanks to my editors on the two editions of this book,
Sue Schumer and Andy Adolfson

CONTENTS

Chapter 2: The Glory of Sports

Chapter 3: Sports and Life

Chapter 5: Sports Classics

PREFACE

"[Sports] can provide many of the same emotional satisfactions as art: the reassuring unities of time and place and action, sudden reversals of fortune and a cathartic close, not to mention the consolations of order and lots of vicarious thrills—and all of this in real time . . . Sports offers a primal drama whose depiction of characters and character require no metaphors, no allegories, no purple prose; a drama in which perfection is not an abstract concept but a palpable goal—a goal as simple as the perfect hit, the perfect shot, the perfect game."

Michiko Kakutani, in the *New York Times Magazine*

"Of course, there are those who learn after the first few times. They grow out of sports. And there are others who were born with the wisdom to know that nothing lasts. These are the truly tough among us, the ones who can live without illusion, or without even the hope of illusion. I am not that grown-up or up-to-date. I am a simpler creature, tied to more primitive patterns and cycles. I need to think something lasts forever, and it might as well be that state of being that is a game; it might as well be that, in a green field, in the sun."

A. Bartlett Giamatti, Former Commissioner of Baseball

CHAPTER 1

The Moment Itself

"Once again the ball was where it should have been—in Jordan's hands with the clock running down." Those are the words of New York Post *writer Kevin Kernan, covering the sixth game of the 1998 National Basketball Association Championship Series between the Chicago Bulls and the Utah Jazz. With 5.2 seconds remaining in the game, Michael Jordan drove toward the basket, pulled up, shot a clean jumper, and the game was over—the Bulls won the game, the series, and their sixth championship.*

That was Jordan's last jumper in the NBA. For one final moment he demonstrated again his unparalleled ability to electrify a crowd and dominate a game. Of Jordan's final shot, Kernan wrote, "Jordan seemed to stay in the air to admire his handiwork."

Perhaps Jordan hoped he could freeze the moment itself *in time.*

Beginning with two selections that pay tribute to the greatest basketball player who ever lived, this chapter offers a look at sports ranging from baseball, basketball, and football to field hockey, track, swimming, rowing, and fishing. Each selection will put you inside the sports moment—the moment itself.

From "Down the Stretch, Michael Decides He'll do It Himself" by Kevin Kernan, *The New York Post,* June 15, 1998. 1998 Copyright, NYP Holdings, Inc. Reprinted with permission from the NEW YORK POST.

PERSPECTIVES

In Beijing Students' Worldview, Jordan Rules

Elisabeth Rosenthal

You Don't Imitate Michael Jordan

David Remnick

From the student dorm room of a Chinese university to the asphalt courts of New York City, fans the world over salute America's king of basketball.

ABOUT THE AUTHOR•ABOUT THE AUTHOR•ABOUT THE AUTHOR•ABOUT THE AUTHOR

Elisabeth Rosenthal is one of the two reporters in the Beijing,[1] China, bureau of the New York Times. *She was born in 1957 and has a bachelor's degree from Stanford University and an MD from Harvard, though she doesn't practice medicine anymore. "I started in journalism as a medical writer and have gradually branched out to other topics," she says.*

Rosenthal adds, "In Beijing, I cover anything and everything—from politics, to movies, to economics, to sports. Most Chinese teenagers I have met are fanatical about Michael Jordan—they have posters, tee-shirts, sneakers, everything—and I'd been trying to think of a creative way to cover the craze. On the morning of the last N.B.A. playoff game last spring I called a student I knew at Beijing University—a young Communist Party member, even—and asked him if I could come watch the game with him and his friends. He said sure, and snuck me into the undergraduate dorm to watch the game."

In Beijing Students' Worldview, Jordan Rules

It was class time at Beijing University, but at 10 this morning seven guys in shorts and T-shirts crowded around a color TV in dorm room 511, a spare cement cubicle decorated with three metal bunkbeds and yesterday's laundry. Nine student "shareholders" had bought the TV last month in anticipation of just such an occasion, and now hoots and jeers filled the air.

"Aya, that Malone he plays dirty."

"Nice ball. Go Rodman!"

"They're losing with three minutes to go. I can't stand it. Hit me with a hammer!"

---

1. Beijing (bā'jing'): capital city of the People's Republic of China.

Minutes later, half a world away, the Chicago Bulls clinched their sixth National Basketball Association championship with a final basket with only five seconds to play. The students jumped to their feet and began a refrain: "Qiao Dan, Qiao Dan, Qiao Dan."

Qiao Dan, of course, is Michael Jordan. Sure, Bill Clinton, president of the world's most powerful nation, is about to visit China. But to the Chinese, Michael Jordan remains America's king.

Mr. Clinton's state visit this month has brought out citizens' interest in all things American, from books to clothes to movie stars. But these all seem like passing fancies compared to the intense passion that Chinese, especially young Chinese, have developed for Michael Jordan and American basketball.

"Michael Jordan is much more famous than Clinton here," said Cheng Qian, 20, a Bulls fan and shareholder in the TV set who is a management major at Beijing University.

The Chinese have named him kongzhong fieren—"space flier." In the last week, businessmen, retired teachers, students, and government officials have all paused to watch him, live on state-run television, as he led the Chicago Bulls to their 4-2 series victory over the Utah Jazz.

When Beijing Meilande Information Company recently asked 1,000 Chinese to name the best-known Americans ever, Michael Jordan came in second, trailing Thomas Edison by just a few percentage points. Behind him were Albert Einstein, Mark Twain and Bill Gates.

On the sidewalks of Jianguomenwai Avenue, vendors sell Michael Jordan posters. In department stores, Michael Jordan books and calendars sit beside those featuring Hong Kong movie stars and the late Chairman Mao.

"Of all American things, basketball is the most popular," said Li Fa, a junior, who could not join the crowd in 511 because he is a Jazz fan. "Everyone knows Michael Jordan."

State television began broadcasting prerecorded NBA games in the early 1990s, and recently switched to live broadcasts. Today, Chinese viewers had three opportunities to see the final playoff game, which the Bulls won 87–86. The first was live at 7:30 A.M., then a taped game at 9 A.M. for late risers, and a replay at 9 P.M.

Chinese are hard pressed to say why they so adore the Bulls and Michael Jordan, who scored 45 points in the final game and was named Most Valuable Player.

"I don't know—because of his skill, and because he alone carries half of the Chicago team," said Li Qixing, 20, another of the TV's shareholders.

American basketball is certainly more colorful than the home-grown variant, where the People's Liberation Army's August 1 team (named for the day the Army was founded) is the reigning champion. In skill and entertainment value, Chinese players are no match for the likes of Dennis Rodman, who played the game with much of his hair dyed green.

Said Han Bai, a junior, sitting on his bunk bed in jeans and a T-shirt, "I couldn't accept this from a Chinese player, but he's an American so we expect it."

And American sportcasts have other attractions.

The students who gathered in 511 on this steamy morning, oohed when they saw Leonardo DiCaprio, star of *Titanic,* sitting at courtside. And, in a room full of male college juniors, the Jazz's cheerleaders, dancing in black leotards, got the thumbs up as well. Heads nodded in approval as Cheng Qian opined,[2] "In this way, the Jazz are better than the Bulls."

---

2. opined: offered an opinion.

ABOUT THE AUTHOR•ABOUT THE AUTHOR•ABOUT THE AUTHOR•ABOUT THE AUTHOR

David Remnick is the editor of The New Yorker *magazine. He began his career as a sportswriter for* The Washington Post. *In 1994 he won a Pulitzer Prize for* Lenin's Tomb: The Last Days of the Soviet Empire. *His other books include* Resurrection: A Struggle for the New Russia, The Devil Problem and Other True Stories, *a collection of essays, and* King of the World, *a biography of prizefighter Mohammed Ali.*

Regarding this essay, Remnick says, "I suppose I decided to write about Michael Jordan's retirement for the same reason that almost everyone else in the world did: it was obvious that with his retirement we were losing someone who was the absolute best at what he did and gave so much pleasure doing it. When I was a very little boy [Boston Celtic] Bill Russell was on his last legs as a player and my father used to tell me this was the greatest player who ever put on shorts. I love my father dearly but children always love to prove their parents wrong once in a while. Michael Jordan did that for me."

You Don't Imitate Michael Jordan

On a late-spring morning last year, while my wife was still asleep and my sons were groggily adjusting their eyes to "Rugrats," I grabbed a basketball out of the coat closet and dribbled up the street to the asphalt courts at Seventy-sixth and Riverside. I don't quite know how to explain such irrational moments except to say that something in the brain must agree that the thrill of playing—the pebbly feel of the ball, the one decent shot among a dozen bricks—overwhelms the foreknowledge of all the pain, the locked back and stinging calves, that surely follows.

It was a beautiful morning for playing: in a minute I'd kicked away the broken bottles and the sun glittered on the river and the cars along the West Side Highway moaned like pigeons. But it was early yet—too early for the full-court crowd. The only middle-aged types around were the ascetic runners joylessly whipping past the fence and on up to Washington Heights. The lithe young shooters and dunkers whom I knew by face and first names were, I safely assumed, still recovering from their Friday revels. They'd show around ten. It was all kids just now—kids eleven, twelve, thirteen years old, boys mostly shooting around.

I shot at a steel backboard with a bunch of kids who were doing what kids do during the Finals. They mimicked everyone on the teams in question—the Utah Jazz and the Chicago Bulls. They aped Scottie Pippen's quick-release jumper in the lane and Ron Harper's downtown heaves. Like earnest A students, a wiry little kid with glasses and his chubby big brother even ran a slo-mo pick-and-roll, à la John Stockton and Karl Malone. They'd absorbed everything; it was just as it had been when I was their age and was trying to imitate Willis Reed's bellowing breaths at the foul line or Dick Barnett's soigné[1] jumper from the deep corners of the court. The curious thing is that none of the boys—not one—imitated Michael Jordan: not the fall-away shot in the lane, not the tongue-dangling drive to the hoop, not even the burlesque ass-waggling back-to-the-basket pivot move that has humiliated a generation of defenders. The kids were not especially reverent; they did a fine job of mocking Dennis Rodman's splay-legged rebounds and a cloddish Luc Longley mistake that had ended with a Keatonesque[2] pratfall. But not Jordan; they wouldn't go there.

I asked why, and they seemed appalled. "You just don't do that," one of them said. "You don't imitate Michael Jordan."

They were kids, with a kid's frame of reference. They couldn't yet know that Jordan was as fierce as Patton, as graceful as Nureyev, as creative as Armstrong—all those grasping similes were not yet theirs. But they knew what they knew. They were New York fans, beaten and disappointed, but also thrilled a thousand times by an incomparable athlete. A few nights later, Michael Jordan won his sixth N.B.A. title and ended his career with a move so exquisite that his defender stumbled in mystification. On the courts the next morning, everyone was talking about it, but no one tried it.

---

1. **soigné** (swän yā): sleek.
2. **Keatonesque:** like Keaton—a reference to Buster Keaton, famous film comedian.

Responding to What You Read

1. In the first selection, what do you think the student in China meant when he commented on Chicago Bull player Dennis Rodman's hair that had been dyed green, "I couldn't accept this from a Chinese player, but he's an American so we expect it"?

2. *Sports Illustrated* writer Phil Taylor has commented that "There is one superhero no comic-book creation can match, and he [wore] number 23 for the Bulls." Using information you learned in the Introduction to Chapter One and in the two selections you just read, give evidence to support Phil Taylor's opinion of Michael Jordan.

3. In the second selection, what is the kid implying when he says, "You just don't do that. You don't imitate Michael Jordan"? What reasons can you think of to explain why kids might not want to try to imitate Jordan?

Writer's Workshop

1. There are a number of colorful, pithy—short; to the point—observations made in the introduction to this chapter and in Elisabeth Rosenthal's article. Here are a few: "Once again, the ball was where it should have been—in the hands of Jordan with the clock running down." "Jordan seemed to stay in the air to admire his handiwork." ". . . dorm room 511, a spare cement cubicle decorated with three metal bunkbeds and yesterday's laundry." The first observation gives a value judgment in a concise, clear, dramatic statement. The second creates a brief, vivid word picture of something impossible—staying frozen in the air, defying gravity. The third uses the word *decorated* in a surprisingly unconventional way.

    Watch a sports event either in person or on television and then create two pithy sentences that capture, in a colorful way, an exciting moment in the contest. Strive for sentences that surprise or perhaps even startle the reader.

2. Elisabeth Rosenthal's article about Chinese students' reactions to Michael Jordan half a continent away is an example of a feature story, a story that covers news from a special angle or point of view. Write a feature story of your own. Attend a sports event at your school or in

your community, but instead of reporting on the game itself, write about a special-interest aspect of the game. Perhaps it will be an interview with a coach or a player or a survey of fan reaction to the event. If you do an interview, take notes as you speak to your subject. In writing your feature, create crisp, original sentences patterned after the ones mentioned in the first assignment above.

Alternate Media Response

Draw Michael Jordan in action on the court. If you're familiar with Jordan, do your drawing from memory. Try to capture the essence of Jordan on the move, in the air. If you're not that familiar with Jordan, look at a videotape of him performing; it's probably not enough to see a still picture. If other students participate in this activity, join together to share your drawings with the class. Create an exhibit paying tribute to Jordan by displaying your drawings on the walls of the room.

Finding Myself: On the Field, in the Gym

Jeannie Ryan

An all-star athlete takes up a new sport, and she finds it isn't easy.

ABOUT THE AUTHOR•ABOUT THE AUTHOR•ABOUT THE AUTHOR•ABOUT THE AUTHOR

Jeannie Ryan was born in 1967. In high school she played field hockey, basketball, and track, and was captain of all three teams. She also was awarded All-League honors in all three sports. She was chosen Female Athlete of the Year for her high school and All Decade (the 1980s) athlete by her county newspaper for field hockey. In addition, she won her school's English award at graduation. Since high school, Ryan has received a bachelor's degree in English from Boston College and a master's degree from New York University. While at Boston College, she played lacrosse. Currently, she is working on a doctorate degree in educational administration.

Ryan remembers her high-school days with great fondness because of her involvement in athletics. "Those experiences inspired me to become a teacher and coach," she says. "My teachers and coaches tried to make learning relevant for me, and I try to do the same for my students now. Though my mother, often dismayed at the muddy cleats and dirty uniforms, threatened on many occasions to send me to finishing school, I maintain that a sound mind and sound body are a natural pair, just as the terms student *and* athlete *are."*

Finding Myself: On the Field, in the Gym

Coach Ely said that I'd know when it was right. I'd be able to feel it. My wrist would snap as my knees straightened and I'd land in the same spot from which I'd left the floor. "As you follow through, pretend that you are trying to reach those two front hooks where the net is connected to the rim," he would explain. Then I would be shooting the ball with my finger tips, not heaving it with my palm. "It is a basketball, Jeannie, not a shot put." The jump shot was more than just two points illuminated on a scoreboard according to Coach Ely. It was an art form and a discipline.

Madame Kedron said that I would know when I was becoming a French scholar because then I would read the French writings of Balzac and the words would make sense to me, in French. I would no longer need to translate my way through a piece of writing. Stephanie Geesey said that I'd know when a boy really, really liked me because he would keep his eyes closed longer than me when we were kissing.

Who developed all of these rules? Couldn't I be a natural athlete? Was I expected to really look for those two front hooks on the rim in the middle of a game? Other girls would be waving to their boyfriends in the bleachers and I was going to be waving to two brown, rusted, metal hooks. And did I really want to be a French scholar? Why wasn't receiving A's in French IV Enriched enough of an accomplishment? So what if I was a translator? And what if he never closed his eyes? I'm in no way opposed to rules. But the rules of high school always eluded me. Maybe that explains my affinity to the playing field; *there,* there were rules.

After completing a 2–18 season with the Hastings High girls basketball team, Coach Ely decided to take me under his wing. Since I was one of the younger girls on the team, I guess Coach thought he could mold me into a decent player. I had had less time to develop bad habits, he explained. He issued end-of-the-season report cards to our team and mine read, "JEANNIE: Your weaknesses include your jumpshot, your foul shot, dribbling, and upper body strength. Your strength is your attitude." Nice to have only one strength, and it isn't even a basketball skill. Although I wasn't thrilled with this post-season assessment of my skills, I reminded myself that field hockey was my primary sport. I was going to attend two summer camps and I was invited to play in a spring league. Hoops were over and I was ready to concentrate on my sport, hockey.

Attached to my report card was an application to a basketball summer league. Coach explained that it was a competitive league and most of the girls would be much better than I was. If I was serious about improving, he would get me in. I had a difficult time believing that I was so poor a player that I needed connections to drive an hour in mid-July to play ball in a hot gymnasium. But leagues for girls were a new development, and this league was really the only one around. He managed to get me signed up.

At 9:00 A.M. on a Saturday morning, Coach Ely called and told me to get my hightops on. This wasn't a new thing—he called all the time. He took me to a gym to sign me up for a Nautilus program, he took me to see Syracuse play St. John's at Madison Square Garden, and he took me to local gyms when he knew we could sneak in. I never met a man who knew so many custodians. This morning he bypassed any good-morning greeting and snapped, "Pascack Valley gym, 10:30, be ready to play and bring Amy and Sue." Now this was the challenge. It was tough enough to roll myself out of bed and get excited about listening to this man yell "Keep your elbow in!" for most of the morning, but convincing Amy and Sue to join me was also a problem. "Listen, I'll buy you lunch. We'll go for an hour . . . you don't know that, it could be fun . . . okay, then do it for me. I have to play in this league and I don't want to embarrass myself . . . Thanks. You'll pick me up? Okay."

Sue eventually succumbed to my pressure and she even called Amy for me. When she picked me up she handed me a baked ham and told me to get in the back seat. "Here, hold this. We have to get it over to my mom's friend. Her mother died and my mom wants us to leave this with her. It's on the way." Eventually, we entered the town of Hillsdale and my palms began to sweat. Pascack Valley High School always had a great team. They were the kind of team that won so often that there was no wall space in their gym, just banner after banner. League champs. County champs. State champs. We used to call their gym the forest because once you entered, you were engulfed by all these green felt banners. Those inanimate pieces of fabric managed to intimidate me every time I came out of the locker room. And, somehow, Coach Ely managed to intensify that fear. On this particular Saturday, Coach had two guests with him. Two former stars from P.V. strolled in while I was stretching. They were in college now on basketball scholarships. I guess they were home for the weekend.

I slid down the gymnasium wall and my head snapped back against the cinder block. Why wasn't I out with Stephanie Geesey looking at prom dresses? At least I was with Amy and Sue. But Amy had this huge knee brace and she looked tough because of it. A brace like that makes people wonder how good you could be without that piece of hardware on your leg. And Sue knew how to shoot. She kept her elbow in and snapped her wrist. I stretched. I reached out to touch my left foot, and then my right. Quietly, one of the scholarship girls asked me, "Do you shoot, or just stretch?" What I did couldn't be called shooting compared to what I had been observing. This girl could shoot like Coach Ely. Better, actually. She knew how to use the backboard on bank shots, and she tossed up these graceful underhand layups. But the most impressive thing she did didn't even involve the hoop. She took two basketballs and stood on the baseline. She sprinted down the court slamming those two balls simultaneously on the hardwood. Even the forest of banners couldn't absorb the pounding vibration. At half court, she switched to an alternating rhythm, but still with two balls, LEFT, RIGHT, LEFT, RIGHT. Then she got creative and started making up patterns, LEFT, LEFT, RIGHT, RIGHT, LEFT, LEFT, RIGHT, RIGHT.

She paused at the other end of the court, knowing that she had an audience. She yelled down to her friend, "Let's do figure-eight drills." The friend had just gone 12 for 12 from the foul line and I was pleased to see her stop shooting. But the best thing of all was that I could do figure-eight drills. The trick was to relax your upper body. When you do dribbling drills, you have to sway a little bit, and give with the ball. I was tempted to leave my prime viewing position on the gym floor at this point. I had been doing ball-handling drills in my basement for months now. I could do this.

Absolutely unbelievable. Janet started doing figure-eights with two balls. She even told her friend that sometimes she pretended that her left hand was chasing her right. That made her work at top speed. Maybe if I pretended that I wasn't in this gym on a beautiful spring morning . . . Maybe if I clicked my hightops together three times . . . "How 'bout you get your act together and start warming up?" hissed Coach Ely. He yanked my hand and I heard a rip. Part of the honey glaze from that ham had dripped onto my shorts and when I was pulled up, a small portion of my shorts remained virtually cemented to the gym floor. At least some of the tension was broken.

We divided up into two teams. The awesome dribbler was on my team so I was relieved of any point-guard responsibilities. I set a few picks and tried to stay out of the way. A really nice pick was set for me and I found myself open on the baseline. I raised my hands to signal that I was open, and to show where I wanted to receive the pass. I had watched girls do that at a summer camp, and it seemed to make sense. By the time I had my target set, the pass skimmed my middle finger and landed in the bleachers. No one said "Good try," and no one patted me on the shoulder. Janet shook her head as if to say, "I'm in for a long afternoon." Fortunately, several Pascack Valley girls showed up ready to play. It was easier to get lost in the crowd if we played five on five. I could hold my own defensively and I could just pass a lot on offense.

We broke up our game, picked new teams and agreed to start again in ten minutes. I ran into a bathroom stall and stood still while tears burned down my flushed face. I hated those girls. I would never go to a field hockey field and try to exploit really weak players. How is this little workout session helping me? And how is it helping them? Some of the new arrivals had followed me into the locker room to get their sneakers. Janet did her best to explain to them who Amy, Sue, and I were: "Oh, John Ely brought them down from Hastings High School with him. They seem nice enough but they can barely catch. It's weird. John said one of them was the scoring leader in Bergen County for field hockey. She's absolutely petrified to shoot a basketball." I left the bathroom and found the entrance to the gym. Janet and the other girls never knew that I was in the locker room. I hated Coach Ely. I resented that he would tell them about the field hockey stuff. It always baffled him that I could manage to send a hockey ball into a goal cage at least once or twice a game, but I couldn't manage to send a big leather orange sphere through a net once in a while.

Coach Ely was scowling at me from across the gym. I knew what was bothering him. The problem was that it bothered him more than me. I tried, again, to explain, "Coach, I don't mind that I don't score a lot. We have some really tall people on our team. I'll pass to them. My position on the field hockey field is left inner. I'm on the forward line. It is part of the job description to score a lot. For now, in this sport, I'd rather pass."

"Now, Jeannie, are you trying to tell me that there is no thrill associated with scoring? You were just doing your duty?"

"Well, no. I mean, of course not. Like this one time, at Wayne Hills. We tied in regulation play. But it was a state tournament game so we had a shoot-out. Five players from each team would go one on one with the goalie. I had practiced this so often and I really wanted this goal. A Wayne Hills girl went first and she made it, and then I was up. The ref blew the whistle signaling that my ten seconds had begun. I lunged at the ball and sent it ten yards ahead. People on the sidelines gasped a little. They thought that the little pass to myself was my shot. You only have ten seconds, you need to gain some more ground quickly. You were only allowed one shot. No follow ups. No rebounds. So I pulled my stick back and I was ready to drive but I could see those huge white goalie pads. She had cut off my angle. I hesitated and stopped my drive right before I made contact. I seemed to scare her, or startle her. She rested back on her heels, and then I knew I was okay. Once the goalie plants her feet, you can get a step on her. I pulled the ball back diagonally across my body and I accelerated right. Then I let go a firm push pass to the lower left hand corner." I was so embarrassed when I finished talking. Coach Ely had a big grin on his face. I resented him even more for laughing at me.

"Tell me another one, Jeannie."

"Another what?"

"You know, a scoring moment."

"Listen, it's really different in hockey. I didn't mean to get all caught up in my glory days of the past season. Will you rebound for me?" I had almost forgotten that I was still in the P.V. gym.

"No, I won't rebound for you. I want to hear about another goal."

"Fine." I had heard so many of his dumb stories: The time he got hurt in college and missed most of the season . . . the time he first dunked a basketball. He could deal with one more of my "moments."

"County finals against Old Tappan. We were down one to nothing, and it was the end of the second half. A girl from their team kicked the ball so we received a penalty corner. Chris stood behind Laurel and me at the top of the shooting circle. When the ball was hit, Laurel and I bolted to the mouth of the goal. You had to keep your feet facing the goal and you could look over your shoulder to see if the shot had been taken. You couldn't turn all the way around or it was an obstruction and you lost the ball. Chris settled the ball and drove it. She had a beautiful drive, but this one was headed right for the goalie's pads. As the ball passed me I stuck out my stick. I didn't want to stop the ball, and I didn't even want to really hit it, but I had to try to redirect it. It skimmed off the tip of my stick, and skimmed the net. Overtime!"

"Don't you want that same thrill on the basketball court? Couldn't it be the same way?" begged Coach.

"No. What I didn't include in those moments of glory was that we lost both of those games. I just told you about a state game and a county game. My memory doesn't immediately recall that empty feeling on the bus ride home that everybody talked about. And I don't picture the seniors' teary eyes. I remember my teammates hugging me after I scored. And I remember Laurel landing on my foot after we leaped up and gave each other a high five, but, you know, my foot didn't even hurt until I got home. And at the Old Tappan game, I remember everybody asking who scored, me or Chris? And I know that some people think that I robbed her of that goal. What are you supposed to do in the scoring circle? Wait to see if the ball goes in on its own or drive it home yourself? The man from the paper called that night to ask me about the game and about scoring. I told him that Chris always does such a great job of settling the ball and sending it in to the circle. I told him that he had to print that. Coach D. told me that it was as important for our team that I score as it was that P. J., our goalie, not let the other team score. But people always manage to see scorers as ball hogs or glory hounds. Sure, there's no greater feeling, but I'd never steal someone's goal. How could you do that?"

"Wow, Jeannie, I didn't realize you. . ."

"I mean, there I am on the bus and our season is over. But I'm still on cloud nine because I never scored in one of those shootouts before. Everyone else is crying, except me, and I'm feeling so guilty about it. Now I have the option to pass. This team can succeed without me putting the ball in the net. And you are insisting that I chuck the ball. I don't want to steal other people's shots!"

"Aw, Jeannie, who thinks about that? In one game there might be a mismatch and Amy will have four inches on the girl she is guarding. And then in the next game the team plays a zone. On any given night, someone is going to have to take charge and lead the team offensively. When you are the member of a five-player team, you owe it to your teammates to square up to the basket and be a threat. You don't even look at the hoop. Your defender plays way off of you and double teams Sue or Amy. That isn't fair."

"Well, then, it isn't fair. Okay. I'll try to be more of a threat. I think if we were patient enough, though, Sue would eventually get open and we could get her the ball."

"Get on the court and play. Don't think about every shot. Just play. Turn your brain off and react. You want to be exactly eight feet four inches from the hoop and you want to be on the baseline and you want your teammates to throw you the perfect pass to set up this perfect shot. When are you going to realize that you need to adapt to the situation? It's just like that goal that put your team into overtime. React."

So much for the ten-minute break. The ball-handling maverick was on the other team now. I wound up guarding her. She was so explosive. Her head went left so my hands and my body followed her fake. Then she planted her outside foot and cut right. Before I could turn around she had released the ball at the foul line for two points. Everything she did was fast. She had me beat and she pulled up for the jump shot. A simple concept. I wiped my sweaty palms on the bottom of my hightops. A dumb ritual that I picked up at a camp. I was embarrassed that I did it. It sort of said, "Now that I've corrected my traction problem, I'll be able to take you."

During the next series, Janet pushed the ball through her legs as she drove to the hoop. Somehow she hit her opposite knee as she performed this move and the ball lay unguarded at mid-court. Instinctively I ran to grab it and threw an outlet pass to my teammate. I ran out wide to fill the left lane on the fast break. As often occurs in a pickup game, no one from Janet's team wasted the energy to race down the easy lay-up. I stood confused near the foul line. My teammate threw a poor, dribbly pass that was at my ankles when I bent down to retrieve it. I tucked in my elbow, used my legs to get some power behind my shot, snapped my wrist, and held my follow-through. I was staring kind of unconsciously at those two front hooks when the ball floated down through the net. It all went so slowly, as if the game came to a halt and we were suddenly playing under water.

I don't really know why but I let out a moan and then I heard Coach Ely yell, "Wow, brother!"

"I think that was it!"

"No, Jeannie. Don't think, just know. That was a jump shot. Remember how it felt. Don't forget that feeling. You'll feel it again. You see what can happen when you don't think. You were unsure about the shot, and you just let it fly."

"I think that my feet left the ground together. One wasn't farther forward than the other." My heart was beating so fast it was difficult to speak but I wanted to.

"Don't ruin it. Don't analyze it to death. It is a feeling that you don't have to express. Just experience it. Just enjoy it."

Responding to What You Read

1. How does the narrator's success in field hockey compare with her ability in basketball?

2. What is it that the narrator finally learns about shooting a basketball?

Writer's Workshop

This piece of writing works well because it is totally frank and honest and because it is extremely detailed. Ryan shares both her triumphs and her frustrations. She puts the reader right on the hockey field with her during a crucial game and right on the basketball court as she struggles to help her team.

Choose a sport or recreational activity familiar to you. Focus on a particular moment in that sport or activity and write a narrative in which you describe the physical action in the present tense. Include all the details that capture what that moment is really like. The more details you include, the more you will be able to make that moment come alive.

Pitcher

Robert Francis

A poet looks at what being a pitcher is all about.

ABOUT THE AUTHOR•ABOUT THE AUTHOR•ABOUT THE AUTHOR•ABOUT THE AUTHOR

*R*obert Francis was born in 1901 and lived most of his life in Amherst, Massachusetts. His Collected Poems (1936–1976) *brings together seven previous volumes of poetry. He won the Academy of American Poets Fellowship in 1984. Francis died in 1987.*

Although he was not well known by the general public, Francis was highly regarded among his peers. In addition to poems, Francis published an autobiography titled The Trouble with Francis *and a collection of his journals titled* Traveling in America.

Pitcher

His art is eccentricity,[1] his aim
How not to hit the mark he seems to aim at,

His passion how to avoid the obvious,
His technique how to vary the avoidance.

5   The others throw to be comprehended. He
Throws to be a moment misunderstood.

---

1. eccentricity: a deviation from an accepted or established pattern.

Yet not too much. Not errant,[2] arrant,[3] wild,
But every seeming aberration[4] willed.

Not to, yet still, still to communicate
10   Making the batter understand too late.

Responding to What You Read

Write no more than three sentences explaining, in your own words, exactly
what this poem is saying about being a baseball pitcher.

Writer's Workshop

Surely no sportswriter would describe pitching the way
poet Robert Francis does in "The Pitcher." Poets delight
in expressing ideas in unusual, creative ways. Using
"The Pitcher" for inspiration, write a poem that
describes an aspect of sport in a new way. Try to write
five sets of two lines (couplets) as Francis did.

---

2. errant: traveling outside the proper path; moving about aimlessly.

3. arrant: without moderation, extreme.

4. aberration: a departure from standard behavior.

PERSPECTIVES

The Passer

George Abbe

In the Pocket

James Dickey

These two poems offer startling imagery to describe a perfectly thrown pass. What other insights might these poems offer?

ABOUT THE AUTHOR●ABOUT THE AUTHOR●ABOUT THE AUTHOR●ABOUT THE AUTHOR

George Abbe was born in 1911 in New England and grew up there. He has won the Shelley Memorial Award, presented by the Poetry Society of America. His poems have appeared in many periodicals and anthologies and on records. He has taught at Yale, Columbia, and Mt. Holyoke and at numerous writers' conferences throughout the United States. He once said that while good poetry "is the most demanding of the arts, it is also the most rewarding."

The Passer

Dropping back with the ball ripe in my palm,
grained and firm as the flesh of a living charm,
I taper and coil myself down, raise arm to fake,
running a little, seeing my targets emerge
5   like quail above a wheat field's golden lake.

In boyhood I saw my mother knit my warmth
with needles that were straight. I learned to feel
the passage of the bullet through the bore,[1]
its vein of flight between my heart and deer
10   whose terror took the pulse of my hot will.

I learned how wild geese slice arcs from hanging pear
of autumn noon; how the thought of love cleaves home,
and fists, with fury's ray, can lay a weakness bare,
and instinct's eye can mine fish under foam.

---

1. bore: the inside diameter of a gun barrel.

15   So as I run and weigh, measure and test,
        the light kindles on helmets, the angry leap;
        but secretly, coolly, as though stretching a hand to his chest,
        I lay the ball in the arms of my planing end,
        as true as metal, as deftly as surgeon's wrist.

ABOUT THE AUTHOR•ABOUT THE AUTHOR•ABOUT THE AUTHOR•ABOUT THE AUTHOR

J*ames Dickey, who was born in Atlanta, Georgia, in 1923, was a college football and track star who graduated* magna cum laude *from Vanderbilt University. Dickey wrote several novels, including the well-known* Deliverance, *and published many volumes of poetry. Much of Dickey's writing, including "In the Pocket," explores themes of struggle and conflict.*

According to Lance Morrow writing in Time *magazine, several months before Dickey's death in 1997 Dickey told a friend, "I had a dream last night. I was back in high school playing football. I scored three touchdowns, including the winning touchdown, and I ended up with the most beautiful girl in the school. I said to her, 'This is the most wonderful day of my life. Too bad it's only a dream.' And she said, 'Yes, but in the dream it's real.'"*

In the Pocket

Going backward

All of me and some

Of my friends are forming a shell   my arm is looking

Everywhere and some are breaking

5   In   breaking down

And out   breaking

Across, and one is going deep   deeper

Than my arm   Where is Number One hooking

Into the violent green alive

10   With linebackers?   I cannot find him he cannot beat

His man   I fall back more

Into the pocket   it is raging and breaking

Number Two has disappeared into the chalk

Of the sideline   Number Three is cutting with half

15   A step of grace   my friends are crumbling

Around me the wrong color

Is looming   hands are coming

Up and over between

My arm and Number Three: throw it hit him in

20   the middle

Of his enemies   hit move scramble

Before death and the ground

Come up LEAP STAND KILL DIE STRIKE

Now.

Responding to What You Read

1. Write a paragraph about what both these poems say about being a passer in football. Include two-line references from each poem.

2. Why do you think James Dickey arranged "In the Pocket" on the page the way he did, and why did he include almost no punctuation until the end?

Writer's Workshop

A **simile** compares two dissimilar objects using the words "like" or "as." Notice how in "The Passer" George Abbe refers to his targets for a football pass being "like quail above a wheat field's golden lake." This is an example of a simile.

A **metaphor** compares two dissimilar objects but doesn't use the words "like" or "as." In the second stanza of "The Passer," Abbe compares the direct flight of a football from quarterback to receiver to knitting "needles that were straight" and to a bullet that goes directly to a deer. These lines are examples of metaphors.

Write two short paragraphs or poems in which you describe a very specific, narrow moment in a sports event *in terms of something else*, as Abbe did in "The Passer." In one paragraph or poem, create at least one simile. In the other, create at least one metaphor.

Alternate Media Response

Do a drawing or painting of either of the two passers from these poems. Work to capture the mood or tone conveyed in the poem you choose. If you wish to draw both passers, keep in mind that the poems are strikingly different in tone and intensity and, therefore, your illustrations of the passers should be too.

Eight-Oared Crew

Harry Sylvester

Competing in sports often involves making difficult choices. Is winning the only goal?

ABOUT THE AUTHOR•ABOUT THE AUTHOR•ABOUT THE AUTHOR•ABOUT THE AUTHOR

Harry Sylvester was born in Brooklyn, New York, in 1908. He attended the University of Notre Dame, receiving his B.A. in 1930. He worked for several New York newspapers for a few years before deciding to devote full time to writing short stories and novels. He contributed short stories to Commonweal, Collier's, Cosmopolitan, Esquire, *and the* Atlantic Monthly, *and published a collection of short stories titled* All Your Idols. *His novels include* Big Football Man, Dearly Beloved, Moon Gaffney, *and* The Golden Girl.

Eight-Oared Crew

Dusk lay on the river, making all things its own color. Lights had begun to appear in the other boathouses but where Al Leyden—at thirty-eight, the "Old Man"—stood on the landing, there was only the growing shadow, quick-deepening now that the sun had gone out of sight behind the west bank of the Hudson. The shell, moving leisurely toward the landing, was only a darker shadow when it docked. Leyden stood apart from the crew, the mood of the evening heavy in him.

The crew swung the shell out of the water at Kip Grant's command and marched it past Leyden. In the blue light they looked like some giant insect, the shell held over their heads. Kip Grant walked by them, silent now and no longer harrying the crew. Too silent, Leyden thought, but he felt no better for knowing the reason for that silence toward the crew of sophomores.

He touched Kip on the arm and the coxswain turned to him. "How was it?" Leyden said.

In the dusk he could barely see the slight shrug of the other's shoulders. "I don't know. Their form is still good—when they don't have to turn on the heat." He paused and said, again: "What they'll do in the race, I don't know. They learned too quickly. . . ."

Leyden nodded.

"My brother and some friends are in town for the race," Kip said. "Mind if I run into town for an hour or so?"

"Go ahead," Leyden said. He almost added: "Don't make your going too obvious," but with Grant that wasn't necessary, Leyden knew. These boys from the school's traditional families were mentally precocious . . .

Leyden watched Kip Grant go into the coaches' room to dress. Grant had begun to do this after Leyden had made the change in the crews. It was not a good thing, Leyden knew, for crew and coxswain to be so sharply divided as they were. Regret stirred in him again at having made that change, but in his mind he knew that he had done the right thing. He came from poor people himself. Even if the university was or had been a "rich man's school," Leyden felt that he himself must be just. His sense of justice lay on him now like a weight. He went wearily up the wooden stairs to his own room.

Two years ago the university had gone out and got some scholarship men to bolster up the football team, which had been bad for three years in a row. They were good boys, the new scholarship men, intelligent enough to get by the stiff entrance exams, but hailing from mine and mill and with names new to the school: Kowalik, Leary and Pivarnik; Granski, Lisbon and Guttman; the Slavs already replacing the Irish among the athletes.

None of them had ever seen a shell; some of them had never seen a river before coming to the school. They came out for crew in the winter of their freshman year and Leyden had watched them that first day in the barge, with the ice still on the river; watched them with pride and with foreboding.

Leyden had two freshman crews that year and the football coach complained that he was keeping the scholarship men from spring practice. So Leyden let them go for spring football practice and they had returned to him after it and said that they still wanted to row. So Leyden had let them row. . . . It was too late to mold them, or some of them, into the freshman crew that would compete at Poughkeepsie that year. So Leyden had let the scholarship men row alone, as a unit . . . and Leyden saw then the thing that might happen.

Leyden had been an athlete and a coach long enough to know that any great team, whether it be a crew or a football eleven, is more than half accident. The unbelievable and precise coordination that made a team great, as a team, was largely beyond the ability of any coach to create. He could develop it once the accident had occurred but he could not create it.

What Leyden had seen was that eight of the scholarship men had or were part of the curious accident of coordination that might make a great crew. He knew, guiltily, that they, for all their crudeness, could beat the freshman crew already formed. And even when that crew was a close second at Poughkeepsie, Leyden still felt that he had been less than just. Rowing was the traditional sport at the university and, partly by accident, partly by design, the crew was almost always composed of names old in the school's history. Leyden wondered just how much this had affected his judgment.

The next spring he had left the scholarship men together as a unit, as the junior varsity, and he had gone about the always difficult business of making a new crew of some of last year's varsity and some of the freshmen. It was not better than an average crew although it had a great coxswain, the senior, Kip Grant. It was a traditional crew in that it had the old names, Carteret, Grant, Morgan, Fairlee. It won one sprint race, was second in two others, and last in a longer race.

That spring it took Leyden a long time to do the thing he felt compelled to do. In May, for the first time, he had the varsity and junior varsity meet in the brush along the river. The junior varsity, the scholarship men, won by a little. They won by a bow a week later, despite having lost their form in the middle of the race. Then, they won by two lengths in a three-mile race with the varsity.

Leyden did then the thing he had to do. He called the varsity together. "The junior varsity," he told them, "has beaten you, decisively. If you want to row at Poughkeepsie as the varsity, go ahead. . . . Knowing you as I do, I don't think you'll want to go to Poughkeepsie that way. The better way is to race the junior varsity the Poughkeepsie distance, four miles . . . and if they beat you, let them go—as the varsity. Tell me tomorrow how you want to go to Poughkeepsie."

So their captain, Jim Fairlee, had come and told Leyden quite gravely
that they would go to Poughkeepsie only if they could beat the junior
varsity. And they had raced and the junior varsity, stroked by Kowalik, had
won by three lengths.

They needed a coxswain and Leyden had asked Kip Grant to go into
their boat. And Kip had consented to but he hadn't liked it or them. And so
Leyden's varsity was the eight scholarship men and Kip Grant, third
generation of his family to sit in one of the university shells.

His dislike for the men he handled the tiller grips for was not
unreasonable. They had displaced his friends, had broken a long tradition
of which he was a part. Alumni had protested privately and Kip's brothers
had even urged him not to sit in the varsity shell. They had done so half
humorously, but Kip knew how they felt. He knew, too, how Leyden felt
and the weight of the justice that lay heavy on Leyden. . . .

His brothers were waiting for him now in the private dining room they
always had the evening before the race. When he opened the door of the
room they were yelling at him:

"The kid himself!"

"Say, Kip, is it really true you had to learn to speak Polish?"

In a way he didn't hear them. For he had seen her face. Among the
other women there, among the tall Old Blues, it stood out quietly, as Kip
expected that it always might. He greeted the others and sat beside her—
Mary Adams, his friend since childhood, now the girl he was going to
marry. She took his hand under the table and was silent until the others
had stopped shouting at Kip.

"Sure," he kept telling them, "we'll win in a breeze."

"They'll blow up in your face under the bridge," Ad Grant said. "I was
watching them from the bank this afternoon through glasses."

"They'll row those other crews into the river," Kip said.
Their antagonism, however friendly, did something to him. For the first
time, and in surprise, he felt as though he were really part of his crew. . . .

They let him alone after a while and he was able to slip out with Mary
Adams. The side streets of the town were quiet under the old trees, the
wind from the river rich with spring.

"You seem quiet," Mary Adams said. "I had thought you'd be more
nervous with the race so close."

"As I get older I suppose I conceal things better," he said. "If the race has made me nervous, something else has made me quiet. Something else besides you." His hand tightened on her arm. "You can always make me quiet. Just being near you."

"It makes me very happy, Kip," she said.

"The other thing," he went on gravely, "is that I've suddenly realized I've been dishonest. I've snooted those men on the crew when I should have tried to know them better. Why I did, I don't know. They're good men."

"I understand," she said quietly. "I suppose it would have been more honest for you to have resigned from the squad or stroked your—own people on the junior varsity."

"My own people," Kip said. There was an edge to his tone. "They rode me tonight. And they're apt to go haywire and fire Al Leyden after the race."

"I think not," she said. "Coming down in the train, they agreed they'd just let him know that they wanted him not to do anything like it again."

"Even if they win," Kip said.

"None of them expect you to win tomorrow," she said.

An old car squeaked to a stop near them. It had Pennsylvania license plates. A head with a battered hat on it poked out one window and spoke unintelligibly to them. Kip went closer to the car and Mary stood on the curb.

"You know where this faller, Pete Kowalik, he stay at? Faller what row in front in bast crew on here?"

From the curb, Mary saw Kip straighten. "I imagine it's a bit late to see him. All the crew men are in bed."

"All day long, most last night, we drive this flivver," the voice went on in a singsong. "Stop every garage on road, by damn. Pete Kowalick, he be worried about us. Couldn't phone him, eider, I bet."

"They wouldn't call him to the phone at this time of night," Kip said. He moved back to the curb. Mary touched his arm. "These people—" she hesitated. "They've come a long way. You could take a message to Kowalik. He's your stroke, isn't he?"

"I suppose," he said, "I'll be a snob until I die." He walked back to the old car, which was refusing to start. "I'll see Kowalik—if not tonight, first thing in the morning, I can take a message to him."

"You just tell him that his brother Joe got here all hokay and that Malie Stefansik, he come too, and we both be there tomorrow, yalling like hell! Say, who are you, mister? Your face, it—"

"I'm one of the mangers," Kip said. He turned away.

"I feel better at your having done that," Mary Adams said.

"I feel better myself." They walked a while in silence.

"Something still bothers you," Mary said.

"I know. I don't think we'll win tomorrow. I had to say it in front of the others, but the men are still green for all their power and natural ability."

"No," she said. "It's just the night that makes you think so." She turned to him in the shadow and he kissed her, feeling some old tension in him become lost in another one, renewed. He broke from her. "I have to get back," he said. At the hotel she pressed his hand. "Until after the race," she said.

The boathouse was in darkness when Kip got there. Going up the wooden stairs to the dormitory where the crews slept, the only light he could see was from the crack under the door of Al Leyden's room. Kip was a long time getting to sleep.

After breakfast, Kip said to Kowalik: "I'd like to speak to you on the float." The tall boy looked his surprise but followed Kip outside.

"I ran into your brother last night in town," Kip said. "He had trouble getting here, but he wanted to let you know that he had arrived."

Kowalik looked at once grateful and amused. "Thanks a lot, Grant. I'm glad to hear about my brother getting here all right. But when you called me over here I thought you had something important to say about the race."

"No," Kip said. He turned away, flushing a little. Was he at fault or they? he thought. Was he a snob or were they crude? He had not wanted the others to know that he had spoken even that intimately to Kowalik. Strangely, though, he felt once more his new kinship with the crew, a relation delayed and now hastened by the attitude of his brothers and friends, by the chance meeting with Kowalik's brother, by Mary Adams's quiet words.

A manager came and told Kip that Leyden would like to see him. He found the coach in his room with the crossed oars on the wall. One of them, Kip knew, had been used by Ad Grant six years ago. "Close the door," Leyden said. "Sit down."

"Guess you didn't sleep much," Kip said. "Saw your light on when I came in."

"I never do the night before a race. The crew did, though."

"They all look good," Kip said. His words fell hollowly into a silence created by Leyden's looking away. When he turned to Kip again, Leyden's face showed his weariness.

"They might win," Leyden said, "but probably they won't."

Kip nodded once.

"They have the stuff," Leyden said, "a lot of it. And guts. They just haven't rowed long enough. They'll try too hard and go to pieces."

"It's a touch late to substitute the jayvee for them," Kip said. "I don't mean to be a wise guy," he added quickly.

"I know," Leyden said. "I made my decision and I'm going to stand by it. About the job I don't have to worry. Your brothers and old man Calder of the crew committee phoned me last night while you were away and said that no matter what happened my job was safe. So it's not me. It's those kids. You don't like them. I can see your point even though I come from the same kind of people they do. But I let them win their place, didn't I?"

"You don't have to talk me into anything," Kip said. "I've changed some. It would be hard to tell you why. But I'll do all I can for them. And I want to win myself. It's my last chance. I'm the only one in the family that never sat in a winning boat at least once at Poughkeepsie."

Leyden nodded. "It's not their last chance," he said. "That's why I called you in here. They have two more big years. What I ask is this. If they win, all right. If they lose, that's all right, too, in a way, although none of us like to lose. But bring them in a crew—an eight-oared varsity crew." He paused and the two men looked at each other. "You know what I mean," Leyden said. "If they go to pieces today they may never get together again, this year or any other. I don't know what you may have to do . . . but bring them in right—for their sake and the school's . . . if not for anyone else's."

The river was like glass, the stake boats hardly moving in it. Kip's crew had the outside lane, the fastest but also the roughest if the river kicked up. Also the nearest to the line of yachts at the finish.

The referee called: "Ready all?" and the California cox raised his hand. Kowalik and Guttman cursed at the delay. "Steady," Kip said. It was the first word he had spoken outside of commands since leaving the boathouse. He looked down the line of them and pride in them and what was left of his vanity of class fought in him. They stared at him and formed a curious foreshortened design of white on bronze: the sweatbands sharp against their dark faces, the adhesive tape strapped to their bellies, the heavy wool socks.

"Ready all?" the referee said again and no hand was raised. The little cannon boomed and Kip's "Row!" was lost in its echoes, in the sudden rush of waters as the oars bent in the swift, tremendous beat of the racing start. Something had begun to flow in Kip like his blood, but swifter and more subtle, so that he let them come out of the racing start only gradually, his hands beating out the stroke with the tiller grips at 40 before he consciously knew how high the beat was.

Already they had a quarter on the others and the lead grew rapidly, was over a length before the mile mark.

"Bring it down! Down, you madmen!" Kip yelled. Something in their eyes dismayed him. They were trying too hard, almost as though they were trying to escape something. . . . He felt older than they . . . but kept shouting at them until they dropped their beat. Still open water showed between them and Navy and California, leading the others.

"Leary—you're shooting your slide!" Kip yelled. Under the excitement, he could marvel at the power they were getting in spite of their form, worse than usual. He saw that Navy was coming up and, with the edge of his eyes, caught the flash of orange-tipped oars. Syracuse making an early bid. "We're not getting much run," he thought. "That's where the bad form counts."

"Get together!" he barked. There was blood on the lips of Lisbon and Guttman. "They're trying too hard," he thought. "If I yell too much they'll blow up."

The beat was up again, he realized, and wondered vaguely whether he was taking the stroke from Kowalik or Kowalik from him. This annoyed him as did their passing the two-mile mark without his knowing it.

"Down, down, you lugs!" he yelled. His voice had risen higher than usual. They eyed him fearfully. They still led, but in dropping the beat they lost ground and Navy's bow was almost even with them, and Syracuse and California less than a length behind.

Kip knew that this crew was in no mood for subtleties, whether of thought or action. He saw the bridge ahead and that decided him, "All right," he called. "Bring it up." He felt that thrill of their tremendous power move through the frail boat and he saw, with pride, the lead begin to grow again. They liked that, he saw, letting them go all out.

"Give it to them!" he called. "Give it to them! Break their damned hearts!"

They liked to hear him talk that way. They had never heard him do it before. Some of them were even grinning. They led by open water again. Something like a coldness dropped on Kip and was gone, and the noise of many voices. They had passed the bridge and the third mile.

Kip turned a little. They had over a length on Syracuse. The others were strung out, Navy and California at Syracuse's bow.

Leary was shooting his slide again, Guttman getting his oar out of the water too fast. "Steady," Kip called, afraid to say more. Still the cedar shell fled like a thing alive, still the long oars bit deeply into the river, shoveling the water back.

Seven bombs had gone off on the bridge when they went under it to tell those at the finish that the crew in the seventh lane was leading. So they would be ready for him, Kip knew, on the yacht. And he would be ready for them. He would bring his crew aboard with him and see how his brothers liked that!

Exultation beat up in him. Half a mile now. The crew's bodies, sheeted in sweat, gleamed strangely in the twilight. The line of yachts was opening on either side. They were in, Kip thought. "Pick it up," he called. "Pick it up!"

They drove the blades deep, the great bodies bent. "We're in!" he kept thinking in time with the beat of his tiller grips. "We're in! We're in!" The shell trembled as it tore through the water.

Then they blew. Guttman had taken his oar out of the water too soon, had bothered the No. 6 in front of him and made him catch a crab. Leary, shooting his slide, losing power, almost caught one. What he screamed at them, Kip never knew. But when he saw that the bow oar was catching when Kowalik, the stroke, was taking his blade from the water, he knew that it was all over. What boat first slid by them, he did not know. He saw only the strained faces, the terrible confusion in the waist of the shell, and Kowalik's efforts to keep rowing, to pass the rhythm back to the others. The other shells slipped by like ghosts in the deepening twilight.

"Get together," he said mechanically. Pathetically, they were trying to. The shell had almost lost headway.

People were yelling on the yachts but one voice, out of a megaphone, pierced to Kip's ears. "Leave those punks by themselves," Ad Grant was yelling from the bow of the yacht. Kip turned. They were abreast his brother's yacht, *Cormorant*. He could see them in the bow, yelling and gesturing to him. "Jump in and swim over here," Ad said.

The full meaning of it all came to Kip in a rush. He should abandon these men before him as a last, contemptuous gesture and sign that they did not belong or deserve to belong to that long tradition of which he and his brothers were a part. In doing so, he would appease his brothers and take some of the edge off their sarcasm tonight. His anger and scorn of the crew returned to him, strong, and Kip half rose to ease himself over the side of the shell. He remembered what Leyden had asked, with curious foresight, of himself—to bring them in an eight-oared crew, so that they would be fully such in the coming years. To hell with them, he thought, and to hell with Leyden. All of them had humiliated him.

Pathetically, they were still rowing, their oars clashing under the sound of the whistles which were already blowing for the winning crew. From his half-crouch, Kip turned to go over the side. He saw them in the bow of the *Cormorant* again . . . this time saw Mary Adams, a little apart from the others as he always liked to think of her. She was shaking her head, almost sadly. When he turned she waved her hand—for him to go on.

He had sat in the shell again before he knew he had done so. Why? he thought and felt stupid. This is silly, he tried to tell himself, but he saw the years that were to come, for them, and some strong, nameless excitement passed over him and left him weak and clearheaded. Sarcasm could never hurt him as much as he had the power to hurt these men before him.

"Way enough!" he called. They looked at him, startled. "Way enough!" His voice bit. The oars came out of the water, hung poised for his command. He made his voice as casual, as even as he could. "Now get together," he said, as though they were just out for a practice paddle. "You've been going like a bunch of washwomen."

"Ready—" he said. Their faces had grown almost composed. He felt pleasantly the sense of his own power, heard Ad Grant's voice through the megaphone, but did not hear Ad's words. . . . "Row!" Kip said. The eight oars took the water like a machine.

Ahead the whistles were screaming for a Navy crew that had come up in the dusk to beat Syracuse and California. And that dusk filled the river, turning the shells into shadows. But those who happened to be looking saw a curious sight—last by almost an eighth of a mile, but moving with a rhythm precise and sure, with unbelievable power; last now, but rich with great promise, an eight-oared varsity shell came home.

Responding to What You Read:

1. In all fiction there is a **conflict**. What is the conflict that Kip Grant faces in this short story?

2. "Leyden had been an athlete and a coach long enough to know that any great team, whether it be a crew or a football eleven, is more than half accident. The unbelievable and precise coordination that made a team great, as a team, was largely beyond the ability of any coach to create. He could develop it once the accident had occurred but he could not create it." Explain in your own words the point that is being made in this quotation. Have you ever witnessed or been a part of a similar phenomenon? Sports writers and commentators use a special word to describe this phenomenon. Do you know what it is?

3. What did Leyden mean in his words to Kip Grant, "Bring them in a crew—an eight-oared varsity crew"?

Writer's Workshop

Writing fiction is no easy task. To do the job well, a writer has to create believable characters and put them in an interesting situation that involves conflict. Good writers work hard to create conflicts that are compelling and that deliver more than the reader might have expected.

Using "Eight-Oared Crew" for inspiration, write a short story, or part of a story, that centers on a sports event. Create a conflict, as Harry Sylvester did, that explores something more than simply winning or losing.

PERSPECTIVES

The Four-Minute Mile

Sir Roger Bannister

Running the New York City Marathon

Caroline Wood Richards

Two runners, each in different ways, confront the moment itself—an opportunity "to do one thing supremely well."

ABOUT THE AUTHOR•ABOUT THE AUTHOR•ABOUT THE AUTHOR•ABOUT THE AUTHOR

Sir Roger Bannister was born in 1929. On June 5, 1954, he startled the world by being the first person ever to run a mile in under four minutes. For this accomplishment Sports Illustrated named him Sportsman of the Year. Bannister, who at age 25 was already a doctor when he ran that race, gave up athletics and became a full-time neurologist. He was knighted in 1975 and has served as Master of Pembroke College of Oxford University in England.

The Four-Minute Mile

I expected that the summer of 1975 would be my last competitive season. It was certain to be a big year in athletics. There would be the Empire Games in Vancouver, the European Games in Berne, and hopes were running high of a four-minute mile.

The great change that now came over my running was that I no longer trained and raced alone. Perhaps I had mellowed a little and was becoming more sociable. Every day between twelve-thirty and one-thirty I trained on a track in Paddington and had a quick lunch before returning to hospital.[1] We called ourselves the Paddington Lunch Time Club. We came from all parts of London and our common bond was a love of running.

I felt extremely happy in the friendships I made there, as we shared the hard work of repetitive quarter-miles and sprints. These training sessions came to mean almost as much to me as had those at the Oxford track. I could now identify myself more intimately with the failure and success of other runners.

In my hardest training Chris Brasher was with me, and he made the task very much lighter. On Friday evenings he took me along to Chelsea Barracks where his coach, Franz Stampfl, held a training session. At weekends Chris Chataway would join us, and in this friendly atmosphere the very severe training we did became most enjoyable.

---

1. hospital: St. Mary's Hospital Medical School, London, where Bannister was a student at the time.

In December, 1953, we started a new intensive course of training and ran several times a week a series of ten consecutive quarter-miles, each in 66 seconds. Through January and February we gradually speeded them up, keeping to an interval of two minutes between each. By April we could manage them in 61 seconds, but however hard we tried it did not seem possible to reach our target of 60 seconds. We were stuck, or as Chris Brasher expressed it—"bogged down." The training had ceased to do us any good and we needed a change.

Chris Brasher and I drove up to Scotland overnight for a few days' climbing. We turned into the Pass of Glencoe as the sun crept above the horizon at dawn. A misty curtain drew back from the mountains and the "sun's sleepless eye" cast a fresh cold light on the world. The air was calm and fragrant, and the colors of sunrise were mirrored in peaty pools on the moor. Soon the sun was up and we were off climbing. The weekend was a complete mental and physical change. It probably did us more harm than good physically. We climbed hard for the four days we were there, using the wrong muscles in slow and jerking movements.

There was an element of danger too. I remember Chris falling a short way when leading a climb up a rock face depressingly named "Jericho's Wall." Luckily he did not hurt himself. We were both worried lest a sprained ankle might set our training back by several weeks.

After three days our minds turned to running again. We suddenly became alarmed at the thought of taking any more risks, and decided to return. We had slept little, our meals had been irregular. But when we tried to run those quarter-miles again, the time came down to 59 seconds!

It was now less than three weeks to the Oxford University versus A.A.A.[2] race, the first opportunity of the year for us to attack the four-minute mile. Chris Chataway had decided to join Chris Brasher and myself in the A.A.A. team. He doubted his ability to run a three quarter-mile in three minutes, but he generously offered to attempt it.

I had now abandoned the severe training of the previous months and was concentrating entirely on gaining speed and freshness. I had to learn to release in four short minutes the energy I usually spent in half an hour's training. Each training session took on a special significance as the day of the Oxford race drew near. It felt a privilege and joy each time I ran a trial on the track.

---

2. A.A.A.: Amateur Athletic Association.

There was no longer any need for my mind to force my limbs to run faster—my body became a unity in motion much greater than the sum of its component parts. I never thought of length of stride or style, or even my judgment of pace. All this had become automatically ingrained. In this way a singleness of drive could be achieved, leaving my mind free from the task of directing operations so that it could fix itself on the great objective ahead. There was more enjoyment in my running than ever before, a new health and vigor. It was as if all my muscles were a part of a perfectly tuned machine. I felt fresh now at the end of each training session.

On April 24 I ran a three-quarter-mile trial in three minutes at Motspur Park with Chataway. I led for the first two laps and we both returned exactly the same time. Four days later I ran a last solo three-quarter-mile trial at Paddington. Norris McWhirter, who had been my patient timekeeper through most of 1953, came over to hold the watch.

The energy of the twins, Norris and Ross McWhirter, was boundless. For them nothing was too much trouble, and they accepted my challenge joyfully. After running together in Oxford as sprinters they carried their partnership into journalism, keeping me posted of the performances of my overseas rivals. They often drove me to athletics meetings, so that I arrived with no fuss, never a minute too soon or too late. Sometimes I was not sure whether it was Norris or Ross who held the watch or drove the car, but I knew that either could be relied upon.

For the trial at Paddington there was as usual a high wind blowing. I would have given almost anything to be able to shirk the test that would tell me with ruthless accuracy what my chances were of achieving a four-minute mile at Oxford. I felt that 2 minutes 59.9 seconds for the three-quarter-mile in a solo training run meant 3 minutes 59.9 seconds in a mile race. A time of 3 minutes 0.1 second would mean 4 minutes 0.1 second for the mile—just the difference between success and failure. The watch recorded a time of 2 minutes 59.9 seconds! I felt a little sick afterward and had the taste of nervousness in my mouth. My speedy recovery within five minutes suggested that I had been holding something back. Two days later at Paddington I ran a 1 minute 54 second half-mile quite easily, after a late night, and then took five days' complete rest before the race.

I had been training daily since the previous November, and now that the crisis was approaching I barely knew what to do with myself. I spent most of the time imagining I was developing a cold and wondering if the gale-force winds would ever drop. The day before the race I slipped on a highly polished hospital floor and spent the rest of the day limping. Each night in the week before the race there came a moment when I saw myself at the starting line. My whole body would grow nervous and tremble. I ran the race over in my mind. Then I would calm myself and sometimes get off to sleep.

Next day was Thursday, May 6, 1954. I went into the hospital as usual, and at eleven o'clock I was sharpening my spikes on a grindstone in the laboratory. Someone passing said, "You don't really think that's going to make any difference, do you?"

I knew the weather conditions made the chances of success practically nil. Yet all day I was taking the usual precautions for the race, feeling at the same time that they would prove useless.

I decided to travel up to Oxford alone because I wanted to think quietly. I took an early train deliberately, opened a carriage door, and, quite by chance, there was Franz Stampfl inside. I was delighted to see him, as a friend with the sort of attractive cheerful personality I badly needed at that moment. Through Chris Brasher, Franz had been in touch with my training program, but my own connection with him was slight.

I would have liked his advice and help at this moment, but could not bring myself to ask him. It was as if now, at the end of my running career, I was being forced to admit that coaches were necessary after all, and that I had been wrong to think that the athlete could be sufficient unto himself.

In my mind there lurked the memory of an earlier occasion when I had visited a coach. He had expounded his views on my running and suggested a whole series of changes. The following week I read a newspaper article he wrote about my plans, claiming to be my adviser for the 1952 Olympics. This experience made me inclined to move slowly.

But Franz is not like this. He has no wish to turn the athlete into a machine working at his dictation. We shared a common view of athletics as a means of "recreation" of each individual, as a result of the liberation and expression of the latent power within him. Franz is an artist who can see beauty in human struggle and achievement.

We talked, almost impersonally, about the problem I faced. In my mind I had settled this as the day when, with every ounce of strength I possessed, I would attempt to run the four-minute mile. A wind of gale force was blowing which would slow me up by a second a lap. In order to succeed I must run not merely a four-minute mile, but the equivalent of a 3 minute 56 second mile in calm weather.

I had reached my peak physically and psychologically. There would never be another day like it. I had to drive myself to the limit of my power without the stimulus of competitive opposition. This was my first race for eight months and all this time I had been storing nervous energy. If I tried and failed I should be dejected, and my chances would be less on any later attempt. Yet it seemed that the high wind was going to make it impossible.

I had almost decided when I entered the carriage at Paddington that unless the wind dropped soon I would postpone the attempt. I would just run an easy mile in Oxford and make the attempt on the next possible occasion ten days later at the White City in London.

Franz understood my apprehension. He thought I was capable of running a mile in 3 minutes 56 seconds, or 3:57, so he could argue convincingly that it was worthwhile making the attempt. "With the proper motivation, that is, a good reason for wanting to do it," he said, "your mind can overcome any sort of adversity. In any case the wind might drop. I remember J. J. Barry in Ireland. He ran a 4 minute 8 second mile without any training or even proper food—simply because he had the will to run. Later in America, where he was given every facility and encouragement, he never ran a fast race. In any case, what if this were your only chance?"

He had won his point. Racing has always been more of a mental than a physical problem to me. He went on talking about athletes and performances, but I heard no more. The dilemma was not banished from my mind, and the idea left uppermost was that this might be my only chance. "How would you ever forgive yourself if you rejected it?" I thought, as the train arrived in Oxford. As it happened, ten days later it was just as windy!

I was met at the station by Charles Wenden, a great friend from my early days in Oxford, who drove me straight down to Iffley Road. The wind was almost gale force. Together we walked round the deserted track. The St. George's flag on a nearby church stood out from the flagpole. The attempt seemed hopeless, yet for some unknown reason I tried out both pairs of spikes. I had a new pair which were specially made for me on the instructions of a climber and fell walker,[3] Eustace Thomas of Manchester. Some weeks before he had come up to London and together we worked out modifications which

---

3. **fell walker:** hiker.

would reduce the weight of each running shoe from six to four ounces. This saving in weight might well mean the difference between success and failure.

Still undecided, I drove back to Charles Wenden's home for lunch. On this day, as on many others, I was glad of the peace which I found there. Although both he and his wife Eileen knew the importance of the decision that had to be made, and cared about it as much as I did myself, it was treated by common consent as a question to be settled later.

The immediate problem was to prepare a suitable lunch, and to see that the children, Felicity and Sally, ate theirs. Absorbed in watching the endless small routine of running a home and family, I could forget some of my apprehensions. Charles Wenden had been one of the ex-service students in Oxford after the war, and some of my earliest running had been in his company. Later his house had become a second home for me during my research studies in Oxford, and the calm efficiency of Eileen had often helped to still my own restless worries. Never was this factor so important as on this day.

In the afternoon I called on Chris Chataway. At the moment the sun was shining, and he lay stretched on the window seat. He smiled and said, just as I knew he would, "The day could be a lot worse, couldn't it? Just now it's fine. The forecast says the wind may drop toward evening. Let's not decide until five o'clock."

I spent the afternoon watching from the window the swaying of the leaves. "The wind's hopeless," said Joe Binks on the way down to the track. At five-fifteen there was a shower of rain. The wind blew strongly, but now came in gusts, as if uncertain. As Brasher, Chataway, and I warmed up, we knew the eyes of the spectators were on us; they were hoping that the wind would drop just a little—if not enough to run a four-minute mile, enough to make the attempt.

Failure is as exciting to watch as success, provided the effort is absolutely genuine and complete. But the spectators fail to understand— and how can they know—the mental agony through which an athlete must pass before he can give his maximum effort. And how rarely, if he is built as I am, he can give it.

No one tried to persuade me. The decision was mine alone, and the moment was getting closer. As we lined up for the start I glanced at the flag again. It fluttered more gently now, and the scene from Shaw's *Saint Joan* flashed through my mind, how she, at her desperate moment, waited for the wind to change. Yes, the wind was dropping slightly. This was the moment when I made my decision. The attempt was on.

There was complete silence on the ground . . . a false start . . . I felt angry that precious moments during the lull in the wind might be slipping by. The gun fired a second time . . . Brasher went into the lead and I slipped in effortlessly behind him, feeling tremendously full of running. My legs seemed to meet no resistance at all, as if propelled by some unknown force.

We seemed to be going so slowly! Impatiently I shouted "Faster!" But Brasher kept his head and did not change the pace. I went on worrying until I heard the first lap time, 57.5 seconds. In the excitement my knowledge of pace had deserted me. Brasher could have run the first quarter in 55 seconds without my realizing it, because I felt so full of running, but I should have had to pay for it later. Instead, he had made success possible.

At one and a half laps I was still worrying about the pace. A voice shouting "Relax" penetrated to me above the noise of the crowd. I learned afterward it was Stampfl's. Unconsciously I obeyed. If the speed was wrong it was too late to do anything about it, so why worry? I was relaxing so much that my mind seemed almost detached from my body. There was no strain.

I barely noticed the half-mile, passed in 1 minute 58 seconds, nor when, round the next bend, Chataway went into the lead. At three-quarters of a mile the effort was still barely perceptible; the time was 3 minutes 0.7 second, and by now the crowd was roaring. Somehow I had to run that last lap in 59 seconds. Chataway led round the next bend and then I pounced past him at the beginning of the back straight, three hundred yards from the finish.

I had a moment of mixed joy and anguish, when my mind took over. It raced well ahead of my body and drew my body compellingly forward. I felt that the moment of a lifetime had come. There was no pain, only a great unity of movement and aim. The world seemed to stand still, or did not exist. The only reality was the next two hundred yards of track under my feet. The tape meant finality—extinction perhaps.

I felt at that moment that it was my chance to do one thing supremely well. I drove on, impelled by a combination of fear and pride. The air I breathed filled me with the spirit of the track where I had run my first race. The noise in my ears was that of the faithful Oxford crowd. Their hope and encouragement gave me greater strength. I had now turned the last bend and there were only fifty yards more.

My body had long since exhausted all its energy, but it went on running just the same. The physical overdraft came only from greater willpower. This was the crucial moment when my legs were strong enough to carry me over the last few yards as they could never have done in previous years. With five yards to go the tape seemed almost to recede. Would I ever reach it?

Those last few seconds seemed never-ending. The faint line of the finishing tape stood ahead as a haven of peace, after the struggle. The arms of the world were waiting to receive me if only I reached the tape without slackening my speed. If I faltered, there would be no arms to hold me and the world would be a cold, forbidding place, because I had been so close. I leaped at the tape like a man taking his last spring to save himself from the chasm that threatens to engulf him.

My effort was over and I collapsed almost unconscious, with an arm on either side of me. It was only then that real pain overtook me. I felt like an exploded flashlight with no will to live; I just went on existing in the most passive physical state without being quite conscious. Blood surged from my muscles and seemed to fell me. It was if all my limbs were caught in an ever-tightening vise. I knew that I had done it before I even heard the time. I was too close to have failed, unless my legs had played strange tricks at the finish by slowing me down and not telling my tiring brain that they had done so.

The stop-watches held the answer. The announcement came—"Result of one mile . . . time, three minutes"—the rest lost in the roar of excitement. I grabbed Brasher and Chataway, and together we scampered round the track in a burst of spontaneous joy. We had done it—the three of us!

We shared a place where no man had yet ventured—secured for all time, however fast men might run miles in future. We had done it where we wanted, when we wanted, how we wanted, in our first attempt of the year. In the wonderful joy my pain was forgotten and I wanted to prolong those precious moments of realization.

I felt suddenly and gloriously free of the burden of athletic ambition that I had been carrying for years. No words could be invented for such supreme happiness, eclipsing all other feelings. I thought at that moment I could never reach such a climax of single-mindedness. I felt bewildered and overpowered. I knew it would be some time before I caught up with myself.

Caroline Wood Richards was born in 1973. She graduated from Bates College and Teachers College of Columbia University in New York City. As poet Robert Frost recommended, she combines her vocation and her avocation by teaching high-school English while still finding time to run with her husband and sometimes with her students. Regarding preparing for the New York City Marathon, she says, "The body really fuels the mind. Training for a long-term goal such as a marathon allowed me to see tangible results in my body that gave me the confidence to run the race and meet the challenge of 26.2 miles." About this piece of writing, she says, "I looked forward to the opportunity to reflect on the marathon. The writing allowed me to re-run the race, solidify and preserve my thoughts and feelings on this great personal accomplishment."

Running the New York City Marathon

The official time clock at mile twenty-two reads three hours and forty-five minutes. An anonymous runner to my left and I are joking about how it's going to be really rough to cover the last four miles in fifteen minutes in order to reach the desired four-hour finish. We run together for a hundred or so yards and then he gets lost in the crowd as we turn a corner, and I wonder whether the reason I don't see him is that he's been able to pick up his pace. I know it is crazy, but I still hold out hope to reach Tavern on the Green pretty close to four hours after I crossed the starting line at the Verazanno Narrows Bridge.

Not long after mile twenty-two, I am having a hard time keeping myself together. I am fighting to keep my facial muscles from contorting and my breathing becoming unregulated. I can feel my shoulders creeping toward my ears in two mounds of tension. From somewhere inside me a rational voice is saying, "Not now. Not now," and I repeat this to myself over and over.

I am running the New York Marathon! I am here! After months of training, long runs in both the heat of August and the chill of October, pre-dawn runs navigating cars, cyclists and wild animals, trips to the knee doctor, and countless moments of exhilaration and doubt, I have arrived and not only am I fine, but I feel good. The thought of realizing my goal is overwhelming me to the point of tears and yet part of me knows that to get emotional here and now will ruin the rest of the run for me. That by allowing the sobs that are catching in my throat to break free, I will lose the precious rhythm which I am so lucky to have.

Instead, I take some Gatorade from a well-wishing middle-school student in a rain slicker and retreat inward, away from the crowd, because interacting with them is too real and is draining too much of my energy. I mentally re-run the early miles of the race (when adrenaline and blood sugar were both in abundance) that for me were so exhilarating. I hope that this activity will eat up some of the time it will take my fiancé running-partner and me to cover the remaining miles.

The start of the race was like nothing I have ever seen before. A sea of people in all directions, nervously self-absorbed yet friendly. I both love and hate every one of the eight minutes it takes my fiancé and me to cross the start line. I draw energy from my fellow runners and also from the heli-copters swarming above us. It's exciting and I'm scared, but I am pumped. I am ready! I have worked hard for this, and know that I will do it well.

Brooklyn is the first borough off the bridge and it will become one of my favorite parts of the race. The pack of runners is very thick, but the pace is good. The crowd is incredible. People are everywhere and they call my name, which I have written on my shirt, as I run by. "Go, Caroline!" "Come on, Caroline!" "CaRoLine!" Children are on their parents' shoulders and almost everyone has a hand extended to give us high fives as we go past. Somewhere on a street lined with beautiful brownstones, some guys have The Village People's hit song "YMCA" blaring from their stereo system and I forget that I am not out on the dance floor and my arms shoot above my head and do the appropriate letter formations as I charge up a hill. Everyone in my immediate vicinity is singing and dancing and I am disappointed when the beat of the music fades in the distance.

Coming off the 59th Street Bridge from Queens into Manhattan is like nothing else in this world. The roar of thousands catches me and carries me like a hero all the way up First Avenue from 59th Street to the Willis Avenue Bridge. Countless arches of colored balloons cross First Avenue and I know that somewhere up there around 83rd Street, my parents and friends are watching for me. People are lined up fifteen deep carrying balloons and signs, holding out orange wedges and water, and shouting encouraging remarks as we run by. The thought resonating in my head with every pound of my sneaker and every cheer from the fans is that this is my ticker tape parade.

Only a narrow portion of the Willis Avenue Bridge is carpeted to lessen the impact of feet on steel, and the pace is slow. Concerned about my time, and frustrated by the delay, I shoot off to the right and around the slow-moving pack. I see that a blind runner, keeping his course by a rubber band strung between himself and his guide runner, is slowing the pace; and I am at the same time ashamed at my impatience and wondrous at what it must be like to train and run the New York City Marathon with a disability. I know I can do it, I know that it is attainable, but now I can't find the 25-mile marker and by *my* calculations I should have long since *bolted* by it. I come out of my reflections to hear the crowd shouting at me and urging me to the finish. They are behind me, and their encouragement combined with my will and desire to realize a long-term goal force me to put one tired but exhilarated foot in front of the other.

I pick up the pace as I round the corner from 59th Street into Central Park and grab Bart's hand in anticipation of the finish which we have practiced on our last few training runs. We sprint, or try to, up and then down the hill to the finish and throw our joined hands in the air as we cross the line. As intensely personal as long distance running is, we have done this together. Not only have I learned what I am capable of and what I can endure, I have had someone with whom to grow and share. Together and alone we have conquered something which neither of us thought possible.

Responding to What You Read

1. What physical and emotional feelings do both Roger Bannister and Caroline Wood Richards experience as they run?

2. Why did Roger Bannister feel that a three-quarter-mile race run in 2 minutes 59.9 seconds was vastly different from the same race run in 3 minutes 0.1 second?

3. After the record was broken, Bannister says, "We had done it—the three of us!" What do you think he means? Did Caroline Wood Richards have a similar feeling? Explain.

Writer's Workshop

In a **comparison-and-contrast essay,** the writer looks for comparisons (similarities) between two things as well as contrasts (differences). Write an essay in which you compare and contrast Bannister's and Richards's narratives. Before starting to write, first identify the similarities between the two accounts. Then identify the differences. Decide whether your essay will focus on the similarities or the differences or both. Then compose a **thesis statement** that explains the central points you want to make. As you write the essay, use your thesis statement as a guide to organize your ideas.

Alternate Media Response

Create a video that runs no more than two minutes and that captures some small moment taken from either of these first-person accounts of running in competition. Shoot the video from the narrator's point of view. Let the viewer see what the runner sees. Include a voice-over narrator to tell what the runner is feeling in this segment of the run—using the exact narration from the text for this purpose.

Jump Shot

Richard Peck

The critical moment in a basketball game, repeated over and over at both ends of the court, is slowed down here, so that you can see what it is made of.

ABOUT THE AUTHOR•ABOUT THE AUTHOR•ABOUT THE AUTHOR•ABOUT THE AUTHOR

Richard Peck is a prolific writer of poems, short stories, and novels, often directed at adolescents. His novels include Are You in the House Alone? and Father Figure, *both of which were chosen as Best Books for Young Adults by the American Library Association.*

Peck, a former teacher, was born in 1934 and presently lives in New York City. He often sits in coffee shops near schools to listen in on teenage conversation to help him create realistic dialogue in his fiction.

Jump Shot

Lithe,[1] quicker than the ball itself;
Spinning through the blocking forearms,
Hands like stars, spread to suspend
The ball from five, and only five,
5   Magic fingerprints.

---

1. lithe: flexible and graceful.

The rebound resounding down the pole
And into asphalt, pounded hard by sneakers
Raggedier than the missing-tooth grimaces.

10   Grimaces. No smiles here. Concentration.
Movement. The calculation.
The arch-back leap. And off the rim again.
Once in ten the satisfying swoosh.

And no time wasted to enjoy it.
Grasp that globe and keep it dribbling:
15   Elbows were meant for eyesockets;
Work it up higher than hands,
Higher than the grab of gravity.

Working, each man for himself,
Yet neatly, neatly weaving in the pattern.

Responding to What You Read:

1. A **theme** in a piece of writing is its main idea. What do you think is the main idea in "Jump Shot"?

2. Identify a **simile** and a **metaphor** in the first stanza and a metaphor in the fourth stanza. Explain what two things are being compared in the simile and the metaphors.

3. **Alliteration** is a poetic device in which the author uses similar consonant sounds in a row. Identify several examples of alliteration in this poem.

Writer's Workshop

Write a **free-verse poem** (no rhyme, no regular rhythm or meter) in which you capture one aspect—like the jump shot in basketball—of one sport. Include at least two striking comparisons between dissimilar things, using either similes or metaphors.

PERSPECTIVES

400-meter Freestyle

Maxine Kumin

In the Swim

Alexis Collins

Two swimmers. Two races. Catch the excitement as they shoot through the water, hit the wall, flip, push off, and surge to the finish.

ABOUT THE AUTHOR•ABOUT THE AUTHOR•ABOUT THE AUTHOR•ABOUT THE AUTHOR

Maxine Kumin was born in Philadelphia, Pennsylvania, in 1925. She was educated at Radcliffe College in Cambridge, Massachusetts. She won the Pulitzer Prize for Poetry in 1973 and served as the poetry consultant to the Library of Congress as well as Poet Laureate of New Hampshire. She has taught at Washington University, Brandeis, and Columbia. The New York Times Book Review *says of her writing, "Her poems become increasingly unforgettable, indispensable . . .Thoreau would commend her honesty, the precision of her language and her occasional moral allegory."* The San Francisco Examiner and Chronicle *calls Kumin ". . . a poet whose certain voice and command of her craft free her to actually look at the world—and reconnect us to it." Kumin has published poetry, short stories, and essays about country living. Her* Selected Poems, 1960-1990 *was published in 1997.*

Kumin became interested in writing poetry when she was a high-school student. Later, at Radcliffe, she showed some of her poems to an instructor, who belittled her efforts. Kumin was so stung by the criticism that she didn't attempt another poem for several years. By 1953, however, Kumin experienced some success publishing what she refers to as "light verse" in such popular magazines as Saturday Evening Post *and* Cosmopolitan. *Her career as a poet received a major boost in 1957 when she enrolled in a poetry workshop at the Boston Center for Adult Education. Her professor in the workshop was John Holmes, an important literary figure of the time. Through Holmes, Kumin was introduced to fellow poet Anne Sexton, who became a close friend. Critics credit Holmes and Sexton with providing the influence and inspiration that has made Kumin one of the leading poets of contemporary America.*

Kumin prefers verse forms that impose rigid structures on poetry, and she admits that the more difficult the poem is to write, the more she enjoys it. The following poem, "400-meter Freestyle," is an excellent example of Kumin's love for structure.

400-meter Freestyle

THE GUN full swing the swimmer catapults and cracks

                                                          s

                                                          i

                                                          x

5   feet away onto that perfect glass he catches at

       a

n

       d

       throws behind him scoop after scoop cunningly moving

10   t

                                                          h

                                                          e

       water back to move him forward. Thrift is his wonderful

       s

15   e

       c

       ret; he has schooled out all extravagance. No muscle

                                                          r

                                                          i

20   p

       ples without compensation wrist cock to heel snap to

       h

i

       s

25   mobile mouth that siphons in the air that nurtures

                                                          h

                                                          i

                                                          m

       at half an inch above sea level so to speak.

30   T

       h

       e

astonishing whites of the soles of his feet rise
                                                    a
35   n
                                                    d
salute us on the turns. He flips, converts, and is gone
a
l
40   l
in one. We watch him for signs. His arms are steady at
                                                    t
                                                      h
                                                    e
45   catch, his cadent feet tick in the stretch, they know
t
h
  e
lesson well. Lungs know, too; he does not list for
50   a
                                                      i
                                                    r
he drives along on little sips carefully expended
b
55   u
  t
that plum red heart pumps hard cries hurt how soon
                                                    i
                                                      t
60   s
near one more and makes its final surge   TIME: 4:25:9

┌───┐
ABOUT THE AUTHOR•ABOUT THE AUTHOR•ABOUT THE AUTHOR•ABOUT THE AUTHOR

Alexis Collins was born in 1982. She began swimming when she was four years old. When she wrote this personal account as a sophomore in high school she had already been swimming competitively for nine years. Her events are the 200-meter individual medley and the 200-meter backstroke. She swims for her high school and also for the Cougars of Montclair, New Jersey. Alexis says, "As I got older I realized that this was the sport I excelled in, so I decided to continue with it. I am really glad that I stayed with swimming because I feel that I have the will and desire to go far in life with it."
└───┘

In the Swim

"If it is to be, it's up to me." Those nine words softly chant in my head as I stand behind my lane. My mind is filled with nervousness and determination. I take one deep breath and look up to the ceiling to crack my neck. My stomach cramps up and I crack my knuckles as a nervous reaction. I watch as the girl in the heat before mine steps up to the block. "Swimmers, step up, 200 individual medley, listen to the starter. Take your mark." Simultaneously all eight girls bend down and grab the block. "Bee-eeee-eee-eee-eee-ppp." The buzzer screams and echoes in my mind. I watch as the girls fly in the air and disappear into the cool water. As they come up to take their first stroke I think to myself, "Oh God, I'm next."

I look around and the girls in my heat are waiting impatiently behind their blocks. As I peel off the three layers of clothing I am wearing, to keep me warm and keep my muscles relaxed, I can't think of anything else except the words, "If it is to be, it's up to me."

Suddenly a flashback overwhelms my mind. I see my old coach Ed standing on the deck in front of my group. He yells, "If it is to be . . ." We yell back, ". . . it's up to me!"

As I walk up to the block, my friend Lisa comes up to me and says, "Good luck. You're gonna do fine . . . besides, it's only eight laps!" I look at the swimmers in the water and say to myself, "Ugh . . . they're only on backstroke. I want to get this over with."

I adjust my goggles and bend down to touch the floor. I turn to my left to see who I will be swimming against. I think to myself, "Wow, she is pretty big. I hope she's slow." I turn to my right and see my friend Kara, whom I used to swim with. "Come on, Lex, you can do it . . . you can beat her," I tell myself. I look up to the stands to see my mother's nervous face. She smiles and bows her head slightly, to show approval.

Sooner than I know, the starter says, "Swimmers step up." I get on the block. As a tradition I clap my hands three times to break the other swimmers' concentration. (Another benefit is that it makes my hands a little numb. I like them numb because when they hit the water, the water slips off them faster.) "200 individual medley, listen to the starter. Take your mark." My left foot moves to the edge of the block; my right foot remains at the back. My head drops down between my legs. "Bee-eee-eee-eee-eee-ppp!" Almost immediately, my body is in the air.

The cool water flows over my head and back. I take the first stroke as my arms instinctively pull me forward and my legs push me through the water. I touch the wall and as I turn I see my friend Kara ahead of me. As hard as I pull I can't seem to catch up to her.

I hit the wall going into my third lap. As I push off, my arms are tired and feel like someone has punched my shoulders a thousand times. But those words, still chanting in my head, keep me going: "If it is to be, it's up to me." I make the turn for my second lap of backstroke and I am ahead of Kara now. As I pull faster and faster, my stomach feels a little nauseous and I want to stop.

●   ●   ●   ●

Last summer I attended my first swim camp, in Florida. I was nervous at first but then my sister told me that this was a "once-in-a-lifetime" chance and I had to go.

While I was there, I heard about a tryout to do an English Channel expedition. It would involve taking a trip with ten strangers to try to break the world record for a relay in the English Channel between England and France. My friends decided to try out and so did I. It took a little convincing, but after a while my parents gave me permission.

We began the tryouts on a Monday and they lasted one week. They told us that for the next seven days we were to do what they said. If they said "Jump!" we were to say, "How high?"

We ran three miles every morning beginning at 6:30 A.M. At 8:30 we had breakfast. Then we swam for an hour and a half straight. This time, from 9:00 A.M. to 10:30 A.M., was to be our "thinking time" as we swam, explained Bud, our Channel coach. "This is the time you take to decide if you really want to be here or if this is just a waste of time," he said. He told us that if we stopped at any point in the hour and a half of swimming, our tryout was finished.

Then we got out of the pool and formed two straight lines. We threw a ten-pound medicine ball back and forth to a partner. This went on for twenty minutes.

Then we had to tread water for ten minutes.

Our morning workout was done.

We had an hour rest before our classroom session. During classroom we would watch videos on how our strokes should be. We had motivational speakers come and talk to us.

After classroom we had lunch. Then we sat in a five-foot-deep circular pool. Over a number of days the temperature was lowered to 40 degrees, which was the closest to the Channel temperature they could get.

We also had a drill where Coach Bud blew his whistle and we had to hold our breaths for thirty seconds to build up our endurance.

After the cold pool we would go to afternoon practice for an hour. At this time we practiced our strokes and techniques, to increase our endurance.

I didn't make the cut. I didn't get to go to the English Channel. But I enjoyed camp and worked hard the whole time I was there.

•   •   •   •

I make the turn for my fifth lap, which is the breast stroke, my worst. My lungs hurt and my legs are dragging. But all I can think of is Coach Ed's mantra: "If it is to be, it's up to me." As I put my head underwater with each stroke, I can see out of the corners of my eyes that I am ahead of everyone. I think, "Come on, you've got it, pull faster." I grab the wall and spring off for my sixth lap, the last lap of the breast stroke. My head begins to feel heavy and everything aches.

Pushing off the wall for freestyle, my final two laps, I see my coach and teammates on the side of the deck. My coach is standing with both arms in the air. In one hand is a stopwatch and, in the other, his clipboard. My teammates are cheering for me; they are all rapidly swaying their arms from left to right, urging me on. I suddenly start kicking faster because I know by their gestures that I am going to get a good time.

The wall is in reaching distance now and my heart has stopped. All of my nervousness has been replaced by anticipation. I have been swimming and practicing for almost twelve years, for moments just like these.

I glide into the wall and look up at the scoreboard. "Lane 4, 1st place, time 2:10.43."

A smile breaks over my face and I think, "Yes! . . . My best time!" I look over at Kara and her face shows disappointment. I reach over the lane, smile, and say, "Good job." I reach for a handshake and she gives me a hug. "Good job, how did you go that fast?" Kara asks me. I think to myself, "If it is to be, it's up to me." But I say nothing, and, instead, just smile.

Responding to What You Read

1. How does the shape of "400-meter Freestyle"—the way the poem looks on the page—reflect its subject matter?

2. Why do you think the poet in "400-meter Freestyle" omits punctuation in the last several lines of the poem?

3. In "In the Swim," what does Alexis Collins do mentally to help her stay focused as she swims in the race? Do you think this principle applies to all sports? Explain.

Writer's Workshop

"400-meter Freestyle" is a **concrete poem**; its appearance on the page *concretely*—visually— communicates its subject matter. The poet E. E. Cummings once wrote a famous concrete poem about autumn, a poem in which the words seem to drift down the page like leaves in fall. Try to write your own concrete poem about any subject—not necessarily sports. Keep your poem short and focused on a single image.

PERSPECTIVES

Fishing

William Wordsworth

Instruction in the Art

Philip Booth

Two poets, more than a century apart, reveal that fishing is timeless—in more ways than one.

William Wordsworth is considered one of the greatest of England's romantic poets. He lived from 1770 to 1850, spending most of his life in England's Lake District. He was made poet laureate of his country in 1843. Tourists today go to the Lake District in northern England to see its beauty and to visit historical attractions dedicated to Wordsworth.

Fishing

We were a noisy crew; the sun in heaven
Beheld not vales[1] more beautiful than ours;
Nor saw a band in happiness and joy
Richer, or worthier of the ground they trod.
5   I could record with no reluctant voice
The woods of autumn, and their hazel bowers,[2]
With milk-white clusters hung; the rod and line,
True symbol of hope's foolishness, whose strong
And unreproved[3] enchantment led us on
10   By rocks and pools shut out from every star,
All the green summer, to forlorn cascades[4]
Among the windings[5] hid of mountain brooks.

---

1. **vales:** valleys.
2. **hazel bowers:** branches of hazel trees (a type of birch), forming a kind of enclosure.
3. **unreproved:** uncensored, unchallenged.
4. **forlorn cascades:** lonely, little waterfalls.
5. **windings:** curved or sinuous courses.

Philip Booth was born in New Hampshire in 1925. He was educated at Dartmouth College, where Robert Frost was one of his freshman-year teachers, and at Columbia University. He was a founder of the graduate Creative Writing Program at Syracuse University. His book Pairs, *published in 1994, was his ninth work published by Penguin Books. Poet Stanley Kunitz says that Booth has "quietly and unostentatiously made himself master of a province . . . In his deep-rooted sense of place, the probity of his spirit, the integrity of his art, I find an essential beauty."*

Instruction in the Art
"Take a Boy Fishing"

Boy, the giant beauty
that you cast for lies
upstream in this same current
that you wade. Men wise
5   with love have wintered
on the iron bridge, dreamed
opening day, and tied
their hatful of bright
artificial flies.

10   This is an old one, boy,
not in memory struck
at a false cast. No, nor
felt the quick-set hook.
The snags are ragged

15 with lost lures, hair and
 gold; even icons shaped
 like a woman, this beauty
 never took.

 Boy, cast lightly. Long
20 and lightly where the shallow
 split tongue of current
 undercuts the meadow;
 in that spun pool
 where blue flowers overhang
25 the bank, by first light
 a few quiet men at last
 have seen the shadow.

 We only guess, boy,
 by the stream-run shape
30 of steelheads, or a rainbow
 beached in winter sleep.
 Such forms lose color
 in the creel; men file
 barbs not toward food
35 or trophies, but for luck
 they cannot keep.

 Boy, the giant beauty
 that you cast for lies
 upstream. I pray you patience
40 for that tug and rise,
 the risen image
 that outleaps the rapids
 in one illimitable
 arc: to praise,
45 but not to prize.

Responding to What You Read

1. In Wordsworth's poem, how are the fishing rod and line "true symbols of hope's foolishness"?

2. **Diction** refers to a writer's word choice. How does Booth's choice of words—or diction—contribute to the **tone** and **mood** of "Instruction in the Art"?

Writer's Workshop

Tone and mood work closely together in literature. Words help create the tone of a selection and the tone, in turn, helps create the mood. A bright, lilting tone will create a happy, cheerful mood. A lofty, solemn tone will create a serious mood. Write a short poem or prose description on any subject. Try to reproduce the delicate, quiet tone and warm, reverential mood that Booth achieves in "Instruction in the Art."

Alternate Media Response

Choose any medium other than writing and create something that evokes the feelings of either or both of these poems. For example, you might draw a picture, build a diorama, or sing a song. Present your project to the class and ask students to evaluate how well you have captured the spirit of the poem(s).

CHAPTER 2

The Glory of Sports

To many people, the focus of sports is the glory that players achieve on playing fields, but the glory of sports can extend far beyond the playing fields. True sports greats often are remembered for achievements beyond their skill at the game. This chapter offers selections about the glory of sports both on and off the field.

Lou Gehrig and Jackie Robinson thrilled baseball fans with their skills. But off the field they also inspired millions of people—Gehrig in the courageous way in which he faced a crippling and ultimately fatal disease, and Robinson through his courage in the face of hostility from teammates and fans as he broke the color barrier in baseball.

The women on a Massachusetts high-school basketball team find that glory is more than skill on the court. For them, glory is about local recognition, teammates, and friendships—memories that they will carry with them throughout their lives.

A sky diver finds glory in the attempt, a football star basks in the glory of the moment, and a businessman sees glory in the past.

Define your own concept of the glory of sports as you read about these athletes and others—different people achieving their own glories.

Baseball's Great Experiment: Jackie Robinson and His Legacy

Jules Tygiel

America had just fought and won a war against powers that stood for bigotry and racism. Now, it was time for the country to practice the ideals that thousands had died for.

ABOUT THE AUTHOR•ABOUT THE AUTHOR•ABOUT THE AUTHOR•ABOUT THE AUTHOR

Jules Tygiel is a leading authority on Jackie Robinson. He is the author of Baseball's Great Experiment: Jackie Robinson and His Legacy, *published in 1983, from which this excerpt comes, and* The Jackie Robinson Reader: Perspectives on an American Hero, *published in 1997. Tygiel is professor of history at San Francisco State University.*

Baseball's Great Experiment: Jackie Robinson and His Legacy

Opening Day of the baseball season was always a festive occasion in Jersey City on the banks of the Passaic River. Each year Mayor Frank Hague closed the schools and required all city employees to purchase tickets, guaranteeing a sellout for the hometown Giants of the International League. The Giants sold 52,000 tickets to Roosevelt Stadium, double the ball park capacity. For those who could not be squeezed into the arena, Mayor Hague staged an annual pre-game jamboree. Jersey City students regaled the crowd outside the stadium with exhibitions of running, jumping, and acrobatics, while two bands provided musical entertainment.

On April 18, 1946, the air crackled with a special electricity. Hague's extravaganza marked the start of the first minor league baseball season since the end of the war. But this did not fully account for the added tension and excitement. Nor could it explain why people from nearby New York City had burrowed through the Hudson Tubes[1] for the event. Others had arrived from Philadelphia, Baltimore, and even greater distances to witness this contest. Most striking was the large number of blacks in the crowd, many undoubtedly attending a minor league baseball game for the first time. In the small area reserved for reporters chaotic conditions prevailed. "The press box was as crowded as the subway during rush hours," wrote one of its denizens[2] in the Montreal *Gazette*. On the field photographers "seemed to be under everybody's feet." The focus of their attention was a handsome, broad-shouldered athlete in the uniform of the visiting Montreal Royals. When he batted in the first inning, he would be the first black man in the twentieth century to play in organized baseball. Jackie Robinson was about to shatter the color barrier.

"This in a way is another Emancipation Day for the Negro race," wrote sportswriter Baz O'Meara of Montreal's *Daily Star*, "a day that Abraham Lincoln would like." Wendell Smith, the black sportswriter of the Pittsburgh *Courier* who had recommended Robinson to Brooklyn Dodger President Branch Rickey, reported, "Everyone sensed the significance of the occasion as Robinson . . . marched with the Montreal team to deep centerfield for the raising of the Stars and Stripes and the 'Star-Spangled Banner.' We sang lustily and freely for this was a great day." And in the playing area, the black ballplayer partook in the ceremonies "with a lump in my throat and my heart beating rapidly, my stomach feeling as if it were full of feverish fireflies with claws on their feet."

Six months had passed since Rickey had surprised the nation by signing Robinson to play for the Dodgers' top farm club. It had been a period of intense speculation about the wisdom of Rickey's action. Many predicted that the effort to integrate baseball would prove abortive,[3] undermined by opposition from players and fans, or by Robinson's own inadequacies as a ballplayer. Renowned as a collegiate football and track star, Robinson had played only one season in professional baseball with the Kansas City Monarchs of the Negro National League. Upon

---

1. Hudson Tubes: subway tunnels under the Hudson River.

2. denizens: inhabitants.

3. abortive: unsuccessful.

Robinson's husky, inexperienced shoulders rested the fate of desegregation in baseball.

Robinson's experiences in spring training had dampened optimism. Compelled to endure the indignities of the Jim Crow[4] South, barred by racism from many ballparks, and plagued by a sore arm, Robinson had performed poorly in exhibition games. One reporter suggested that had he been white, the Royals would have dropped him immediately. Other experts also expressed grave doubts. Jim Semler, owner of the New York Black Yankees, commented before the opener, "The pace in the IL is very fast. . . . I doubt that Robinson will hit the kind of pitching they'll be dishing up to him." And Negro League veteran Willie Wells predicted, "It's going to take him a couple of months to get used to International League pitching."

Robinson, the second Montreal batter, waited anxiously as "Boss" Hague threw out the first ball and leadoff hitter Marvin Rackley advanced to the plate. Rackley, a speedy center fielder from South Carolina, grounded out to the shortstop. Robinson then strode to the batter's box, his pigeon-toed gait enhancing the image of nervousness. His thick neck and tightly muscled frame seemed more appropriate to his earlier gridiron exploits than to the baseball diamond.

Many had speculated about the crowd reaction. Smith watched anxiously from the press box to see "whether the fears which had been so often expressed were real or imagined." In the stands Jackie's wife, Rachel, wandered through the aisles, too nervous to remain in her seat. "You worry more when you are not participating than when you are participating," she later explained, "so I carried the anxiety for Jack." Standing at home plate, Jackie Robinson avoided looking at the spectators, "for fear I would see only Negroes applauding—that the white fans would be sitting stony-faced or yelling epithets."[5] The capacity crowd responded with a polite, if unenthusiastic, welcome.

Robinson's knees felt rubbery; his palms, he recalled, seemed "too moist to grip the bat." Warren Sandell, a promising young left-hander, opposed him on the mound. For five pitches Robinson did not swing and the count ran to three and two. On the next pitch, Robinson hit a bouncing ball to

---

4. Jim Crow: (from the name of a stereotype black in a musical act) discrimination against blacks by legal enforcement or traditional approval.
5. epithets: abuse and insults

the shortstop who easily retired him at first base. Robinson returned to the dugout accompanied by another round of applause. He had broken the ice.

Neither side scored in the first inning. In the second the Royals tallied twice on a prodigious home run by right fielder Red Durrett. Robinson returned to the plate in the third inning. Sandell had walked the first batter and surrendered a single to the second. With two men on base and nobody out, the Giants expected Robinson, already acknowledged as a master bunter, to sacrifice. Sandell threw a letter-high fastball, a difficult pitch to lay down. But Robinson did not bunt. The crowd heard "an explosive crack as bat and ball met and the ball glistened brilliantly in the afternoon sun as it went hurtling high and far over the left field fence," 330 feet away. In his second at-bat in the International League, Robinson had hit a three-run home run.

Robinson trotted around the bases with a broad smile on his face. As he rounded third, Manager Clay Hopper, the Mississippian who reportedly had begged Rickey not to put Robinson on his team, gave him a pat on the back. "That's the way to hit 'em, Jackie," exclaimed Rackley in his southern drawl. All of the players in the dugout rose to greet him, and John Wright, a black pitcher recruited to room with Robinson, laughed in delight. In the crowded press box, Wendell Smith turned to Joe Bostic of the *Amsterdam News* and the two black reporters "laughed and smiled. . . . Our hearts beat just a little faster and the thrill ran through us like champagne bubbles." Most of their white colleagues seemed equally pleased, though one swore softly, according to one account, and "there were some very long faces in the gathering" as well.

The black second baseman's day had just begun. In the fifth inning, with the score 6–0, Robinson faced Giant relief pitcher Phil Oates. The "dark dasher," as Canadian sportswriters came to call Robinson, bunted expertly and outraced the throw "with something to spare." During spring training Rickey had urged the fleet-footed Robinson "to run those bases like lightning. . . . Worry the daylights out of the pitchers." Robinson faked a start for second base on the first pitch. On the next he took off, easily stealing the base. Robinson danced off second in the unnerving style that would become his trademark. Tom Tatum, the Montreal batter, hit a ground ball to third. Robinson stepped backwards, but as the Jersey City fielder released the ball, he broke for third, narrowly beating the return throw.

Robinson had stolen second base and bluffed his way to third. He now determined to steal home to complete the cycle. He took a long lead, prompting Oates to throw to third to hold him on base. On the pitch he started toward home plate, only to stop halfway and dash back. The crowd, viewing the Robinson magic for the first time, roared. On the second pitch, Robinson accelerated again, causing Oates to halt his pitching motion in mid-delivery. Oates had balked and the umpire waved Robinson in to score. Earlier Robinson had struck with power; now he had engineered a run with speed. The spectators, delighted with the daring display of baserunning, went wild, screaming, laughing, and stamping their feet. Blacks and whites, Royal fans and Giant fans, baseball buffs and those there to witness history, all joined in the ensuing pandemonium.[6]

One flaw marred Robinson's performance. "By manner of proving that he was only human after all," according to one reporter, Robinson scarred his debut with a fielding error in the bottom of the inning. Acting as middleman in a double play, he unleashed an errant throw that allowed the Giants to score their only run. Otherwise, Robinson affirmed his reputation as an exceptional fielder.

In the seventh inning, Robinson triggered yet another Royal rally. He singled sharply to right field, promptly stole another base, and scored on a triple by Johnny Jorgenson. Before the inning had ended two more runs crossed the plate to increase the Royal lead to 10–1. In the eighth frame Robinson again bunted safely, his fourth hit in the contest. Although he did not steal any bases, he scrambled from first to third on an infield hit. Once again he unveiled his act, dashing back and forth along the baseline as the pitcher wound up. Hub Andrews, the third Jersey City pitcher, coped with this tactic no better than his predecessor. Andrews balked and for the second time in the game umpires awarded Robinson home plate. According to a true baseball aficionado,[7] this established "some kind of a record for an opening night game."

The Royals won the game 14–1. Montreal pitcher Barney DeForge threw an effortless eight-hitter and Durrett clubbed two home runs. But, as the Pittsburgh *Courier's* front-page headline gleefully announced, JACKIE "STOLE THE SHOW." "He did everything but help the ushers seat the crowd," crowed Bostic. In five trips to the plate Robinson made four hits, including a three-run home run, scored four times, and drove in three runs. He also stole two bases and scored twice by provoking the pitcher to balk.

---

6. **pandemonium:** confusion, wild uproar.
7. **aficionado:** fan.

"Eloquent as they were, the cold figures of the box score do not tell the whole story," indicated the *New York Times* reporter in an assessment that proved prophetic of Robinson's baseball career. "He looked as well as acted the part of a real baseball player."

"This would have been a big day for any man," reported the *Times,* "but under the special circumstances, it was a tremendous feat." Joe Bostic, who accompanied his story in the *Amsterdam News* with a minute-by-minute account of Robinson's feats in the game, waxed lyrical. "Baseball took up the cudgel[8] for Democracy," wrote Bostic, "and an unassuming, but superlative Negro boy ascended the heights of excellence to prove the rightness of the experiment. And prove it in the only correct crucible[9] for such an experiment—the crucible of white hot competition."

Responding to What You Read

1. Why was there such a crowd on opening day at Roosevelt Stadium in Jersey City, New Jersey?

2. Why was Jackie Robinson's first hit in the International League so startling?

3. Suppose that Robinson had struck out each time he came to bat. What effect do you think this would have had on his career? on the careers of other African Americans in professional sports?

Writer's Workshop

Attend a sporting event at your school. Report it accurately in an article, including quotations from at least three different people, including a coach and at least one player, on aspects of the game.

---

8. cudgel: a short, heavy club.

9. crucible: a place where forces interact to produce change; a vessel used for melting substances that require great heat.

PERSPECTIVES

Take the Plunge

Gloria Emerson

Sky Diving

Richmond Lattimore

These authors provide two perspectives on sky diving—one from the air and one from the ground. What similarities do both find in the event?

ABOUT THE AUTHOR•ABOUT THE AUTHOR•ABOUT THE AUTHOR•ABOUT THE AUTHOR

*G*loria Emerson covered four wars, including Vietnam, for the New York Times. *Later, she lived in the Gaza Strip in the Middle East to witness and understand Palestinian resistance to Israeli occupation; her book* Gaza *tells of her experiences there. Emerson's book on the Vietnam War and its effects on America,* Winners and Losers, *won a National Book Award in 1978.*

Take the Plunge

It was usually men who asked me why I did it. Some were amused, others puzzled. I didn't mind the jokes in the newspaper office where I worked about whether I left the building by window, roof or in the elevator. The truth is that I was an unlikely person to jump out of an airplane, being neither graceful, daring nor self-possessed. I had a bad back, uncertain ankles, and could not drive with competence because of deficient depth perception and a fear of all buses coming toward me. A friend joked that if I broke any bones I would have to be shot because I would never mend.

I never knew why I did it. It was in May, a bright and dull May, the last May that made me want to feel reckless. But there was nothing to do then at the beginning of a decade that changed almost everything. I could not wait that May for the Sixties to unroll. I worked in women's news; my stories came out like little cookies. I wanted to be brave about something, not just about love, or a root canal, or writing that the shoes at Arnold Constable looked strangely sad.

Once I read of men who had to run so far it burned their chests to breathe. But I could not run very far. Jumping from a plane, which required no talent or endurance, seemed perfect. I wanted to feel the big, puzzling lump on my back that they promised was a parachute, to take serious strides in the absurd black boots that I believed all generals wore.

I wanted all of it: the rising of a tiny plane with the door off, the earth rushing away, the plunge, the slap of the wind, my hands on the back straps, the huge curve of white silk above me, the drift through the space we call sky.

It looked pale green that morning I fell into it, not the baby blue I expected. I must have been crying; my cheeks were wet. Only the thumps of a wild heart made noise; I did not know how to keep it quiet.

That May, that May my mind was as clear as clay. I did not have the imagination to perceive the risks, to understand that if the wind grew nasty I might be electrocuted on high-tension wires, smashed on a roof, drowned in water, hanged in a tree. I was sure nothing would happen, because my intentions were so good, just as young soldiers start out certain of their safety because they know nothing.

Friends drove me to Orange, Massachusetts, seventy miles west of Boston, for the opening of the first U.S. sports parachuting center, where I was to perform. It was the creation, the passion, of a Princetonian and an ex-Marine named Jacques Istel, who organized the first U.S. jumping team in 1956. Parachuting was "as safe as swimming," he kept saying, calling it the "world's most stimulating and soul-satisfying sport." His center was for competitions and the teaching of sky diving. Instead of hurtling toward the earth, sky divers maintain a swan-dive position, using the air as a cushion to support them while they maneuver with leg and arm movements until the ripcord must be pulled.

None of that stuff was expected from any of us in the little beginners class. We were only to jump, after brief but intense instruction, with Istel's newly designed parachute, to show that any dope could do it. It was a parachute with a thirty-two-foot canopy; a large cutout hole funneled escaping air. You steered with two wooden knobs instead of having to pull hard on the back straps, or risers. The new parachute increased lateral speed, slowed down the rate of descent, reduced oscillation. We were told we could even land standing up but that we should bend our knees and lean to one side. The beginners jumped at eight A.M., the expert skydivers performed their dazzling tricks later when a crowd came.

Two of us boarded a Cessna 180 that lovely morning, the wind no more than a trickle. I was not myself, no longer thin and no longer fast. The jump suit, the equipment, the helmet, the boots, had made me into someone thick and clumsy, moving as strangely as if they had put me underwater and said I must walk. It was hard to bend, to sit, to stand up. I did not like the man with me; he was eager and composed. I wanted to smoke, to go to the bathroom, but there were many straps around me that I did not understand. At twenty-three hundred feet, the hateful, happy man went out, making a dumb thumbs-up sign.

When my turn came, I suddenly felt a stab of pain for all the forgotten soldiers who balked and were kicked out, perhaps shot, for their panic and for delaying the troops. I was hooked to a static line, an automatic opening device, which made it impossible to lie down or tie myself to something. The drillmaster could not hear all that I shouted at him. But he knew the signs of mutiny and removed my arms from his neck. He took me to the doorway, sat me down, and yelled "Go!" or "Now!" or "Out!" There was nothing to do but be punched by the wind, which knocked the spit from my mouth, reach for the wing strut, hold on hard, kick back the feet so weighted and helpless in those boots, and let go. The parachute opened with a plop, as Istel had sworn to me that it would. When my eyelids opened as well, I saw the white gloves on my hands were old ones from Saks Fifth Avenue, gloves I wore with summer dresses. There was dribble on my chin; my eyes and nose were leaking. I wiped everything with the gloves.

There was no noise; the racket of the plane and wind had gone away. The cold and sweet stillness seemed an astonishing, undreamed-of gift. Then I saw what I had never seen before, will never see again; endless sky and earth in colors and textures no one had ever described. Only then did the parachute become a most lovable and docile toy: this wooden knob to go left, this wooden knob to go right. The pleasure of being there, the drifting and the calm, rose to a fever; I wanted to stay pinned in the air and stop the ground from coming closer. The target was a huge arrow in a sandpit. I was cross to see it, afraid of nothing now, for even the wind was kind and the trees looked soft. I landed on my feet in the pit with a bump, then sat down for a bit. Later that day I was taken over to meet General James Gavin, who had led the 82nd Airborne in the D-Day landing at Normandy. Perhaps it was to prove to him that the least promising pupil, the gawkiest, could jump. It did not matter that I stumbled and fell before him in those boots, which walked with a will of their own. Later, Mr. Istel's mother wrote me a charming note of congratulations. Everyone at the center was pleased; in fact, I am sure they were surprised. Perhaps this is what I had in mind all the time.

ABOUT THE AUTHOR•ABOUT THE AUTHOR•ABOUT THE AUTHOR•ABOUT THE AUTHOR

*R*ichmond Lattimore was born in 1906. His books of poetry include Sestina for a Far-Off Summer *and his translations of* The Iliad *and* The Odyssey. *He was the recipient of the National Institute of Arts and Letters Award. Lattimore died in 1984.*

Sky Diving

They step from the high plane and begin to tumble
down. Below is the painted ground, above
is bare sky. They do not fumble
with the catch, but only fall; drop sheer; begin to move

5   in the breakless void; stretch and turn, freed
from pressure; stand in weightless air
and softly walk across their own speed;
gather and group, these dropping bundles, where

the neighbor in the sky stands, reach touch
10   and clasp hands, separate and swim
back to station (did swimmer ever shear such
thin water?) falling still. Now at last pull the slim

cord. Parasols bloom in the air, slow
the swift sky fall. Collapsed tents cover
15   the ground. They rise up, plain people now.
Their little sky-time is over.

Responding to What You Read

1. What are some of the reasons Gloria Emerson gives for wanting to sky dive? At the end of the essay, what does she think might have been her reason all along?

2. How do the perspectives about sky diving differ in Emerson's and Lattimore's pieces? Explain your answer.

Writer's Workshop

Attempt a sporting activity—not a dangerous or risky one—that you haven't tried before or at which you haven't been very successful when you did try. It could be running and shooting in field hockey, or trying to hit a golf or tennis ball. Then report in a short essay of three or four paragraphs exactly what the activity was like. Be sure to include as many specific details as possible, as Gloria Emerson did.

Alternate Media Response

Find a medium—painting? music?—in which you can create the feeling of drifting through the air that each of these pieces of writing evokes.

Why I Play the Game

Morgan McCarthy

Life without teamwork would be pretty difficult. What does teamwork mean to this writer?

ABOUT THE AUTHOR•ABOUT THE AUTHOR•ABOUT THE AUTHOR•ABOUT THE AUTHOR

Morgan McCarthy was born in 1980. In high school she received three varsity letters in field hockey, three in softball, and four in winter track. She was one of three tri-captains for field hockey during her senior year and was named to the All-County field hockey team as a center midfielder in both her junior and senior years as well as receiving recognition at the state level. In 1999, Morgan McCarthy was honored by the National Association for Girls and Women in Sport. Currently she is a student at Vanderbilt University.

Why I Play the Game

The first thing that my Advanced Placement English teacher warned us about writing college essays was that colleges did not want to see stories about sports, and "the big game." He spoke of the cliché which surrounded the mere idea of writing about such events, and quickly moved on to discuss our homework for that evening. I cannot, however, think of an experience in my life which has been more significant to me than belonging to a team like the one that I've been lucky enough to be a part of for the past four years.

I glanced up at the scoreboard, not knowing what to wish for. It was the county semi-finals and there were two minutes left in regulation time. The score was tied at one goal apiece. I swallowed, and prayed for our defense to send the ball up.

I heard the referee counting down from ten seconds, and I realized that we had made it to overtime. At the sound of the whistle I forced my legs to jog off the field, ignoring the burning from sixty minutes of non-stop field hockey. I reached the sideline, dropped my stick to the ground, and, hands on my hips, gazed at the brilliant sky while I struggled to regain my breath. I heard my coach as if she were speaking through a tin can, her voice echoing dimly in my ears.

"Girls, you must remember why you're here. How you got here. Each and every one of you knows . . . ."

Why was I there, on that uncharacteristically warm November afternoon, praying to anyone who would listen, running up and down a field until I felt as if my legs were two dead weights and my heart wanted to give out? I smiled as I remembered the answer. The most simple and natural human emotion that existed, of course. I loved the game. I loved banging the dirt and grass out of my cleats at the end of practice. I loved my stick, taped and retaped too many times, adorned with stickers of every size, shape, and variety imaginable. Most importantly, I loved my team. I loved being a part of a group of people who were so very different, so totally individual, yet so willing to become one. We were a team of 17 girls joined not by 17 red and black plaid kilts, but by the dread of sprints at the end of a long practice, and the thrill of victory in games that we weren't supposed to win.

There were two minutes left before we were to start overtime. I reached for my green water bottle, covered in permanent marker letters from my hockey pals. Missy, our goalie, quietly moved beside me, and then placed her goalie glove on top of my head, causing my bandana to slide out of place. She reached over to pull it back into place, as she giggled under her goalie equipment. And as I had done so many times before, I reached my hand out to hold her mask in place, while I poured ice water into her mouth through the bars which protected her face. I took another sip, and then placed the bottle on the bench. Missy and I had begun this sport together four years before as good friends, and over the four years we had grown even closer. Four years of sweat, smiles, and tears had bonded us for life.

A whistle jolted me back to the present. I grabbed Missy's hand, and Elizabeth held mine. We whispered our poem, *If there was ever a time to dare, to make a difference, to embark on something worth doing, the time is now* . . . . 17 girls joined by 17 sets of callused hands and tangled fingers bowed their heads in unison. Another whistle, and then the team, led by the three captains, two other girls and me, jogged onto the field with a new-found burst of energy.

Three ten-minute overtimes later, the game was still tied. The team that was waiting to play after us stood at the fence, rooting against us, afraid of possibly facing us. Their cheers for our opponents were drowned out by the reckless cheers erupting from our fans. With every step I took, I felt a sharp pain following the path of the Nike swoosh along my cleat, but, unwilling to stop, I ignored it.

I was fighting for a chance at the county title. I was battling for it, in fact. And in the end, it was my team—our team—that shed the tears of victory in the warm grass. We had earned a chance to be county champs. And the next week, we would take that chance, and once again, I would be reminded of why I played the game.

Responding to What You Read

1. What are the specific reasons Morgan McCarthy gives for "playing the game"?

2. The headnote to this selection points out that life would be difficult without teamwork. Keep in mind that teamwork extends beyond the playing fields. Do you agree or disagree with this? Explain your position.

Writer's Workshop

As any good writer does, Morgan McCarthy *names things* in this piece of writing. List as many specific details as you can that McCarthy includes in her essay to capture what playing the game of field hockey is like for her.

Then, write a similar essay, of similar length, about some sporting experience you have had—even if you didn't like it—and include all the key specific details. Make us feel as if we are there.

PERSPECTIVES

Lou Gehrig—An American Hero

Paul Gallico

Great Day for Baseball in the 90s

Harvey Araton

In 1939, baseball-great Lou Gehrig set a record for consecutive games played. In 1995, a more recent baseball-great, Cal Ripken, Jr., broke that record.

Lou Gehrig—An American Hero

Out by the flagpole in center field of the Yankee Stadium, the ball park which during the glittering Golden Decade was the home of the greatest slugging team baseball had ever known, there stands a newly erected bronze plaque.

On it in relief is the bust of a man wearing a baseball cap and uniform. And the inscription reads:

Henry Louis Gehrig. June 19, 1903-June 2, 1941. A man, a gentleman, and a great ball player, whose amazing record of 2,130 consecutive games should stand for all time. This memorial is a tribute from the Yankee players to their beloved captain and teammate, July 4, 1941.

Henry Louis Gehrig was born at 179th Street and Amsterdam Avenue, Manhattan, on June 19, 1903. His father, Henry Gehrig, was an artisan, an ironworker; that is, he made ornamental grilles for doors and railings and balustrades—when he could get work at his trade. When he couldn't, he did odd jobs, until he landed a steady job as a janitor. Christina Gehrig, the mother, was a solid German hausfrau who knew her place in life was the kitchen, and her duty to feed and look after her family.

His early home life was European in the sense that less affection was shown Lou than is usual in, let us say, a typical American home. In the German home, the father is king, and among the poorer people who are engaged in a constant struggle for existence there is little time for a senti-mental relationship between parents and children. Henry Louis was no stranger to corporal punishment at the hands of his father.

Early in life he became imbued with a sense of his own worthlessness which he never overcame to the end of his days. He just never understood how he could possibly be any good, or how anybody could really love him. When he married, he used to break his wife's heart with the constant reproaches he cast at himself. Her most difficult task was to build in him some slight sense of true worth.

As a man, his greatest handicap was that he was supersensitive, shy, self-accusing, quick to take hurt and slow to recover therefrom.

His boyhood was responsible for this. He was a big boy for his age, and slow-witted. Smaller kids would gang up and chase him. They called him "chicken heart," threw stones at him, chased him away from their games, hooted his ineptness at things that came naturally to them.

Eventually, he won some measure of tolerance. He swam with the other boys off the old coal barge in the Harlem River near the High Bridge, got chased by cops and once was even arrested for swimming without trunks. There was a fine scandal in the Gehrig household when Pop had to come down to the police station and bring him home. Their boy in jail already! A bummer he was becoming with them good-for-nothing loafers. Louie got a good smacking.

But when he was fourteen, America entered the First World War and the inevitable witch-hunts spread even to his neighborhood. His old folks were Germans, and Germans were enemies. That terrible time, too, had its effect on the character of the boy. Added to his poverty and awkwardness, it drove him still farther away from his own kind, pitched him still lower in his own estimation.

There was nothing at which he was very good: neither studies nor baseball. He was an undistinguished fifth wheel on the P.S. 132 ball team, a left-handed catcher who couldn't hit the length of his cap, a chicken heart who was so ball-shy at the plate that even when he reached college he had to be cured of batting with one foot practically in the dugout.

But no matter what the atmosphere of the Gehrig home or the handicaps of poverty, one thing must not be forgotten. Mama Gehrig was insistent that her Louie avail himself of the great opportunity provided by this new land— education. Poor they might be, and insignificant in the social scale, but he had the same opportunity to become educated as the richest boy in the land.

And so when Gehrig was graduated from P. S. 132, instead of being sent out to find work to augment the meager family budget, he entered New York's famous High School of Commerce at 65th Street near Amsterdam Avenue.

Commerce was a long distance from upper Amsterdam Avenue, but his parents provided him with carfare, or he walked or hitched on delivery wagons. He had his lunch box and a nickel for a bottle of milk in the General Organization lunchroom.

The rebuffs he suffered as a boy when he tried to play with the kids on the block had already had their effect upon him. Oliver Gintel, now a prosperous furrier in New York, writes:

"In my first year at Commerce, I was trying to get a berth on the soccer team. In practice one day, I kicked the ball accidentally towards a huskily built boy who booted the thing nonchalantly almost the length of the practice field.

"I approached him to try out for the team. He refused, stating that he wasn't good at athletics, and besides, his mother wouldn't give him permission. Later I went to work on him in earnest and eventually Lou did make the team, playing for three seasons as halfback. We won the winter championship for three successive years while he was a member of the team."

Apparently, Lou managed to convert his parents to the importance of sport in the life of an American boy, for he also played on the football team and returned to his first love, baseball. But the curious thing was that, whereas he was a brilliant soccer player and a capable prospect on the football field, he was a poor performer on the diamond. He was made a first baseman, and in his first year batted only .150.

But here entered two factors that were to follow him through life. The first was his own dogged persistence and his desire to learn and improve himself, and the second was the faith in him that somehow, in spite of his clumsiness and awkwardness, he inspired in the men who taught the game.

Harry Kane, coach of the Commerce baseball team, was the first of these, and Gehrig always gave him full credit for correcting his early faults as a hitter. Day after day, Kane would take the boy and pitch to him for fifteen-minute stretches. The next year he was already hitting .300.

Then, a crisis overtook the family, one that threatened to bring his education to an end. His father was stricken with some temporary form of paralysis and was no longer able to work.

But brave and determined, Mama Gehrig went to work as a cook and housekeeper for a fraternity house at Columbia University and took in washing on the side.

Young Lou went to work too, after school hours. He got jobs—in butcher shops and grocery stores, running errands, minding kids, delivering papers. And somehow he managed to attend baseball practice as well.

In his final year at Commerce, Gehrig caught his first real glimpses of the world into which he was soon to move. For one thing, he took a part-time job as a waiter in the fraternity house at Columbia where his mother was cooking and housekeeping. And for another he took his first trip away from home, when the then recently born *Daily News* sent the championship Commerce baseball team out to Chicago to play an inter-city game with Lane Tech High.

The New York boys beat the Chicago boys by the score of 12 to 6. Lou Gehrig, the first baseman, didn't get a hit in three times at bat, but the fourth time he appeared at the platter the bases were full and Gehrig poled one over the right field wall and out of the park.

It was a robust clout, and as a result for the first time the shadow of a Great Personage fell athwart the kid player. A reformed pitcher who had come to the New York Yankees from the Boston Red Sox had been hitting a prodigious number of home runs for them. His name, of course, was Babe Ruth. And the newspapers called Lou Gehrig the "Babe Ruth of High Schools."

Babe Ruth! Lou Gehrig! Two names that were to be coupled for so long. And always Babe Ruth first and Lou Gehrig after. Strange that even on his first day of glory he should fall under the great shadow of the Babe. Strange, that is, now that we can see his career as a whole and realize how long Lou Gehrig played in the shadow of Ruth; how long it was before he came into his own, and how tragically short his glory was then.

Lou Gehrig was graduated from Commerce and in 1922 matriculated at Columbia University, aided by a scholarship awarded him, perhaps not for what lay between his ears so much as for his 210 pounds of bone and muscle and the fact that he was willing to give on the field of sport.

Lou Gehrig went out for baseball in the spring and brought the love-light to the eyes of Andy Coakley, Columbia coach and former pitcher for the Philadelphia Athletics. Andy made a pitcher out of him, took up the batting lessons where Kane had left off, and pretty soon Lou Gehrig was poling them high, wide and handsome over the college fences. He hit seven home runs in one season, one of them the longest ever seen at South Field, and batted over .540.

And he won a new name. They called him the "Babe Ruth of Columbia."

A collegian who could sock a baseball as far as Gehrig was hitting them would naturally attract the attention of the major-league scouts, and Paul Kritchell, famous Yankee scout, had seen enough of Gehrig to convince the management that he was worth signing.

Kritchell approached Andy Coakley and Gehrig, but at first all offers were turned down, because to Mama Gehrig a man who did nothing but play games, even if it was for money, was nothing but a loafer and a no-good.

Then for the second time disaster in the form of illness struck at Lou's home and his career, and Gehrig was called upon to make a stern and important choice. Mom Gehrig contracted double pneumonia, Pop Gehrig was still sickly and unable to work, and life closed in on the Gehrigs. Bills and more bills. Not a cent in the house, and nothing coming in.

There has been a considerable discussion as to how much, in cold cash, Lou Gehrig actually cost the New York Yankees. According to Gehrig, he received $500 for making the momentous decision to sign a contract with organized baseball.

That $500 was the biggest sum of money that any of the Gehrigs had ever seen. It came at a time when it was desperately needed. It paid rent and doctors and hospital bills and nurses.

Education or no, Mom was ill and needed attention. That's all there was to it. Kritchell was there at the right time with the contract and the money, and Gehrig signed.

But there were to be many discouraging moments and frustrations before Gehrig heard Miller Huggins, the Yankee manager, say one spring, "All right, Gehrig. Get in there in place of Pipp."

Because for all his big frame, loud voice and quick smile, Lou Gehrig was one of those strange souls who seem born to be frustrated, to have glory and happiness always within their reach, even in their grasp, only to have them snatched away.

Although Gehrig did not realize it, when he was farmed out to Hartford in the Eastern League and then, in 1925, spent a lot of time on the Yankee bench, he was a carefully planned spark plug in the new baseball machine Miller Huggins was building to replace the worn-out one that had won three pennants in 1921-23. Ruth was still the big siege gun, but the rest of the team was getting old. Teams fall apart that way, because most major-league teams are part seasoned veterans and part peppery youngsters. When the veterans go, replacements must be found, and it is in those periods that the big teams will be found out of the money.

But when he chafed on the Yankee bench in 1925, Lou Gehrig, young and ambitious, had no picture of the patient plans of such a master builder of championship ball teams as Miller Huggins. Once, when Huggins was shipping some ivory[1] off to St. Paul, Gehrig begged Hug to send him too. He was asking to be sent from a great major league club back to the minors, so that he might be able to play ball. He was tired of sitting on the bench.

From Huggins he got a lecture he never forgot. "Lou," Hug said, "I'm not going to send you off to St. Paul. You're going to stay right on that bench and learn baseball. You may think you know as much as those fellows out on the field, but you don't. You got a lot to learn, and there's no way to learn it right now except on the bench. Those fellers out there had to do the same thing when they were young. Your turn will come. I want you to sit next to me for a while on the bench. I'll help you."

It put an entirely new light on things for Lou. The bench no longer was a penance and a trial; it became a school. Sitting next to Huggins, Lou learned to appraise every batter who came up to the plate: he memorized the placement of the batter's hits, noted how the infield lined up to handle him. He learned to watch the pitchers: how they pitched, what they pitched, what their strategy was in a tight spot; their mannerisms, little telltale motions toward first—in short, he absorbed anything and everything that would help him to play the game when his time came. Baseball, he discovered, was a painstaking profession, an exhaustive and never-ending study.

Then in May, first baseman Wallie Pipp was beaned in batting practice and became subject to violent headaches. On June first, Gehrig replaced him. Thereafter, for fourteen years and 2,130 consecutive games, he was never off first base, except for one game which he started at shortstop merely to be in the line-up and preserve his great consecutive-games record at a time when he was bent double with lumbago.[2]

From now on the tale of Lou Gehrig is a continuous upward climb to fame and success beyond his dreams. In 1927 he was already daring to challenge Babe Ruth for the home-run championship.

---

1 ivory: baseball slang: players.
2. lumbago: a rheumatic pain around the hips.

In 1926, the American League pitchers were unconvinced about Gehrig's hitting ability and still kept pitching those four wide ones to the Babe in times of crisis. Then Lou would come up and bust the lemon out of the county and there would go your old ball game.

By 1927 word went around the league: "Don't pass the Babe to get at Gehrig. Bad medicine!" So they had to pitch to Babe. And the Babe got sixty home runs. But Lou got the valuable-player award.

Success in full measure now came to Henry Louis Gehrig, the American-born son of immigrant German parents. He had fame, money, popularity, love and companionship, and thanks to his wife Eleanor, even a little self-assurance.

The awkward boy who could neither bat nor field as a youngster had, by his unswerving persistence, his gnawing ambition, his tenacity and iron will power, made himself into the greatest first baseman in the history of organized baseball.

In 1934, Lou won the triple batting championship of the American League and gave it to his league in hitting that year, batting .363, hitting 49 home runs, and driving in 165 runs.

In 1936, Lou was again named the most valuable player in the American League, exactly nine years after he had first achieved this honor. His salary had been mounting steadily, and in 1938 he signed for the largest sum he ever received for playing ball, $39,000.

Toward the end of the last decade, the name, the figure, and above all, the simple engaging personality of Lou Gehrig became welded into the national scene. Came the baseball season, came Gehrig. Came Gehrig, came home runs, triples, doubles, excitement and faultless play around first base. And his consecutive-games record went on and on. Sick or well, he never missed a game.

Lou played with colds. He played with fevers. He played so doubled over with lumbago that it was impossible for him to straighten up, and bent over the plate, he still got himself a single.

In 1934, the year he won the triple crown, he fractured a toe. He played on. He was knocked unconscious by a wild pitch, suffered a concussion that would hospitalize the average man for two weeks. He was at his position the next day and collected four hits. When, late in his career, his hands were X-rayed, they found seventeen assorted fractures that had healed by themselves. He had broken every finger on both hands and some twice, and *hadn't even mentioned it* to anyone.

The fantastic thing about all this is not that he was able to endure the pain of the breaks, strains, sprains, pulled and torn tendons, muscles and ligaments, but that it failed to impair his efficiency. On the contrary, if he had something the matter with him it was the signal for him to try all the harder, so that no one, least of all his own severe conscience, could accuse him of being a handicap to his team while playing in crippled condition.

When, in 1939, Lou Gehrig found himself slow in spring training, he began to punish his body for failure that was unaccountable and drive it harder than ever before.

It had begun before that, the slow tragedy of disintegration. Signs and symptoms had been mistaken. During most of 1938, Gehrig had been on a strict diet. That year had not been a good one for him. In the early winter of 1939 he had taken a $5,000 salary slash. Baseball players are paid by the records they compile. That winter, as usual, Lou and Eleanor went ice skating together. Lou was a fine skater. But, strangely, he kept falling all the time.

The teams went South for the 1939 training season and the sports writers went along with them. And the boys with one accord began sending back stories that must have saddened them to write.

What they saw was not unfamiliar to them. The useful playing lifetime of a top-flight professional athlete is on the average shockingly short. A sports writer is quick to notice the first symptoms of slowing up. They were obvious with Gehrig at St. Petersburg. He was slow afoot, afield and at bat. And while he fought like a rookie to hold his position, no improvement was evident. Sadly the sports writers wrote that the old Iron Horse was running down.

But the players on the Yankee ball club were saying something else. They were close to Gehrig. They noticed things that worried and depressed them. And they had knowledge of their craft and of themselves. One of the things they knew was that a ballplayer slows up gradually. His legs go, imperceptibly at first, then noticeably as he no longer covers the ground in the field that he used to cover. But he doesn't come apart all at one time, and in chunks.

There are grim tales of things that happened in the locker room, and one is macabre with overtones of manly nobility. It tells of Gehrig, dressing, leaning over to lace his spikes and falling forward to the floor, to lie momentarily helpless. And it tells further of tough men with the fine instincts to look away and not to hurt his already tortured soul the more by offering help. Quickly they left the locker room, leaving him to struggle to his feet alone with no eyes to see his weakness.

Few men can have gone through the hell that Gehrig did during those days.

Picture the fear, the worry, the helpless bewilderment that must have filled Lou's soul as he found that he could not bat, could not run, could not field. The strain and terror of it lined his face in a few short months and brought gray to his hair. But it could not force a complaint from his lips.

His performance during the early part of 1939 was pitiful. And yet, so great was the spell cast by his integrity, his honest attempts to please and his service over the long years, that the worst-mannered, worst-tempered and most boorish individual in the world, the baseball fan, forebore to heckle him.

On Sunday, April 30, 1939, the Yankees played the Senators in Washington. Lou Gehrig came to bat four times with runners on base. He failed even to meet the ball, and the Yankees lost.

Monday was an off day. Lou went home. He did a lot of thinking, but he did it to himself. He had the toughest decision of his life to make. But he had to make it alone.

Tuesday, May second, the team met in Detroit to open a series against the Tigers. Joe McCarthy flew in from Buffalo. Lou met him in the dugout and said the fateful words:

"Joe, I always said that when I felt I couldn't help the team any more I would take myself out of the line-up. I guess that time has come."

"When do you want to quit, Lou?" asked McCarthy.

Gehrig looked at him steadily and said, "Now. Put Babe Dahlgren in."

Later, alone in the dugout, he wept.

The record ended at 2,130 games.

The newspapers and the sports world buzzed with the sensation of Lou Gehrig's departure from the Yankee line-up.

At the urging of Eleanor, Lou went to the Mayo Clinic at Rochester, Minnesota, for a checkup.

There was a lull in the news. Then, out of a clear sky the storm burst again. Black headlines tore across the page tops like clouds and lightninged their messages: "GEHRIG HAS INFANTILE PARALYSIS." "GEHRIG FIGHTS PARALYZING ILLNESS."

The New York Yankees released the report of the doctors at the clinic. It was a disease diagnosed as amyotrophic lateral sclerosis, interpreted for the layman as a form of infantile paralysis, and the mystery of the too-sudden decline and passing of Henry Louis Gehrig, perennial Yankee first baseman, was solved.

Before Gehrig came home from the Mayo Clinic, Eleanor went to their family physician, gave him the name of the disease and asked to be told the truth. The doctor knew her well. He said quietly, "I think you can take it. And I think you should know."

Then he told her that her husband could not live more than two years.

Before she could give in to grief and shock for the first and last time, Eleanor phoned to the Mayo Clinic. She had but one question to ask the doctors there. "Have you told my husband?"

Gehrig had so captivated the staff that they had not yet had the heart to tell him the truth, and they so advised Eleanor.

She begged, "Please promise me that you never will. Don't ever let him know. I don't want him to find out."

They promised. Only then did Eleanor permit herself to weep.

The time of weeping was short. Lou came home. He came home full of smiles and jokes, and the girl who met him was smiling and laughing too, though neither noticed that in the laughter of the other there was something feverish.

Lou's cheer was based outwardly on the fact that he hadn't been just an aging ballplayer; that his sudden disintegration had been caused by disease—a disease of which he promised Eleanor he would be cured before he learned to pronounce its name.

Eleanor fought a constant fight to keep the truth from Lou. She had to be on the spot always to answer the telephone; to watch over him so that people did not get to him; to look after the mail before he saw it. Ever present was the menace of the one crackpot who might slip through the shields of love she placed about her husband and tell him that his case was hopeless.

As to what Lou knew, he never told.

On July 4, 1939, there took place the most tragic and touching scene ever enacted on a baseball diamond—the funeral services for Henry Louis Gehrig.

Lou Gehrig attended them in person.

Lou Gehrig Appreciation Day, as it was called, was a gesture of love and appreciation on the part of everyone concerned, a spontaneous reaching out to a man who had been good and kind and decent, to thank him for having been so.

Everyone waited for what he would say. With a curled finger he dashed away the tears that would not stay back, lifted his head and brought his obsequies[3] to their heartbreaking, never-to-be-forgotten finish when he spoke his epitaph:

"For the past two weeks you have been reading about a bad break I got. Yet today I consider myself the luckiest man on the face of the earth . . ."

Epilogue

There is an epilogue, because although the tale of Lou Gehrig—An American Hero—really ends above, he lived for quite a while longer, and perhaps in the simple story of how he lived what time was left to him is to be found his greatest gallantry.

Almost two more years had to pass before the end came to Henry Louis Gehrig, and Eleanor says that during that time he was always laughing, cheerful, interested in everything, impatient only of unasked-for sympathy. In short, he lived his daily life.

But he did more. And here we come to the final bit of heroism. With his doom sealed and his parting inevitable from the woman who had given him the only real happiness he had ever known, he chose to spend his last days in work and service.

Mayor LaGuardia appointed him a city parole commissioner. And so for the next months, as long as he was able to walk even with the assistance of others, Gehrig went daily to his office and did his work. He listened to cases, studied them; he brought to the job his thoroughness and his innate kindness and understanding.

On June 2, 1941, Lou Gehrig died in the arms of his wife in their home in Riverdale, New York.

It is not so much the man whom our weary souls have canonized as the things by which he lived and died. And for the seeing of those we must all of us be very grateful.

---

3. obsequies: funeral or burial rites.

ABOUT THE AUTHOR•ABOUT THE AUTHOR•ABOUT THE AUTHOR•ABOUT THE AUTHOR

*H*arvey Araton is a sports columnist for the New York Times *and co-author of* The Selling of the Green, *an in-depth profile of the Boston Celtics basketball franchise. Remembering the night that Cal Ripken broke Lou Gehrig's record for consecutive games played, Araton says, ". . . I took the train from New York's Penn Station down to Baltimore. . . . The train is how the old time ball players traveled, the sportswriters mixing in the card games and the loud conversations amidst the haze of cigarette smoke. At least that is how I've always imagined it, anyway. Somewhere between Philadelphia and Wilmington, Del., I convinced myself that I was riding that Amtrack train into baseball history, and that I would find a way to work that angle into my column that night.*

"And what a night. Ripken punctuated the occasion by hitting a home run, but it was his ceremonial lap of the field, grabbing the hands of the front-row fans and even the players in the opposing dugout, that worked perfectly into my theme. It fit the trip, the event, which was about perseverance, commitment, about an old-fashioned work ethic and a touching appreciation of the fans who for years had come out to watch Cal Ripken play."

Great Day for Baseball in the 90s

You wanted to be on time getting to the ballpark because you had the feeling that the man of the hour would not be late. You wanted time to relax, to reflect, so the best way to come was the way Iron Horse, Lou Gehrig, did.

Along the industrial rail corridor yesterday, passing through the bowels of Newark and Philadelphia and Wilmington, chugging into Baltimore past the decrepit row homes near the old Memorial Stadium and on into Penn Station, you could imagine what baseball was like when the sporting pulse of major American cities beat inside palaces like Oriole Park at Camden Yards.

Downtown, in front of the beautifully nostalgic ball park, you could see lines of fans pinning buttons to their shirts that said: "I Was There." You could see them sprint toward the box seats to watch batting practice. You could hear Bobby Bonilla admit that his camcorder was battery charged and ready.

Finally, you could see Cal Ripken Jr. hit a 3-0 pitch off California's Shawn Boskie into the left-field seats, and you could, after four and a half innings, watch him lap the field, grabbing hands all the way around, pulling America back into baseball.

President Clinton and Joe DiMaggio and 46,000 flash photographers in the stands had come to observe Ripken merely play the game. Ballplayers once routinely carried such magnetism. Maybe Ripken proved last night they could once more.

By the time Ripken trotted out to shortstop for an experience he would describe to the President as "out of body," there really wasn't much left for Ripken to say. With his light blue eyes sparkling beneath the brim of his black and orange cap, with his gray hair trimmed neatly above his ears, the august sight of Ripken manning his position was worth a thousand words, and 2,131 games.

On the train yesterday afternoon, you also had time to bury the late-inning debate about Ripken's uncompromising pursuit of baseball's most esteemed record. The notion that he equal it, then take a day off, was provocative and smart, but ultimately a tease. Gehrig didn't need Ripken's largess. Mickey Mantle prove immortals are those with the aura, not necessarily the numbers.

Even as a kid, you intuitively knew that. You knew those who argued baseball with statistics didn't know what they were talking about. You knew McCovey and Yastrzemski were dangerous just by looking at them with a bat in their hands. Numbers link players who are generations apart; they don't define them.

What's in this number, 2,131, or whatever it will be before Ripken sits down? By real world standards, Ripken takes five months off and works fewer than four hours a day. By baseball's, he is the essence of equanimity, the root of resolve. While people foretell of baseball's doom because it is out of step with an accelerated pace of life, Ripken somehow became a national hero for being in step with what was mythologized as baseball's ultimate appeal.

"We—baseball—really needed this, and Cal came through," said Orioles first baseman Rafael Palmeiro.

Ripken's countdown has given ballplayers an anchor in not only their post-strike season but in their struggle to prove themselves still relevant. Basketball players and football players and even the occasional tennis player and figure skater have seemed more important the last few years. Barry Bonds and Frank Thomas are superb, but do American children really know who they are?

There are also millions of baby boomers like myself who hear Lou Gehrig's name and immediately conjure up Gary Cooper's face. The irony is that Cooper could have played Ripken too.

The man drove his daughter to her first day of school yesterday morning and last night wore a black T-shirt that said: "2,130 + Hugs and Kisses for Daddy." The Democrats' bid for the family values vote began here, with a man who bats and throws right.

He has played the most physically demanding position for close to 14 years without missing a beat. This summer you saw ballplayers in opposing dugouts stand up to applaud. You saw DiMaggio look down last night from his box and wondered if it felt like the 1940s to him again. You saw all of baseball hold Cal Ripken Jr. up to the country as its champion, as its offering of peace. If Lou Gehrig was respected this much by his peers, then he had every reason to feel like the luckiest man on the face of the earth.

Responding to What You Read

1. What common characteristics do Lou Gehrig and Cal Ripken share?

2. In what ways did writer Harvey Araton put Cal Ripken's reaching 2,131 consecutive games in a context larger than the event itself?

3. Why do you think that, even in the face of a terrible disease, Lou Gehrig said, "Yet today I consider myself the luckiest man on the face of the earth"?

Writer's Workshop

1. Richard Hoffer wrote in the December 1995 issue of *Sports Illustrated*, "Cal Ripken Jr., though he'll surely go into the Hall of Fame as a power-hitting shortstop, is not the greatest baseball player ever, or even of his day. But how could he not be our Sportsman of the Year? He's like the rest of us in our little galaxy—but more so." Using Hoffer's article (titled "Hand It to Cal") or the one you just read, write an essay justifying *Sports Illustrated*'s naming of Ripken as Sportsman of the Year. Be as specific as possible with your "evidence."

2. Paul Gallico calls Lou Gehrig "an American hero." In a brief essay, explain why you think Gallico chose this phrase for Gehrig, and then tell whether you think the label is accurate. Be specific in your support or refutation of Gallico's phrase.

Johnson Is Everywhere, Leaving His Critics to Gape

William C. Rhoden

A football player has a game that legends are made of.

ABOUT THE AUTHOR•ABOUT THE AUTHOR•ABOUT THE AUTHOR•ABOUT THE AUTHOR

William C. Rhoden has been a sports reporter for the New York Times *since 1983. Before that he worked as a copy editor on the paper for the Sunday Week in Review section. Earlier in his career Rhoden had been a columnist for the* Baltimore Sun *and an associate editor of* Ebony. *He is a graduate of Morgan State University in Baltimore. William Rhoden and his family live in Brooklyn, New York.*

Johnson Is Everywhere, Leaving His Critics to Gape

Keyshawn Johnson bailed out a lot of people yesterday. He bailed out a Jets team that showed signs of shrinking from its destiny. He bailed out a defense that turned careless and porous. He even bailed out Curtis Martin, his offensive soul mate, whose second-quarter fumble could have put the Jacksonville Jaguars back in the game.

This was a great day on the strength of Johnson's statistics alone: 9 receptions, matching a Jet post-season record, 121 receiving yards and 2 touchdowns—one on a 21-yard pass play and one on a 10-yard reverse. This was also a performance of Thorpe-like[1] dimensions: Johnson caught the ball, Johnson ran the ball and, at the end of a day when the Jets

---

1. Thorpe-like: a reference to Jim Thorpe (1887–1953). Thorpe, who is an Olympic legend and who played both professional baseball and professional football, is considered by many people to be the greatest athlete of the twentieth century.

continued one of the most spectacular resurrections in pro football history, Johnson even intercepted the ball.

With the Jets holding a 10-point lead, Johnson lined up in the defensive
secondary. When Jaguar quarterback Mark Brunell heaved a last-gasp desperation pass, Johnson went up in a crowd. For the few seconds the ball was in the
air, Johnson was back in a Los Angeles schoolyard playing the football version
of King of the Hill, everyone out for himself. Not Jets. Not Jaguars. The toughest player comes down with the ball. Johnson came down with the ball.

As the Jets came off the field and entered their locker room after their
34-24 victory, Johnson held the intercepted ball like a trophy, an affirma-
tion of everything he has done in three years. The book, the bluntness, the
braggadocio—this ball was the exclamation point to a young career that
shifted upward three speeds yesterday.

"He's a tough kid," Coach Bill Parcells of the Jets said after the game.

"Keyshawn's the man," Martin said.

But the defining play of this game, and maybe of Johnson's three-year
National Football League career, took place in the second quarter. On sec-
ond-and-15 at the Jaguar's 22-yard line, Martin fumbled a handoff.

The ball bounced into the arms of Jacksonville's Chris Hudson, who took
off for the end zone. Hudson was at midfield when, apparently possessed by
some Jets demon of yesteryear, he attempted a lateral. The ball slithered
around on the turf until a streaking green jersey broke in and covered it. The
blur of green was Johnson. He had been blocking on the play when he saw
Hudson carrying the ball and the Jets' championship hopes with it.

"I don't think I'm slow, so I said, 'One thing I'm going to do is run,'"
Johnson said. "If they don't catch him, I'm going to make sure I catch him
somewhere down the line. When he went to lateral the ball, someone batted it, and I was right there, but that comes from hustling. If you don't hustle, you never know. They may have the ball, and the game's in a whole
other situation."

Martin, buried beneath a pile, had no idea his blunder was being erased.
"I didn't know where Keyshawn was," Martin said. "When the ball comes
out, it's like a fish being pulled out of water. You're like: 'Where's it at?
Where's it at?' You can't find that ball and the worst feeling is when you
fumble and people are laying on top of you and you can't get to that ball.
You can't think of anything else."

When Martin found out Johnson had recovered the fumble, he went over to him and expressed his gratitude. "I just said: 'Thanks, man. You bailed me out.' I was elated that we got the ball back."

Johnson's was one of those breakthrough performances that spoke for itself but connected with fans who might never have watched a pro game but who could understand a great performance.

As Johnson left the locker room, Tina Thompson, a classmate of Johnson's at Southern California and now a player for the Houston Comets in the Women's National Basketball Association, congratulated him. For Thompson, the Jets' victory was a revelation. This was her first professional football game and the first time she had paid attention to how Johnson did his job.

"I realized that he was good because I saw him play several games at U.S.C.," Thompson said. "But this was special. He's sort of like one of those Jordanesque type players. Today I watched the details: he was blocking, on the fumble he was all the way in the end zone and sprinted upfield to recover the ball. I was definitely impressed."

Thompson was more familiar with Johnson the human being. She wasn't surprised by the storm he had caused with comments about his team, his teammates, his coaches and the news media. Many turned out to be accurate, if unpopular.

"He's very energetic, a very personable person," she said. "He's just very honest. Sometimes the truth might not be so good."

On a day when Jet fans were delirious with joy, the barbs, the criticism, seemed far, far away; whom Johnson has over for dinner, whom he speaks to, whom he ignores—irrelevant. The day's bottom line was that Johnson pulled the Jets closer to the top of a mountain that two seasons ago seemed unconquerable. He did it with an all-round performance that revealed a level of resolve that had to win over Johnson's most vehement critics. Johnson is not a graceful swan of a receiver who soars and glides. He is an angular, indomitable presence who has often been crowded by scrutiny and critics.

Yesterday Johnson earned just a little more elbow room.

Responding to What You Read

What specific things did Keyshawn Johnson do in this game that caused the sportswriter to call it a "breakthrough game" and "Thorpe-like"?

Writer's Workshop

New York Times columnist William C. Rhoden was assigned to write a feature story on a football game between the New York Jets and the Jacksonville Jaguars, based on whatever he saw that interested him about the game. Rhoden chose Keyshawn Johnson's performance to feature in his column about the game, and this is the article you have just read. Reread the following passage from the article.

"Johnson is not a graceful swan of a receiver who soars and glides. He is an angular, indomitable presence who has often been crowded by scrutiny and critics.

"Yesterday Johnson earned just a little more elbow room."

This passage is a fine example of how a writer crafts language. In a paragraph or two analyze what Rhoden does with language to make those three sentences original and vivid. Consider the images Rhoden creates and the literal and figurative interpretations of those images.

In These Girls, Hope Is a Muscle: A Season in the Life of the Amherst Hurricanes

Madeleine H. Blais

A writer takes you to the girls' state basketball championship game.

ABOUT THE AUTHOR•ABOUT THE AUTHOR•ABOUT THE AUTHOR•ABOUT THE AUTHOR

Madeleine H. Blais *wrote a slightly longer version of this piece for the* New York Times Magazine. *It was later expanded into a book with the same title. Blais, who was born in 1947, has worked as an associate professor of journalism at the University of Massachusetts and has written other works of nonfiction.*

In These Girls, Hope Is a Muscle: A Season in the Life of the Amherst Hurricanes

The voice of the coach rises above the din of shuffling footsteps, loud greetings, the slamming of metal, the thud of books. "Listen up. I want you to check right now. Do you have your uniforms? Your shoes and your socks? Do you have any other items of clothing that might be needed?"

Coach Ron Moyer believes it's possible to pack abstractions along with one's gear, intangibles[1] like "intensity" and "game face" and "consistency" and "defense." As the members of the Amherst Regional High School girls' basketball team prepare to board the Hoop Phi Express on their way to the Centrum in Worcester, more than an hour away from the Massachusetts state championship, he tells them, "Today, I want you to pack your courage."

---

1. intangibles: things that can't actually be touched.

The team is 23–1 going into this game, losing only to Agawam, which, like the Haverhill team they are facing this evening, has some real height. Haverhill, known for aggressive ball, nothing dirty but just short of it, has two girls over six feet nicknamed Twin Towers. Moyer has prepped his team with a couple of specialized plays, the Murphy and the Shoelace, and he tells them: "Expect to play a little football." Amherst girls have a reputation for bring afraid to throw their elbows, but this year they have learned to take the words "finesse team"[2] as an insult. Although Coach has been careful to avoid saying "state championship" to goad his team, last fall he did tell one aging gym rat in town, "I have the two best guards in the state and probably the nation, but it all depends on the girls up front. There's an old saying— 'Guards win games, but forwards win championships.' We'll have to see."

At 6 foot 6, Moyer looms over his players. With a thick cap of graying brown hair and bangs that flop down over his forehead, he resembles a grizzly bear on spindly legs. The girls are more like colts. For Moyer, turning them into a team has nothing to do with breaking their spirit and every-thing to do with harnessing it.

As Jen Pariseau listens to Coach before leaving for Worcester, her legs can't stop twitching. One of the six seniors on the team playing high-school hoop together for the last time, she has thick, dark eyebrows and long, lanky limbs. For her, tonight's game is the perfect revenge, not just against Haverhill but also against some of the rebuffs she suffered as an athlete on the way up. For three years, she played on one of Amherst's Little League teams, the Red Sox. She was pitcher, shortstop and first baseman. When it was time to choose the all-star league, she was told her bunts were not up to par.

Jen's teammates are just as hyped up. Half of them are giving the other half piggybacks. There are lots of hand-slapping and nudges. They swirl around one another, everyone making a private point of touching Jamila Wideman, Jen's co-captain, as if one dark-haired, brown-eyed girl could transmit the power of her playing to all the others. Jamila is an all-America, recipient of more than 150 offers of athletic scholarships. On the court, the strong bones on her face are like a flag demanding to be heeded; she is a study in quickness and confidence, the ball becoming a part of her body. Her nickname is Predator.

---

2. "finesse team": team that relies on quickness and skill rather than brute force.

Jen Pariseau is two-time all-Western Mass, and together the two guards delighted fans all season with the way they delivered the ball to each other, sometimes in a dipsy doo behind the back or between the legs, often in an open shot. JennyandJamila. In Amherst, it's one word.

Coach pauses. He looks as though he is about to rebuke the girls for all the squirming, but he shrugs and gives a big smile. "Let's go." Then, perhaps more to himself than to them: "While we're still young."

Shortly after 5 in the evening, the sky is thick and gray and hooded, the cloud cover a welcome hedge against what has been a bitter New England winter. The bus the girls board is different from the usual.

"Hooked up and smooth," says Jen Pariseau, admiring the special features, including upholstered seats, a toilet, four television sets and a VCR mounted on the ceiling—a definite step up from the yellow tin cans they have taken to every other game. There are some cheerleaders on the bus as well as Tricia Lea, an assistant coach with her own high-school memories about what it was like to go up against those Hillies from Haverhill in their brown and yellow uniforms with the short shorts. "Haverhill. I don't know what they eat up there, but they can be slightly ruthless. Sportsmanship does not run very deep in that town."

A few years back, Coach had trouble convincing players and their families of the seriousness of the commitment to girls' basketball. JennyandJamila remember playing in varsity games five and six years ago when the gym would be empty of spectators except for their parents and maybe a few lost souls who had missed the late bus. Coach remembers girls who would cut practice to go to their boyfriends' games, and once during the playoffs, a team captain left to go on a school-sponsored cultural exchange for three weeks in the former Soviet Union. As far as he's concerned, the current policy could not be clearer. You want cultural exchange? You can have it with Hamp [archrival Northampton].

Tonight, Amherst is sending three "pep" buses to the game, unprecedented support for an athletic event, boys' or girls'. Amherst is a place that tends to prize thought over action, tofu over toughness.[3] It prefers to honor the work of the individual dedicated to a life of monastic scholarship rather

---

3. tofu over toughness: preferring things associated with the niceties of life rather than with the nitty-gritty.

than some noisy group effort. But this season, there were sellout crowds. There was even that ultimate badge: a wary cop on the premises for the first time in the history of a girls' event.

To look at the six seniors on the team, who all appear to be lit from within, one would assume that their lives have been seamless journeys. In fact, as Jen Pariseau puts it, she does not come from a "Dan Quayle kind of family"—and neither do most of the others.

Whatever sadness or disruption they've been dealt, an opposite force follows them onto the court. JennyandJamila have not gone it alone; they have had Kathleen's strong right hand, an almost irresistible force heading toward the basket. She never wastes a motion: the ball is in her hands one second, then quietly dropping through the hoop the next, without dramatics, almost like an afterthought. There's Kristin. Her flushed cheeks are not a sign of exhaustion but of some private fury. When the ball comes curling out of the basket, more often than not it is Kristin who has pushed and shoved her way to the prize.

The only underclass starter, Emily Shore, is so serious about her chance to play with the famous JennyandJamila that she spent the bulk of her summer lifting weights and battling in pickup games on Amherst's cracked and weather-ravaged outdoor courts with a succession of skeptical and then grudgingly appreciative young men.

They have become what every opponent fears most: a team with a mission.

As good as it gets. That is, of course, the exact sentiment the girls feel toward their fancy bus.

"Fasten your seat belts," says Coach. "Beverage service will commence shortly after takeoff. There'll be turbulence coming to Haverhill when the Hurricanes hit Worcester." Then he announces the people to whom he would like them to dedicate the entire season. "And that's to the 140 girls who are now playing youth basketball in Amherst for the first time this year."

Jen Pariseau says she wants to read a letter from Diane Stanton, the mother of Chris Stanton, the star of the boys' basketball team.

"Jenny and Jamila," the letter began. Diane Stanton said she was addressing them because she knew them best, but the letter was for the whole team. "Your existence as a team represents a lot of things to a lot of women like me . . . . As a young girl I remember standing outside the Little League fence and watching the boys and knowing that I could hit and catch better than at least a third of them. When our high-school intramural field hockey team and softball team asked for leagues, we were told flatly— NO, because there was no money . . . . When this group of girl athletes got together to form an intramural basketball team, we were subjected to ridicule and anger from some of the student body . . . . I lost courage, I'm embarrassed to admit, in my junior year and would no longer play intra- mural sports. Part of it was a protest against the failure of my school . . . to recognize that we needed to play as much as boys. I know the struggle."

Coach gives the driver a signal and the vehicle starts to roll. A police car just ahead suddenly activates its lights and in a slow ceremony leads the vehicle to the corner of Main and Triangle Streets, where another officer has been summoned to stop traffic. Coach is beaming and silently thanks his old pal, Capt. Charlie Sherpa, over in the Police Department, for coming through. In addition to being a guidance counselor, Moyer has been the girls' coach off and on since 1961, a task he enjoys because unlike with boys, whose arrogance and confidence often have to be eroded before he can get the team to work, this is all constructive. The way to build a team is to build their individual self-confidence.

The bus heads down Main (a street that is most famous for being the site of the house where Emily Dickinson was born, where she lived, died and wrote her poetry) to the corner of Northeast, where they get to run a red light, turning in front of Fort River Elementary School, then heading out to Route 9, where the escort lasts all the way to the town line. In an instant, the sign that says "Entering Pelham" appears, and in another instant a new one looms ahead that says "Entering Belchertown."

The girls watch the film they had chosen unanimously to pump them for the game—*A League of Their Own.*[4] The six seniors are lost in their own thoughts.

Kim Warner knows her mother, who works in personnel at the University of Massachusetts, will be at the game, plus her two sisters, plus her boyfriend's family. Her father lives in Florida, and although she sends him news accounts of all the games, he has never seen her play. She hasn't seen him since the 10th grade. She plans to go to Westfield State and major

---

4. A League of Their Own: 1992 film about an all-women baseball team and their efforts to succeed.

in early childhood education. On the way to the game, Kim writes a fantasy letter in her head: "Dear Dad, At long last a lot of hard work paid off."

Patri Abad's mother, a bilingual teacher, has to be at work, and although Patri will miss her, she knows that she can count on a large cheering section of friends. She almost didn't get to play this year. During her junior year, she had moved to Chicago with her mother and her new stepfather. Patri, who is Cuban on her father's side and Puerto Rican on her mother's, prayed incessantly to the Virgin. She received constant mail from teammates like Lucia Maraniss, back when Lucia was a gushing eighth grader. "Patri, I will always remember you as one of the wisest, most caring and compassionate people I've ever met. I'm going to miss you very, very, very, very, very, very, very, very, very, very, very, very, very, very much."

Whether it was divine intercession or that 14th "very" from Lucia, the resolve of Patri's mother to stay in Chicago eventually vanished. They returned to the Happy Valley, as Amherst is called, and Patri could finish her senior year as a member of the Hurricanes. She has been accepted at Drew, Clark and the University of Massachusetts, pre-med.

Kristin Marvin, also known as Jolly, Jolly Green and Grace (her teammates have misinterpreted her tenacity as clumsiness), is going to Holy Cross College, pre-med. She likes medicine because it has a strong element of knowability. Her parents were divorced when she was young and she lived with a lot of uncertainty. Her mother has since married a builder whose first wife married Kristin's father, who works in Connecticut and often rushes to the games after work in his business suit. The marital realignment has created a circumstance in which the daughter of her stepfather and stepmother is Kristin's double stepsister.

Coach calls Kathleen Poe his silent assassin—the girl with two distinct personalities. The demure senior with the high grades, with applications at Williams, Haverford, Duke and Dartmouth, is Kathleen; the girl on the court is her ferocious twin, Skippy. He concocted the dichotomy[5] because when Kathleen first started playing she said "Excuse me" all the time and would pause to pick her opponents up off the floor. She wants to be like Jamila: someone you don't want to meet on the court but who will be a good friend off it.

---

5. dichotomy: division of a whole into two distinctly different or contradictory parts.

Jamila plans to study law and African-American studies at Stanford. Like her mother, Judy Wideman, who is in her second year of law school, she hopes to be a defense attorney. As a child of mixed races, she has told interviewers she identifies not with being black or white but with being herself. Still, her bedroom has pictures of Winnie Mandela, Jesse Jackson, and the children of Soweto.[6] After the riot in Los Angeles, she wrote several poems that reflected her feelings.

In "Black," she wrote:

I walk the tightrope between the fires
Does anyone know where I fall through?
Their forked daggers of rage reflect my eye
Their physical destruction passes me by
Why does the fire call me?

Jen is know locally as the best thing that ever happened to Pelham, which is that little twinge on the highway on Route 9. Since Jen was 2 and her brother, Chris, was 4, they have lived with their father, who is a manager of reservoirs and waste treatment in Amherst. She is planning to play ball for Dartmouth and to major in engineering. She turned down Princeton, especially after the recruiter, who made a home visit, would not let her father, who has a stutter, talk.

The door to her room is plastered with Nike inspirational ads. She calls the wall above her bed her "strong women wall," and it is filled with pictures of her favorite role models, including Ann Richards and Toni Morrison.[7] By her bedside, she keeps a clothbound book—given to her by her teammate Rita Powell—in which she writes her favorite quotes, a customized Bartlett's.

Marilyn Monroe: "If I'm going to be alone, I'd rather be by myself."
Colette: "You will do foolish things, but do them with enthusiasm."
Zora Neale Hurston: "The dream is the truth."

---

6. Winnie Mandela . . . Soweto: Winnie Mandela, the wife of South African leader Nelson Madela. Soweto is a group of townships near Johannesburg housing black South Africans.
7. Ann Richards and Toni Morrison: Richards was the first woman governor of Texas. Morrison was the first African-American woman to win the Nobel Prize for Literature.

The team bonding among these six seniors and the 10 younger girls is one reason they have played so well: the sisterhood-is-powerful quest for unity. They have a team song, "Real Love," and they have team trinkets (beaded necklaces with their names and plastic rings and scrunchies with basketballs), team teddy bears, team towels. At team dinners, Jamila's mother carbo-loads them with slivered chicken cooked in garlic and oil and lemon and served on a bed of noodles. The meals often conclude with a dozen or so girls linking arms in a tight circle, swaying, singing, shouting, *"Hoop Phi!"*

Even though they beat Hamp in the Western Mass Regional finals, they weren't really champions—not yet. Do they have what it takes, these sweet-looking girls reared in maple syrup country on land that includes the Robert Frost trail? Playing before a few thousand fans in what is almost your own backyard is nothing compared with a stadium that seats 13,800, where real pros play. Rocking Feiker is one thing, but the Centrum?

When the bus finally pulls in front of the Centrum and it is time to leap off, the girls have faces like masks. To the world, they are a bunch of teenage girls; inside their heads, they are commandos. To the world, these teenagers have pretty names: Patri, Kristin, Jen, Kathleen, Kim, Jamila, Sophie, Jade, Emily J., Emily S., Jan, Lucia, Carrie, Rita, Jessi, Julie. But as far as the girls are concerned, they *are* the codes that encapsulate their rare and superb skills, their specialty plays, their personal styles. They are Cloudy and Cougar and Jones-bones and Gumby and Grace and Skippy and Predator. They are warriors.

The girls crowd into a locker room. With much less commotion than usual, they dress in their baggy knee-length uniforms. They slap hands and stand tall. Meanwhile, the arena is redolent of hot dogs, popcorn, sweat and anticipation, one side of the bleachers filled with their people and the other side with the fans from Haverhill.

The girls walk out wordlessly. They look up.

You have to live in a small town for a while before you can read a crowd, especially in New England, where fences are deep in the soil.[8] But if you've been in a town like Amherst for a while, you can go to an out-of-town game, even one in as imposing and cavernous a facility as the Centrum, and you can feel this sudden lurch of well-being that comes from the soothing familiarity

---

8. **fences are deep in the soil:** people keep their lives and emotions private from others.

of faces that are as much a part of your landscape as falling leaves, as forsythia in season, as rhubarb in June. You scan the rows, and for better, and sometimes for worse, you know who's who. You know whose parents don't talk to whom else and you know why. You know who has had troubles that never get discussed.

You see the lawyer that represented your folks or one of their friends in a land dispute or a custody case. You see the realtor who tried to sell a house next to the landfill to the new kids in town. You see the doctor who was no help for your asthma and the one who was. You see the teacher who declared your baby brother a complete mystery and the teacher who always stops to ask what your remarkable brother is up to now. You know which man is the beloved elementary-school principal, now retired. You recognize the plump-cheeked ladies from the cafeteria who specialize in home-made cinnamon buns for 65 cents. You see your family and you see the fathers and mothers and stepfathers and stepmothers of your teammates. You know whose brother flew in from Chicago for the game; whose step-grandparents came from Minnesota.

But what is most important about all this is how mute it is. The commonality is something that is understood, as tacit as the progression of the summer to fall to winter to spring, and just as comforting.

Usually there is a buzz of cheering at the start of a game, but this time the Amherst crowd is nearly silent as the referee tosses the ball.

The Haverhill center taps the ball backward to her point guard. She comes down the court, swings the ball to the wing, who instantly dishes it inside to the center. Easy lay-up. Amherst blinks first. Two-nothing. In the Haverhill stands, the crowd cheers. It is the only pure cheer they will get.

Within a few seconds, the score is 6–4 Amherst, and something truly remarkable takes place. The Hurricanes enter into a zone where all of them rate all-Americas. It's a kind of controlled frenzy that can overtake a group of athletes under only the most elusive of circumstances. It's not certain what triggers it, perhaps it's Jamila's gentle three-pointer from the wing, or more likely, when Jen drives the baseline and as she swoops beneath the basket like a bird of prey she releases the ball back over her head, placing it like an egg against the backboard and through the hoop. It may have been 10 seconds later when Jamila steals the ball, pushing it down court in a three-on-one break, makes a no-look pass to Jen who just as quickly fires the ball across the lane to Kathleen for an uncontested lay-up. Whatever it is that started it, there is nothing Haverhill can do to stop it, and time-outs repeatedly called for by their hapless coach only fuel Amherst's frenzy further.

Even the sportscasters can't remember a 37 to 0 run in a state championship game. The halftime score is 51–6.

An astonished Amherst can hardly even cheer. One Amherst fan shouts: "Where's Dr. Kevorkian?" Another makes the very un-Amherst comment: "They should bring on the Haverhill boys for the second half."

Among the spectators is Kathleen's father, Donald Poe, an associate professor of psychology at Hampshire College, who saw how her defense, along with that of Kristin and Emily Shore, kept Haverhill's score so low.

When his son, Chris, was an infant, Donald Poe tried to teach him to say "ball" as his first word, until he was told that "b" is a hard sound for a baby. He expected a son to be an athlete, and when Kathleen came along he didn't have that expectation. Yet whenever they go into the yard and she pitches a ball to him, it takes only five minutes before his hand hurts. She throws a heavy ball.

To him, what's important is not that Amherst win, but that the spirit of girls' sports endures. Next year, it doesn't have to be Amherst; it might be Westside in Springfield. Its junior varsity is undefeated. When he was in W. T. Woodson High School in Fairfax, Va., the girls were not allowed to use the boys' gym, which was fancy and varnished with a log in the middle of the floor. The girls had a little back gym, without bleachers. After a game, whenever he saw the little kids asking his daughter for autographs, he was glad to see the girls, pleased that they now had models. But he was just as glad to see the boys asking: to him their respect for the girls' team was just as important.

The final score is 74–36.

After receiving the trophies and after collapsing in one huge hysterical teenage heap, they all stand up. First they sing "Happy Birthday" to Kristin Marvin, who turns 18 this day. Then they extend their arms toward their parents, teachers, brothers, sisters, even to some of those 140 little girls whose parents have allowed them a school night of unprecedented lateness, and in one final act as a team, these girls shout, in the perfect unison that has served them so well on the court, *"Thank you."*

Back in the locker room, Kristin Marvin sucks on orange slices and sloshes water on her face. She then stands on a back bench, raises her right fist, turns to her comrades and shouts: "Holy #@&! We're the *#&*@#

champions!" And then she loses it. For the next half-hour, she throws her-self into the arms of one teammate after another. She cries and hugs, and hugs and cries, and so do they.

Coach keeps knocking at the door, trying to roust the stragglers. Finally, he announces he is coming in, and what greets him is a roomful of girls who return his level gaze with eyes that are rheumy and red as they sputter "last . . . final . . . never again."

He looks right at them and says: "You're wrong. This isn't the last. There will be more basketball." His tone is conversational, almost adult to adult.

"But . . . ." they start to say.

"I promise you. There will be lots more basketball."

Still they regard him with disbelief. They can't decipher his real message, at least not at this moment. They can't fathom how the word "basketball" might have more than one meaning.

Over, the game was over. On the way home, they watched a videotape of the game. Jen was stunned at how it had all fallen into place: We were so fluid it was scary. While they watched themselves, television viewers all over the state were witnessing recaps of the highlights and hearing the verdicts of professional commentators who claimed these girls had wan-dered into the wrong league: They shoulda been playing Calipari's men at U Mass; they coulda taught the Celtics a thing or two.

The girls would hear all that in the days to come, but at this moment they were mostly thinking about the present—when truth itself had become a dream. The bus was going backward, retracing its earlier path, down the Pike back through Palmer, where the only sense of abundance is in the fast-food stores, then through Bondsville with its gin mill and the sunken rusty playground with a metal fence, back through the center of Belchertown, a singularly flat stretch in a town with a singularly unfortunate name, and back in and out of Pelham—thanks to Jen, on the map at last.

Kathleen Poe wished that the whole team could sleep that night in the gym at the high school, the coziest, most homey, softest place she could now imagine, that they could all sink into its floor, become part of it forever. She kept trying out rhymes in her head, phrases popping into her mind like sudden rebounds: top and stop, pride and ride, forever and sever, heart, smart, true, you.

Hoop Phi is of an intangible, untouchable breed.
It satisfies the soul, and a life-long need.
We represented our school, represented our sex,
Now maybe both will get some well-earned respect.

No one really wanted the ride to end. The bare trees, the velvety night air, the cocoon of the bus itself.

At the town line there waited another police escort, this time back into town. The cruiser was once again full of proud, slow ceremony. At the corner of Main and Triangle, the cruiser seemed to lurch right to take the short-cut, back to the school, but then as if that was only a feint, it continued to move forward, so that the girls would be brought through town the long way.

The bus, boisterous in its very bigness, moved past the red-bricked Dickinson homestead with its top-heavy trees, tall and thin with a crown of green: *We're somebody, who are you?*[9] Downtown was almost empty save for a couple of pizza eaters in the front window of Antonio's and a lone worker sweeping in the back shadows of Bart's Ice Cream. As the strobe lights from the cruiser bounced off the storefronts, the bus wheezed past St. Bridget's and the bagel place, turning right, then left, finally pulling into the school parking lot a few minutes shy of midnight.

All of a sudden one of the players shouted: "There are people there, waiting for us!" And, indeed, in the distance was a small crowd standing in the cold and in the dark, clapping.

When the bus came to a stop, Coach stood up. "I promise it won't be mushy. There's just one thing you should know. When you're the state champions, the season never ever ends. I love you. Great job. And now, I'd like everybody else on the bus to please wait so that the team can get off first."

Often the Hurricanes will bound off a bus in a joyous squealing clump. On this night, they rose from their seats, slowly, in silence. *State champs!* For the final time this season, with great care bordering on tenderness, the teammates gathered their stuff, their uniforms, their shoes, their socks, their game faces and their courage. And then in a decision that was never actually articulated but seemed to have evolved as naturally as the parabola

---

9. We're somebody . . . are you?: A reference to a poem by Emily Dickinson that begins "I'm nobody, who are you?"

of a perfect three-pointer, the Hurricanes waited for captain Jen Pariseau to lead the way, which she did, and one by one the rest of the women followed, the captain Jamila Wideman the last of the Hurricanes to step off the bus into the swirling sea of well-wishers and winter coats.

Overhead the sky was as low-hanging and as opaque as it had been earlier in the evening, but it didn't need the stars to make it shine.

Responding to What You Read

1. The action in this selection moves from the town of Amherst to the arena and back again. The author uses specific details to bring those places to life and make the reader feel a certain way. Find specific details describing the bus route to the arena or the atmosphere during the game. What feelings do those details create in you as a reader?

2. Why, to the Amherst fans, was *JennyandJamila* one word?

3. Why does Diane Stanton, mother of the star of the boys' basketball team, write to the girls?

Writer's Workshop

This is an extended assignment. Find some sports activity that will be going on for at least two weeks' time. Now cover it as a journalist, as Madeleine H. Blais did with the Amherst girls' basketball team. Be sure that each locale or setting in your story is carefully described, as Blais did, and make individual people come alive through character sketches that reveal unique aspects of their lives. The word *I* should not appear in your writing unless you are quoting someone else.

Alternate Media Response

Do a video report of a behind-the-scenes look at a sports team in the midst of its season. Aim for a 6 to 7 minute video. You will have to videotape a lot more than 7 minutes of material to be able to produce 6 to 7 minutes of finished product. Focus your video on human-interest issues, as Madeleine H. Blais did in her article.

PERSPECTIVES

From *Rabbit, Run*

John Updike

Ex-Basketball Player

John Updike

The difficult part isn't the playing. It's after the playing is over and you think back.

John Updike, who was born in 1932, has been one of the most prolific and highly regarded American writers of the last 40 years. In addition to literary criticism and other nonfiction, Updike has published novels, short stories, and poems that portray aspects of small-town, middle-class American life. He has won both the Pulitzer Prize and the National Book Award for his work.

The first selection, which is the first chapter from Updike's novel *Rabbit, Run,* introduces the reader to "Rabbit" Angstrom, a former high-school basketball star. The second selection, "Ex-Basketball Player," describes another character who could be Rabbit.

From *Rabbit, Run*

Boys are playing basketball around a telephone pole with a backboard bolted to it. Legs, shouts. The scrape and snap of Keds[1] on loose alley pebbles seems to catapult their voices high into the moist March air blue above the wires. Rabbit Angstrom, coming up the alley in a business suit, stops and watches, though he's twenty-six and six three. So tall, he seems an unlikely rabbit, but the breadth of white face, the pallor of his blue irises, and a nervous flutter under his brief nose as he stabs a cigarette into his mouth partially explain the nickname, which was given to him when he too was a boy. He stands there thinking, the kids keep coming, they keep crowding you up.

His standing there makes the real boys feel strange. Eyeballs slide. They're doing this for their own pleasure, not as a demonstration for some adult walking around town in a double-breasted cocoa suit. It seems funny to them, an adult walking up the alley at all. Where's his car? The cigarette makes it more sinister still. Is this one of those going to offer them cigarettes or money to go out in back of the ice plant with him? They've heard of such things but are not too frightened; there are six of them and one of him.

The ball, rocketing off the crotch of the rim, leaps over the heads of the six and lands at the feet of the one. He catches it on the short bounce with a

---

1. **Keds:** a brand of athletic shoes.

quickness that startles them. As they stare hushed he sights squinting through blue clouds of weed smoke, a suddenly dark silhouette like a smokestack in the afternoon spring sky, setting his feet with care, wiggling the ball with nervousness in front of his chest, one widespread pale hand on top of the ball and the other underneath, jiggling it patiently to get some adjustment in air itself. The moons on his fingernails are big. Then the ball seems to ride up the right lapel of his coat and comes off his shoulder as his knees dip down, and it appears the ball will miss because though he shot from an angle the ball is not going toward the backboard. It was not aimed there. It drops into the circle of the rim, whipping the net with a ladylike whisper. "Hey!" he shouts in pride.

"Luck," one of the kids says.

"Skill," he answers, and asks, "Hey. O.K. if I play?"

There is no response, just puzzled silly looks swapped. Rabbit takes off his coat, folds it nicely, and rests it on a clean ash can lid. Behind him the dungarees begin to scuffle again. He goes into the scrimmaging thick of them for the ball, flips it from two weak white hands, has it in his own. That old stretched-leather feeling makes his whole body go taut, gives his arms wings. It feels like he's reaching down through years to touch this tautness. His arms lift of their own and the rubber ball floats toward the basket from the top of his head. It feels so right he blinks when the ball drops short, and for a second wonders if it went through the hoop without riffling the net. He asks, "Hey whose side am I on?"

In a wordless shuffle two boys are delegated to be his. They stand the other four. Though from the start Rabbit handicaps himself by staying ten feet out from the basket, it is still unfair. Nobody bothers to keep score. The surly silence bothers him. The kids call monosyllables to each other but to him they don't dare a word. As the game goes on he can feel them at his legs, getting hot and mad, trying to trip him, but their tongues are still held. He doesn't want this respect, he wants to tell them there's nothing to getting old, it takes nothing. In ten minutes another boy goes to the other side, so it's just Rabbit Angstrom and one kid standing five. This boy, still midget but already diffident[2] with a kind of rangy ease, is the best of the six; he wears a knitted cap with a green pompom well down over his ears and level with his eyebrows, giving his head a

---

2. **diffident:** hesitant; reserved.

cretinous[3] look. He's a natural. The way he moves sideways without taking any steps, gliding on a blessing: you can tell. The way he waits before he moves. With luck he'll become in time a crack athlete in the high school; Rabbit knows the way. You climb up through the little grades and then get to the top and everybody cheers; with the sweat in your eyebrows you can't see very well and the noise swirls around you and lifts you up, and then you're out, not forgotten at first, just out, and it feels good and cool and free. You're out, and sort of melt, and keep lifting, until you become like to these kids just one more piece of the sky of adults that hangs over them in the town, a piece that for some queer reason has clouded and visited them. They've not forgotten him; worse, they never heard of him. Yet in his time Rabbit was famous through the county; in basketball in his junior year he set a B-league scoring record that in his senior year he broke with a record that was not broken until four years later, that is, four years ago.

He sinks shots one-handed, two-handed, underhanded, flat-footed, and out of the pivot, jump, and set. Flat and soft the ball lifts. That his touch still lives in his hands elates him. He feels liberated from long gloom. But his body is weighty and his breath grows short. It annoys him, that he gets winded. When the five kids not on his side begin to groan and act lazy, and a kid he accidentally knocks down gets up with a blurred face and walks away, Rabbit quits readily. "O.K," he says. "The old man's going."

To the boy on his side, the pompom, he adds, "So long, ace." He feels grateful to the boy, who continued to watch him with disinterested admiration after the others grew sullen, and who cheered him on with exclamations: "God. Great. Gee."

Rabbit picks up his folded coat and carries it in one hand like a letter as he runs. Up the alley. Past the deserted ice plant with its rotting wooden skids on the fallen loading porch. Ash cans, garage doors, fences of chicken wire caging crisscrossing stalks of dead flowers. The month is March. Love makes the air light. Things start anew; Rabbit tastes through sour after-smoke the fresh chance in the air, plucks the pack of cigarettes from his bobbling shirt pocket, and without breaking stride cans it in somebody's open barrel. His upper lip nibbles back from his teeth in self-pleasure. His big suede shoes skim in thumps above the skittering litter of alley gravel.

---

3. cretinous: stupid.

Ex-Basketball Player

Pearl Avenue runs past the high-school lot,
Bends with the trolley tracks, and stops, cut off
Before it has a chance to go two blocks,
At Colonel McComsky Plaza. Berth's Garage
5   Is on the corner facing west, and there,
Most days, you'll find Flick Webb, who helps Berth out.

Flick stands tall among the idiot pumps—
Five on a side, the old bubble-head style,
Their rubber elbows hanging loose and low.
10   One's nostrils are two S's, and his eyes
An E and O. And one is squat, without
A head at all—more of a football type.

Once Flick played for the high-school team, the Wizards.
He was good: in fact, the best. In '46
15   He bucketed three hundred ninety points,
A county record still. The ball loved Flick.
I saw him rack up thirty-eight or forty
In one home game. His hands were like wild birds.

He never learned a trade, he just sells gas,
20   Checks oil, and changes flats. Once in a while,
As a gag, he dribbles an inner tube,
But most of us remember anyway.
His hands are fine and nervous on the lug wrench.
It makes no difference to the lug wrench, though.

25   Off work, he hangs around Mae's Luncheonette.
Grease-grey and kind of coiled, he plays pinball,
Sips lemon cokes, and smokes those thin cigars;
Flick seldom speaks to Mae, just sits and nods
Beyond her face towards bright applauding tiers
30   Of Necco Wafers, Nibs, and Juju Beads.

Responding to What You Read

1. In the selection from *Rabbit, Run*, why do you think the author has set the story in the month of March?

2. What is Rabbit's mood at the end of the excerpt?

3. Find similarities and differences between Rabbit and Flick, and describe them in your own words. Quote lines from *Rabbit, Run* or "Ex-Basketball Player" to support your descriptions.

Writer's Workshop

1. Recall from earlier in this book that **tone** in a piece of writing is the author's attitude toward the subject matter. Remember that there can be comical tones, happy tones, and mournful or sad tones. Identify several tones in the selection from *Rabbit, Run* and explain why you feel Updike is conveying that particular tone. In other words, what words or images help create the tone?

   Then identify the tone or tones evident in "Ex-Basketball Player" and cite your evidence for what you say.

2. Compare and contrast these two John Updike works. A key thing to watch for will be similarities and differences in the tone.

Alternate Media Response

Draw Rabbit as he appears in any moment of the prose selection. Then draw Flick Webb among the "idiot pumps" at the gas station. Have the two drawings reflect the two different tones found in these pieces.

PERSPECTIVES

The Sprinters

Lillian Morrison

To an Athlete Dying Young

A. E. Housman

Two poets consider the joy runners bring to spectators and the ways spectators honor these runners.

Lillian Morrison is the author of several volumes of poetry, and her own work is in several anthologies. She says, "I love rhythms, the body movement implicit in poetry, explicit in sports, sometimes a kind of transcendence and beauty one wants to catch. One turns naturally to poetry to express these things."

The Sprinters

The gun explodes them.
Pummeling, pistoning they fly
In time's face.
A go at the limit,
5   A terrible try
To smash the ticking glass,
Outpace the beat
That runs, that streaks away
Tireless, and faster than they.

10   Beside ourselves
(It is for us they run!)
We shout and pound the stands
For one to win
Loving him, whose hard
15   Grace-driven stride
Most mocks the clock
And almost breaks the bands
Which lock us in.

A. *E. Housman lived from 1859 to 1936. He published only two collections of poems while he was alive,* A Shropshire Lad *and* Last Poems. *Critic Basil Davenport said, "Housman is the author of some of the most moving verse in the English language. Twice, a quarter of a century apart, he spoke for all rejected lovers, for young men killed in battle, for those who are homesick for some land of no return, for those to whom the very beauty of earth is a reminder of its evanescence. His poems, deeply melancholy in mood, are all of a chiseled perfection in form, achieving the most exquisite harmonies by the simplest means."*

To an Athlete Dying Young

The time you won your town the race
We chaired you through the market place;
Man and boy stood cheering by,
And home we brought you shoulder-high.

5   Today, the road all runners come,
Shoulder-high we bring you home,
And set you at your threshold down,
Townsman of a stiller town.

Smart lad, to slip betimes away
10   From fields where glory does not stay
And early though the laurel[1] grows
It withers quicker than the rose.

---

1. laurel: an evergreen shrub or tree, the leaves of which symbolize victory.

Eyes the shady night has shut
Cannot see the record cut,
15   And silence sounds no worse than cheers
After earth has stopped the ears:

Now you will not swell the rout[2]
Of lads that wore their honors out,
Runners whom renown outran
20   And the name died before the man.

Responding to What You Read

1. Usually we think of a person shooting or "exploding" a gun. How can a gun "explode" the sprinters, as Lillian Morrison writes?

2. According to Morrison, how can a runner fly "in time's face"?

3. What is the speaker referring to in stanza two of Housman's poem when he describes the lad as a "Townsman of a stiller town"?

4. In stanza three of Housman's poem, why does the speaker refer to the lad as "smart" in dying young? Support your answer with references to the poem.

Writer's Workshop

This section of the book is called "The Glory of Sports." Write a poem, with or without figurative language, about something "glorious" that you have seen or read about in sports.

---

2. rout: a disorderly retreat.

CHAPTER 3

Sports and Life

Sporting events may take place in a small arena, but sports in general cannot escape the larger arena of life.

Two athletes who achieved glory at Columbia University are tested by a real-life illness that enters their fairy-tale existence.

Two baseball superstars use their fame to focus attention on life issues more complicated than curve balls.

A boy discovers that the softball game he is playing in is not a "game" at all, but rather a contest of moral beliefs.

A group of women, a major-league pitcher, and some amateur hockey players escape the daily routine of the real world for a brief period of time.

This chapter includes selections about athletes, as well as ordinary people, who make a critical connection between sports *and* life. *As you read about them, think about how their sports experiences relate to larger issues.*

From Columbia, an Athletes' Romance, in Sickness and in Laughter

Ira Berkow

A "fairy-tale romance" takes a different turn.

Ira Berkow is a sports columnist and feature writer for the New York Times. *He has written a dozen books, the most recent a memoir:* To the Hoop: The Seasons of a Basketball Life. *His awards and honors include being a finalist for the Pulitzer Prize for Distinguished Commentary.*

Regarding "From Columbia, an Athletes' Romance, In Sickness and in Laughter," Berkow says, "I spent a morning with Mike and Kathleen. Then there were many calls, to people in their lives. The coach in Rhode Island, a coach at Columbia. Not all phone interviews see the light of day in a finished piece but they all contribute to the foundation of a piece.

"Sometimes I go to a site to report about it. I didn't need to visit and write about a past scene for this story. It was enough for me to create that scene in the house, with him in the bed."

From Columbia, an Athletes' Romance, in Sickness and in Laughter

It had all the ingredients of a fairy-tale romance. They are from ethnic working-class families but attended an Ivy League school, entering Columbia University at the same time, in the fall of 1989. He becomes a two-time all-Ivy League wide receiver in football and makes the dean's list; she is an all-academic Ivy point guard in basketball. They meet, don't connect, then fall in love after they happen to take a course together as juniors, History of Ancient Mesopotamia.

After graduating, he remains in New York to do research at a local hospital, she travels to Europe to play pro basketball for a season in Austria. They carry on a long-distance relationship, but when she returns to New York, he is off to the University of North Carolina to study for a Ph.D. in biochemistry.

Still, they are bound, as the poets say, in their hearts. They arrange to see each other with 21-day-advance plane reservations, for more inexpensive fares. Finally, at age 27, they decide to marry this July 24. Kathleen, at 5 feet 6^1/$_2$ inches, blonde and blue-eyed, buys a wedding dress but cannot reveal the details of it ("an old Irish superstition," she says). Mike, dark-haired and a strapping 6-2 and 185 pounds, will wear a black tuxedo, and endure the relatives' tapping of glasses with silverware, indicating he must kiss the bride—an Italian custom.

Originally, Mike Sardo and Kathleen Johnson were to be wed in the backyard of her parents' two-bedroom house in Scarborough, Maine, but the site was recently switched to a nearby church, which, among other things, would lend easier access for Mike's wheelchair.

At the end of last April, out of the blue, Mike began to feel weak. On a Saturday afternoon, he had returned home from the gym in Chapel Hill, N.C., after working out in his regular routine, lifting weights and running five miles through the streets. In his apartment, he felt a terrible pain in his back.

"It was like someone twisting something in my spine," he said.

At first he was told by doctors that it was probably just a back problem.

"They gave me these huge horse pills," he said. "Didn't help."

A few days later, he was admitted to the emergency room. Doctors decided because of his low blood count to keep him in the hospital for a battery of tests, including a bone marrow biopsy.

That night Mike spoke with Kathleen by telephone and told her about the tests. He said he was short of breath, sometimes having to stop after walking only 10 feet, and the pain in his back was excruciating. The test results would be learned the next day, on May 2.

When Kathleen hung up the phone with Mike from the hospital, she was puzzled at his condition, and worried.

"Mike always had such a high threshold of pain," she recalled. "I remember him suffering injuries from football—like broken ribs—and just going on, never complaining."

Mike and Kathleen had dreams for the future—Mike wants to be on the faculty of a university and teach and do research in biology or biochemistry, Kathleen hopes to get a Ph.D. in women's studies and create women's studies courses for high schools. In the meantime, though, they have been struggling financially in the early stages of their careers.

So late the next morning, when Mike was wheeled back into his room in the University of North Carolina Hospital after taking blood tests, he was surprised to see Kathleen sitting beside his empty bed.

"What are you doing here?" he said.

"You didn't think I'd let you stay in the hospital by yourself, did you?" she said.

"But it must have cost you a fortune."

"I'm a schoolteacher," she said, "I've got money to burn."

Later that afternoon, they got the results of the tests. The news was not good. "You have a rare case of acute lymphatic leukemia," Mike was told. "Cancer in the spine."

He was stunned, and disbelieving. "I never imagined something like that could happen to me," he said.

Then he began to sort it out. "I thought that there'd be chemotherapy and radiation and I'd get through it," Mike said. "I'd done research in cancer and just realized that it was a freak accident, that some cells went haywire. I figured I'd be all right after a while."

Kathleen wasn't sure what to think. She knew, though, what she was going to do.

"I'm staying here," she said.

They had planned for Kathleen to move in with Mike, but later in the year. "Well," he said, leaning forward to kiss her, "now we'll be in the same area code again."

Staying Warm In the Winter

Laughter for Mike and Kathleen has been a big part of their lives together. Which is the way they came to enjoy each other, the way they get through these days—and nights.

"Mike was distinctive on campus," Kathleen said, "because he'd always wear shorts—even in wintertime. Coat and shorts."

"It was warm in the classrooms," Mike explained. "She'd always wear a pretty hat, usually a red or a black woolen hat with a little brim, but they didn't cover her ears. She'd wear them just because they'd match her sweater or coat. Wouldn't keep her warm."

For the holidays, they returned home from North Carolina to visit their parents, Kathleen to Maine, Mike to Long Island, and then met up in Mike's parents' home in Bethpage, where they would spend the turn of the year, before returning to Chapel Hill. Mike's leukemia is in remission, but early next week he and Kathleen will go to Memorial Sloan-Kettering Cancer Center in Manhattan to see if doctors there can unravel the mystery of why his legs are in their present condition—or whether cancer is at the root of it. His legs fill with fluid and are so heavy that—along with loss of strength in his upper body—he cannot lift them to move from bed to chair.

At his parents' home now, Mike, nearly bald after chemotherapy treatments, lay in a bed under blue covers beside the bay window in the family living room adorned with bright Christmas decorations. Kathleen was seated nearby, her hair longer than shoulder length, and wore a purple turtleneck sweater, jeans and thick-soled black boots. The couple banter easily.

"We met when we were juniors," Kathleen said. "And I saw him right after the Harvard game and complimented him on having played well. He said, 'Thanks,' and blew me off."

"I didn't blow you off," he protested.

"Well, he was upset that they had lost," she said.

"We met when we were freshmen," he said, and then turned to a guest in the room. "But she doesn't remember. My roommate had wanted to date her. Didn't happen, though. I remember it because I remember she was beautiful."

In their senior year, Kathleen helped pay tuition by checking identification cards in the school's Dodge Physical Fitness Center on weekday mornings. Mike used to watch game films in the mornings or get his various injuries worked on.

"I'd come by and talk to her before going to class," Mike said. "She was a captive audience."

"Once I got to know Mike," Kathleen said, "I found him to be the kindest guy I'd ever met. He never brags, and he's got so much to brag about. Like when we first started dating, he never talked about himself. I'd have guys who'd practically read their résumé to me. Not Mike. And he's funny. Nice looking, too, which doesn't hurt."

Kathleen taught history to inner-city high-school girls at St. Michael's Academy in Manhattan until Mike became ill. After moving in with Mike, she managed to get a teaching job at a middle school in Raleigh, 45 miles from Chapel Hill. Before leaving for work in the morning, Kathleen prepares breakfast for Mike and puts it at his bedside, and then leaves school in time to feed him a late lunch. He uses a catheter. His father, John, a carpenter and bricklayer who has a small construction crew, has built a ramp into his Chapel Hill apartment to enable access for Mike's wheelchair.

Her salary, plus Mike's $14,000 grant from the university, and as much help as their parents can manage—they are both schoolteachers—has put a drain on all of them financially and emotionally. They need home nursing care when Kathleen is at work. Other expenses not covered by insurance are mounting.

A fund was started by John Reeves, the director of athletics at Columbia; Wally Halas, the former men's basketball coach at Columbia and current associate director of the Institute for International Sport, based at the University of Rhode Island; and Tony Apallaro, a former Columbia baseball player and classmate of Mike's.

"I'm from the same hometown as Kathleen—Worcester, Mass.," Halas said. (The Johnsons still live part time in Worcester and teach elementary school nearby.) "I knew her family—her dad, Bob, was a fine basketball player at Fitchburg State. And I got to know Mike at Columbia. Two wonderful kids, from lunch-pail families. I mean, they both worked hard to get the grades to go to Columbia and worked hard every day to improve themselves once they were there."

In fact, Sardo is the first in his immediate family to attend college. "And now," Halas added, "they're in this thing. It's a tough blow, but maybe they can take something from what they learned in sports. Coaches always say you have to fight through a hard situation."

Just Remembering the Good Games

Mike's mind drifts periodically to his days as a football player, remembering the good games with pleasure, such as catching 13 passes against Cornell to set a Columbia record for receptions, or the following week against Brown making a 40-yard touchdown catch in the third quarter to put the Lions ahead in a game they went on to win.

"I think of some of the bad games, games that we either lost or in which I didn't do so well, like when we were down by 7 points to Harvard and had a chance to tie at the end of the game, and there was a mix-up on a fourth-down pass pattern," he said. "I replay those. When I do"—he smiled—"the results always improve. But I also think how strange it is, how you can be seemingly healthy at one point, and very quickly it changes."

While Kathleen says that Mike is good at any sport, he disputes it. "I've had to work at all of them," he said. "But this thing can get very frustrating. When you can't be independent. When you can't get into the chair from the bed by yourself."

From May to early September last year, Mike was weak and unsure of his footing, but he was able to be relatively independent. That changed on Labor Day when, he said, "my legs stopped working."

"I couldn't stand without holding onto something," he said. It has continued that way since.

"Mike almost never gets mad," Kathleen said, smiling. "The only times he does is when he can't do something he could do even a week earlier. Like get into a chair by himself."

"And then I curse and scream," Mike said. "I have to vent. It takes about five minutes. And I'm back to normal."

What does Kathleen do in those moments? "I leave the room," she said. "When it gets quiet in there, I go back."

"And then," Mike said, "we laugh."

He says he feels bad that she has to serve virtually as a nurse, helping him even in indiscreet moments.

"He's such a good patient," she said. "I want to do it."

One of the hardest things to deal with, Kathleen said, is to see Mike make some progress, then regress.

"After solving one problem," she said, "there just seems to be another one, and another. There's an infection, a blood transfusion, one leg swells, then the other. And when we're alone in the middle of the night, and something happens, it's so maddening because we aren't sure if we're doing the right thing. And at those points I feel overwhelmed."

Like the night he began to shake violently and sweat in his chair. She moved him into the bed, and he continued shaking. She brought water, applied cold compresses. And then he passed out.

"I was feeling so tired, so frustrated," she said, "and I sat down and began to cry."

But later, always, she added, "We're able to laugh again."

They also argue, which is one of the sustaining elements of their loving relationship.

"We're opposite in so many ways," Kathleen said. "He's from New York, I'm from Massachusetts. He's a Knick fan, I'm a Celtic fan. He's Yankees, I'm Red Sox, he's Jets, I'm for the Patriots. He loves junk food, and I'm into health foods. And our families are so different. My family is Irish and kind of low-key and quiet. His family is Italian and, when I first came around, I thought they were hollering at each other, but I learned that they're just having a conversation."

And the couple are competitive. "But I'm super-competitive," Kathleen said.

Once they played one-on-one basketball. "I'm not really a basketball player, but I won," Mike said.

"I let him win," Kathleen said.

"Oh, please."

"I wasn't having my best day, and besides, I knew you'd be upset if you lost to a girl. Big mistake."

"Somebody who majored in history ought to get it straight," he said.

"History has many sides—it depends on who you talk to."

"I admit I backed you into the basket—but when we played shooting games you crushed me," he confessed.

And then Mike told a story of when the two went to a bar last summer in Chapel Hill that has a regulation basket inside. Kathleen was shooting free throws and two guys came by and called "next." Ground rules are that you relinquish your place when you miss.

"How many have you made in a row," one of the guys said, "four or five?"

"How about 68," Kathleen said.

And she had.

Mike was watching nearby. "Then Kathleen hit about five more in a row and quit," he recalled. "These guys were watching with their eyes wide."

Two Families Become Closer

Though the future husband and wife have their rooting and ethnic differences, the families appear to have no such conflicts.

"Kathleen's family loves Mike," said Tony Apallaro, a former college roommate of Mike's and still one of his best friends, "and the same is true for Mike's family about Kathleen. And Mike's illness, and how Kathleen has responded, seems to have even brought everyone closer together."

Mike and Kathleen hope that by July the mysteries of his leg problems will be solved and that he will be walking again, or at least regain much of his independence.

And their immediate plans after the wedding? "A honeymoon, of course," Kathleen said.

"Maybe Charlotte," said Mike.

"More like San Francisco," said Kathleen, resisting Mike's little joke, "or Hawaii."

Mike, after all, agreed.

"Yes," he said pulling the blue cover higher on his chest, "we could use a nice change of scenery."

Responding to What You Read

1. Ira Berkow creates a vivid picture of Mike and Kathleen's life together in this selection. What details about their relationship help explain how they are coping with Mike's illness?

2. A friend of the couple says, "It's a tough blow, but maybe they can take something from what they learned in sports. Coaches always say you have to fight through a hard situation." What lessons might Kathleen and Mike have learned from their involvement in sports that can help them cope with Mike's illness?

Writer's Workshop

This **feature story** about Mike Sardo and Kathleen Johnson first appeared in the Sports section of the *New York Times*. Feature stories, sometimes called **news features**, usually focus on people and issues that are in the news. Unlike a news story, which reports the essential facts of a newsworthy event, a feature story goes beyond the facts to present a closer look at the people who are involved or to explore the issues that are raised.

Think of an idea for a feature story that is related to sports in some way. For example, you could do a profile of a classmate who won a state competition, or you could interview people in a neighboring town to learn their reasons for voting down a proposal to build a new athletic stadium. When you write your story, concentrate on presenting details that make the individuals in your story come alive. One way to achieve this goal is to tape conversations you have with your sources and then re-create parts of those conversations as dialogue in the story.

PERSPECTIVES

Clemente!

Kal Wagenheim

Clemente to Sosa, and Beyond

Harvey Araton

Baseball superstars Roberto Clemente and Sammy Sosa are heroes—both on and off the playing field.

ABOUT THE AUTHOR•ABOUT THE AUTHOR•ABOUT THE AUTHOR•ABOUT THE AUTHOR

Kal Wagenheim, a former New York Times correspondent in Puerto Rico, played semi-pro baseball in New Jersey and was offered a contract in the minor leagues. He says, "I was a slick-fielding first baseman, and a long-ball hitter . . . when I hit the ball." He has written several books about Puerto Rico in addition to the biography Clemente from which the following selection is taken.

Clemente!

In a treatise about his own breed, Paul Gallico once said that sports writers are often cynics[1] because they "learn eventually that, while there are no villains, there are no heroes either." But, he warned, "until you make the final discovery that there are only human beings, who are therefore all the more fascinating, you are liable to miss something."

Roberto Clemente Walker[2] of Puerto Rico—the first Latin American to enter baseball's Hall of Fame—was a fascinating human being. And if, as Gallico observes, there are no heroes, there are men who achieve deeds of heroic dimension. Roberto Clemente was one of these gifted few.

"Without question the hardest single thing to do in sport is to hit a baseball," says the great Boston slugger Ted Williams. "A .300 hitter, that rarest of breeds, goes through life with the certainty that he will fail at this job seven out of ten times." A baseball is a sphere with a diameter of $2^7/_8$ inches. The batter stands at home plate and grips a tapering wood cylinder that has a maximum diameter of $2^3/_4$ inches; he tries to defend a strike zone that is approximately seven baseballs wide and eleven high. The pitcher, from $60^1/_2$ feet away, throws the ball at a speed of about 90 miles per hour. As it spins toward the plate—hopping, sinking, or curving—the hitter has four-tenths of one second to decide whether he should let it pass by, jump away to avoid being maimed, or swing. To get "good wood" on it, he must connect squarely

---

1. cynics: fault-finding critics.
2. Roberto Clemente Walker: Roberto Clemente's full name. Walker is his mother's maiden name. Hispanics often use both parents' surnames in their names.

with a ³/₄-inch portion of the ball's round surface—and then hope that none of the nine defensive players catches it. Roberto Clemente had enormous success in this complex, difficult task. In September, 1972, when he smashed his 3,000th hit, he scaled a peak where only ten other men in the hundred-year history of baseball ever set foot. In his eighteen years as a major league player, he made a memorable impact upon a great sport. A lifetime average of .317, four league batting championships, a Most Valuable Player award, and twelve Golden Gloves for superior defensive play are just a few souvenirs that attest to his marvelous talent. During the 1971 World Series, his devastating *tour de force,*[3] witnessed by millions on television, at last evoked the national recognition that he felt was long overdue. Roger Angell, in his superb book *The Summer Game*, says "Now and again—very rarely—we see a man who seems to have met all the demands, challenged all the implacable averages, spurned the mere luck. He has defied baseball, even altered it, and for a time at least the game is truly his." During the 1971 World Series, and on many other occasions, the game was Roberto Clemente's.

But these great moments cost him dearly. Another famous Latin, Enrico Caruso, once said, "To be great, it is necessary to suffer." Roberto Clemente endured severe physical pain and sacrificed a good portion of his life to perfect his skills.

There is much more to a great athlete than the one-dimensional view of his performance on the playing field. Roberto Clemente was a human being like all the rest of us, but when you peel away from each man the frailties that we share, there is a residue[4] that defines each man's uniqueness.

The classical poets of ancient Greece would have rejoiced over Roberto Clemente. Unlike the Goliath-sized supermen of basketball and football, his physique was a nearly perfect match for the "normal" ideal that one sees in time-weathered marble friezes and statues. He was strikingly handsome, with a superbly sculpted body: five feet, eleven inches tall, one hundred and eighty pounds, broad-shouldered with powerful arms and hands, slender of waist, fleet of foot. His simple, traditional values might seem hopelessly naïve to the cynic, but they would have inspired the ancient lyricists. He saw himself as a fine craftsman and viewed his craft, baseball, as deserving of painstaking labor. He believed passionately in the virtue and dignity

---

3. *tour de force:* feat of skill.
4. residue: something that remains after a part is taken.

of hard work. He believed, with equal fervor, that a man should revere his parents, his wife and children, his country, and God. But he was not a docile man. He believed just as fiercely in his personal worth and integrity. "From head to toes, Roberto Clemente is as good as the President of the United States," he proclaimed. "I believe that, and I think every man should believe that about himself."

It was this belief that caused Roberto Clemente to become deeply involved during a period of major social change, the 1950s and 1960s, when black and Spanish-speaking people quickened their pace in the struggle for equality. That long march is far from over, but Clemente's brilliance in his craft and his unyielding demands for respect off the field advanced the cause by great distances. His immense pride in his Puerto Rican heritage and in his blackness inspired many others to hold their own heads high.

Those who knew Roberto Clemente offer an appealing portrait of a remarkable man: a serious artist who wrote his own style of poetry in the air, with powerful strokes of a bat, leaping catches, and breathtaking throws; a man with an enormous well of sentiment, who could inspire tears and could himself be driven to tears by symbolic gestures of kindness and nobility; a man whose temper was quick and terrible like a tropical storm, but who bore no grudge; a man with an almost childlike zest for life, who spoke from the heart and damn the consequences; a man with a very special sense of humor that he shared with only a few friends. But above all, in talking with the people whose lives were touched by Roberto Clemente—in Puerto Rico, in the spring training camp at Bradenton, Florida, in Pittsburgh—one hears of the empathy, the deep concern for others, the concern that moved him one rainy New Year's Eve to fly off on a mission to help others, and to perish in the effort. In her book *Nobody Ever Died of Old Age*, Sharon R. Curtin tells of an elderly woman who "was near the end of her life and had never experienced magic, never challenged the smell of brimstone, never clawed at the limit of human capability." In his all-too-brief life—in those rich, eventful thirty-eight years—Roberto Clemente experienced magic often, and others felt his magic. He knew many people, some for only a brief time, whom he touched very deeply. Through them, he touched me, too.

See the biography of Harvey Araton, on page 93. Regarding "Clemente to Sosa, and Beyond," Araton says, "One of the more rewarding aspects of being a sports columnist is getting the opportunity to simply ask a question that suddenly, without advance notice, unlocks a door, and allows you to step into a story. Such was the case when I went to the Yogi Berra Museum to interview Roberto Clemente Jr., son of the late baseball legend.

"Clemente Jr. was kind enough to share his childhood memories of the worst day of his life, and the strange premonition he had of his father's death. In planning a column, I always try to begin with a point or a premise and hope to be able to support it with reported information.

"When the subjects are as giving as Clemente Jr. was that day, there is the tendency to rush home to the computer, to share one's good fortune with the readers. These are the days when the columns almost write themselves, and when the sports column feels more like a hobby than a job."

Clemente to Sosa, and Beyond

As much as the number he faithfully chose to wear, it was the way Sammy Sosa moved, the way he carried himself, that made Roberto Clemente Jr. think Sosa had something special inside him that was destined to be shared.

It was similar to the way his father galloped from the batter's box, a lasting vision for the oldest of Roberto Clemente's three sons. "We sat along the first-base line at Forbes Field, so we got to see the players as they ran down the line," he said. "To me, my father didn't run, he floated. That was how I as a little kid could tell he was different."

Clemente Jr. was 6 on December 31, 1972, when he walked into the kitchen of his family's Puerto Rico home, looking for his father's plane ticket, a kid's playful habit in trying to delay the inevitable. Except this time, the last time, there was no ticket, no commercial flight. Roberto Clemente was going on a relief mission to earthquake-ravaged Nicaragua. He was going despite what Roberto Jr. says he still believes was a premonition of his father's death.

"I can still remember just feeling that something wasn't right," he said. "I told my mother, 'Don't let Daddy go. That plane's going to crash.' She yelled at me. I ran outside. He came out and said, 'I'll come back soon and we'll play catch.' I told him, 'You're not coming back.'"

Whatever his 6-year-old imagination had conjured up, the reality of that being the last time he would see his father has had a profound ethereal effect on Roberto Clemente Jr. At the All-Star Game last July, long before Sosa chased Mark McGwire deep into September, Clemente and Sosa sought each other out at Coors Field.

"Your father is my hero," Sosa told him. "I wear his number. I watched his films. I studied his swing."

Clemente replied with something he knew was strange to say to someone he hardly knew. "My father's spirit is with you," he said.

That is what Clemente strongly suspected as Sosa, in this of all seasons, emerged from at least a half-dozen other powerhitters' shadows. That is what Clemente decided had to be as he watched Sosa juggle baseball and, eerily, his own relief efforts for a Dominican Republic battered by Hurricane Georges.

Sixty-six home runs, it turned out, were a statistical baton, the passing of a legacy, one No. 21 to another.

After the Latino season of Sosa, Clemente came to the Yogi Berra Museum on the campus of Montclair State University yesterday to show a film and speak about his father to a group that included a baseball team from Essex Catholic High School in nearby East Orange. Most of the players were Hispanic kids who had come through Newark's Roberto Clemente Little League. The team's best pitcher, Arnaldo Mateo, wears No. 21. The coach, Frank Stanco, said Clemente Jr. was, in this case, preaching to the converted.

"They already know what Roberto Clemente did, why he died," Stanco said. "I've been coaching nine years at this school and if I've learned anything, it's that these kids have a fierce Latino baseball pride. Because of Sosa this year, it just came out that much more."

Sosa and Juan Gonzalez and Pedro Martinez and Mariano Rivera and too many more to mention. It gave David Kaplan, the Berra Museum's director, the idea to conduct a Spanish Heritage Month symposium he titled, "From Clemente to Sosa." It was, as much for the purpose of celebration, to examine the extant cultural barriers.

We had an example of one just this week in New York, as the Mets so conveniently by-passed Omar Minaya—Sammy Sosa discoverer—to dust off Frank Cashen as Steve Phillips's temporary replacement. The Mets said they wanted to continue their troubled general manager's program. Who better than his hand-picked assistant?

"I hate to be a spoilsport but there are some important issues to deal with precisely because of the proliferation of the Latino player," said Roberto Gonzalez Echetarria, who teaches Hispanic and comparative literature at Yale and whose book on Cuban baseball will be released next season. He mentioned, for one, the widespread use of Latino youngsters as cheap and, ultimately, disposable talent.

Some players are so essential they wind up speaking, moving, even giving their lives for others. From Clemente to Sosa, the Latino baseball community at least has itself a galvanizing leader for the 21st century. "We've been waiting for someone like my dad, someone like Sammy, for a long, long time," Clemente Jr. said.

Responding to What You Read

1. Reread the Paul Gallico quotation about heroes at the beginning of "Clemente!" In your own words, explain what you think he means.

2. What similarities between Roberto Clemente and Sammy Sosa are pointed out in the selection?

3. Do you agree that Roberto Clemente and Sammy Sosa are worthy choices for heroes? Explain your answer.

Writer's Workshop

In this selection, Araton points out the fierce pride that Latino teens have in their heritage. Write a short essay (two or three paragraphs) about your own sense of heritage. Explain why your heritage is important in your daily life or why it is not important. Support your ideas by including specific incidents or anecdotes from your life that illustrate the influence of your heritage.

The 7-10 Split

John Sayles

Why is making the 7–10 split such a big deal?

ABOUT THE AUTHOR•ABOUT THE AUTHOR•ABOUT THE AUTHOR•ABOUT THE AUTHOR

John Sayles, who was born in 1950, is one of America's leading independent filmmakers. Some of his best known films include Return of the Secaucus Seven, Baby, It's You, The Secret of Roan Inish, and Eight Men Out, about the famous "Black Sox" baseball scandal of the 1920s.

The 7-10 Spilt

If you don't have your own shoes they rent you a pair for fifty cents. None of us are any big athletes, we meet at the lanes once a week, Thursday night. But some of us have our own shoes. Bobbi for instance, she got a pair cause the rented shoes have their size on the heel in a red leather number and Bobbi doesn't want everybody seeing how big her feet are. She's real conscious of things like that, real conscious of her appearance, like you'd expect a hairdresser to be.

We play two teams, four girls each, and take up a pair of lanes. It's Bobbi and Janey and Blanche and me against Rose Teta, Pat and Vi, and Evelyn Chambers. We've worked it out over the years so the sides are pretty even. A lot of the time the result comes down to whether I been on days at the Home or if Blanche is having problems with her corns. She's on her feet all day at the State Office Building cafeteria and sometimes the corns act up. I figure that I roll around 175 if I'm on graveyard but drop down to 140 if I already done my shift in the morning. Janey works with me at the Home and doesn't seem to mind either which way, but she's the youngest of us.

"Mae," she always says to me, "it's all in your head. If you let yourself think you're tired, you'll be tired. All in your head."

That might be so for her, but you get my age and a lot of what used to be in your head goes directly to your legs.

And Janey is just one of those people was born with a lot of pep. Nightshift at the Home, in between bed checks when all the aides and nurses are sitting around the station moaning about how little sleep they got during the day, Janey is always working like crazy on her macramé plant-hangers. She sells them to some hippie store downtown for the extra income. She's a regular little Christmas elf, Janey, her hands never stop moving. It's a wonder to me how she keeps her looks, what with the lack of rest and the load she's been saddled with, the hand she's been dealt in life. She's both mother and father to her little retarded boy, Scooter, and still she keeps her sweet disposition. We always send her up to the desk when the pinspotter jams, cause Al, who runs the lanes and is real slow to fix things, is sweet on her. You can tell because he takes his earplugs out when she talks to him. Al won't do that for just anybody. Of course, he's married and kind of greasy-looking, but you take your compliments where you can.

It's a real good bunch though, and we have a lot of fun. Rose Teta and Vi work together at the Woolworth's and are like sisters, always borrowing each other's clothes and kidding around. They ought to be on TV, those two. . . . Pat is a real serious Catholic, and though she laughs at Rose and Vi she never does it out loud. Pat's gonna pop a seam some day, laughing so hard with her hand clapped over her mouth.

It was just after kidding around with Bobbi that Evelyn walked in and give us the news. We could tell right off something was wrong—she wasn't carrying her ball bag and she looked real tired, didn't have any makeup on. She walks in and says, "I'm sorry I didn't call you, girls, but I just now come to my decision. I won't be playing Thursdays anymore, I'm joining the Seniors' League."

You could of heard a pin drop. Evelyn is the oldest of us, true, and her hair has mostly gone gray, but she's one of the liveliest women I know. She and Janey always used to make fun of the Seniors' League, all the little kids' games they do and how they give out a trophy every time you turn around. Used to say the Seniors' was for people who had given up, that they set the handicaps so high all you had to do to average 200 was to write your name on the scorecard.

Well, we all wanted to know her reasons and tried to talk her out of it. Since she retired from the State last year, bowling was the only time any of us got to see Evelyn and we didn't want to lose her. She's one of those women makes you feel all right about getting older, at least till this Seniors' business come up. We tried every argument we could think of but she'd made up her mind. She nodded down the alley at the AMF machine clacking the pins into place and she says, "I'm the only one here remembers when they used to be a boy behind there, setting them up by hand. You give him a tip at the end of the night, like a golf caddy. I remember when Al had all his teeth, when the hot dogs here had beef in them. I'm the only one here remembers a lot of things and it's time I quit kidding myself and act my age. You girls can get on without me."

Then she said her good-byes to each of us and walked out, tired looking and smaller than I'd remembered her. Wasn't a dry eye in the house.

But, like they say, life must go on. We evened the sides up by having either me or Blanche sit out every other game and keep score. While we were putting on our shoes we tried to figure out who we could get to replace Evelyn and even up the teams again. June Hundley's name was mentioned, and Edie McIntyre and Lorraine DeFillippo. Of course Bobbi had some objection to each of them, but that's just how she is so we didn't listen. Janey didn't say a word all the while, she seemed real depressed.

Janey and Evelyn were really tight. In one way it's hard to figure since there's so much age difference between them, but then again it makes sense. They've both had a real hard row to hoe, Evelyn's husband dying and Janey's running off. And they both had a child with mental problems. Evelyn had her Buddy, who was Mongoloid and lived till he was twenty-seven. She kept him at home the whole while, even when he got big and hard to manage, and loved him like she would a normal child. Never gave up on him. To his dying day Evelyn was trying to teach Buddy to read, used to sit with him for hours with travel brochures. Buddy liked all the color pictures.

And Janey always puts me in mind of that poor Terry on *General Hospital,* or any of the nice ones on the daytime stories who are always going blind or having their men stolen or losing their memories. Just one thing after another—as if having Scooter wasn't enough trouble in one lifetime. Janey has to bring Scooter on Thursdays cause there isn't a babysitter who could handle him. Al allows it cause like I said, he's sweet on her.

There's no keeping Scooter still, he's ten years old, real stocky and wild-eyed, like a little animal out of control. At the Home they'd keep him full of Valium and he'd be in a fog all day, but Janey won't let the school use drugs on him. Says he's at least entitled to his own sensations, and from what I seen from my patients I agree with her. Scooter is all over the lanes, dancing down the gutters, picking the balls up, drawing on score sheets, playing all the pinball and safari-shoot games in the back even when there's no coin in them. Scooter moves faster than those flippers and bumpers ever could, even pinball must seem like a slow game to him. The only thing he does that Al won't stand for is when he goes to the popcorn machine and laps his tongue on the chute where it comes out. He likes the salt and doesn't understand how he might be putting people off their appetite.

Anyhow, you could just look at Janey and tell she was feeling low. She's usually got a lot of color in her cheeks, it glows when she smiles and sets off nice against her hair. Natural blond, not bottled like Bobbi's is. Well, after Evelyn left she was all pale, no color to her at all, and when we started bowling she didn't have the little bounce in her approach like she usually does. One of the things that's fun is watching the different styles the girls bowl. Like I said, Janey usually comes up to the line really bouncy, up on her toes, and lays the ball down so smooth it's almost silent. You're surprised when you hear the pins crash. Rose and Vi both muscle it down the alley, they're as hard on the boards as they are on the pins, and when they miss a spare clean the ball cracks against the back wall so hard it makes you wince. But when they're in the pocket you should see those pins fly, like an explosion. Bobbi uses that heavy ball and can let it go a lot slower—she always freezes in a picture pose on her follow-through, her arm pointing at the headpin, her back leg up in the air, and her head cocked to the side. She looks like a bowling trophy—sometime we'll have her bronzed while she's waiting for her ball to connect. Pat plays by those little arrows on the boards behind the foul line, she doesn't even look at the pins. She's like a machine—same starting spot, same four-and-a-half steps, same little kneeling dip as she lets go, like she's genuflecting. Blanche has this awful hook to her ball, some kind of funny hitch she does with her elbow on her backswing. She has to stand way over to the right to have a shot at the pocket and sometimes when she's tired she'll lay one right in the gutter on her first ball. She gets a lot of action when she connects with that spin, though she leaves the 10-pin over on the right corner a lot and it's hard for her to pick up.

I'm a lefty, so the lanes are grooved in my favor, but I don't know what I look like. The girls say I charge the line too fast and foul sometimes, but I'm not really aware of it.

The other thing with Janey's style is the 7–10 split. It's the hardest to pick up, the two pins standing on opposite sides of the lane, and because Janey throws a real straight ball she sees it a lot. Most people settle for an open frame, hit one or the other of the pins solid and forget about trying to convert, but Janey always tries to pick up. You have to shade the outside of one of the pins perfectly so it either slides directly over to take out the other or bangs off the back wall and nails it on the rebound. Even the pros don't make it very often and there's always a good chance you'll throw a gutter ball and end up missing both pins. But Janey always goes for it, even if we're in a tight game and that one sure pin could make the difference. That's just how she plays it. It drives Bobbi nuts, whenever Janey leaves a 7–10 Bobbi moans and rolls her eyes.

Of course Bobbi is a little competitive with Janey, they're the closest in age and both still on the market. Bobbi is always saying in that high breathy voice of hers that's so surprising coming from such a—well, such a *big* woman—she's always saying, "I just can't under*stand* why Janey doesn't have a man after her. What with all her nice qualities." Like it's some fault of Janey's—like working split shifts at a nursing home and taking care of a kid who makes motorcycle sounds and bounces off the walls all day leaves you much time to go looking for a husband.

Not that Janey doesn't try. She gets herself out to functions at the PNA and the Sons of Italy Hall and Ladies' Nite at Barney's when they let you in free to dance. The trouble is, she's got standards, Janey. Nothing unreasonable, but considering what's available in the way of unattached men, having any standards at all seems crazy. Janey won't have any truck with the married ones or the drinkers, which cuts the field in half to start with. And what's left isn't nothing to set your heart going pitter-pat. When I think of what Janey's up against it makes me appreciate my Earl and the boys, though they're no bargain most of the time. Janey's not getting any younger, of course, and any man interested in her has got to buy Scooter in the same package and that's a lot to ask. But Janey hasn't given up. "There's always an outside chance, Mae," she says. "And even if nothing works out, look at Evelyn. All that she's been through, and she hasn't let it beat her. Nope, you got to keep trying, there's always an outside chance." Like with her 7–10 splits, always trying to pick them up.

But she never made a one of them. All the times she's tried, she's never hit it just right, never got the 7–10 spare. Not a one.

Anyhow, last Thursday after Evelyn left we got into our first string and Janey started out awful. Honey, it was just pitiful to see. None of the girls were really up to form, but Janey was the worst, no bounce in her approach, just walked up flat-footed and dropped the ball with a big thud onto the boards. Turned away from the pins almost before she seen what the ball left, with this pinched look on her face that showed up all the wrinkles she's starting to get. Leaving three, four pins in a cluster on her first ball, then missing the spares. The teams were all out of balance without Evelyn, *we* were all out of balance. Blanche's hook was even worse than usual and Pat couldn't seem to find the right arrows on the boards and I couldn't for the life of me keep behind that foul line. Everyone was real quiet, Rose and Vi weren't joking like always, and the noise of the lanes took over.

Usually I like it, the girls all talking and laughing, that strange bright light all around you, the rumbling and crashing. It reminds me of the Rip Van Winkle story they told in school when I was a girl, how the dwarfs bowling on the green were the cause of thunder and lightning. It's exciting, kind of. But that night with Evelyn gone and the girls so quiet it scared me. The pins sounded real hollow when they were hit, the sound of the bowling balls on the wood was hollow too, sounded like we were the only people left in the lanes. It gave me the creeps and I tried to concentrate on keeping score.

Scooter was drawing all over the score sheet like he always does, making his motorcycle revving noise, but we've gotten used to reading through his scribble and I didn't pay it no mind. All of a sudden Janey reaches over and smacks his hand, real hard. It was like a gunshot, Pat near jumped out of her seat. Usually Janey is the most patient person in the world, she'll explain to Scooter for the millionth time why he shouldn't lick the popcorn chute while she steers him away from it real gentle. I remember how upset she got when she first come to the Home and saw how some of the girls would slap a patient who was mean or just difficult. She always offered to take those patients off their hands, and found some calmer way to deal with them.

But here she'd just smacked Scooter like she really meant it and for once his engine stalled, and he just stood and stared at her like the rest of us did. Then Bobbi's ball finally reached the pocket and broke the spell. Scooter zoomed away and we all found something else to look at.

It put me in mind of when Evelyn's husband Boyd had his stroke and come to the Home for his last days. It was right when they'd moved Janey to the men's ward to help me with the heavy lifting cause the orderlies were so useless. Evelyn would come every night after work and sit by Boyd, and in between checks Janey would go in to keep her company. Boyd was awake a lot of the time but wasn't much company, as he'd had the kind where your motor control goes and all he could say was "ob-bob-bob-bob" or something like that. What impressed Janey most was how Evelyn kept planning this trip to Florida they'd set up before the stroke, as if the rehabilitation was going to make a miracle and Boyd would ever get to leave the Home. She'd ask him questions about what they'd bring or where they'd visit and he'd answer by nodding. Kept him alive for a good six months, planning that trip. "How bout this Parrot Jungle, Boyd," I'd hear when I'd walk by the room to answer a bell, "would you like to stop there?" Then she'd wait for a nod. Janey would come out of that room with a light in her eyes, it was something to see. And honey, three weeks after Boyd went out, didn't Evelyn go and take her Buddy down to Florida all by herself, stopped in every place they'd planned together and sent us all postcards.

Anyhow, the night went on. Sometimes it can get to be work, the bowling, and by the fourth string everybody was looking half dead. Dropping the ball instead of rolling it, bumping it against their legs on the backswing, waving their thumb blisters over the little air vent on the return rack—a real bunch of stiffs. Almost no one was talking and Bobbi had taken out her little mirror and was playing with her hair, a sure sign that she's in a nasty mood. We'd had a few lucky strikes but no one had hit for a double or a turkey and there were open frames all over the place. Everybody was down twenty to forty points from their average and we'd only ordered one round of Cokes and beers. Usually we keep Al hopping cause talking and yelling gets us so thirsty. When I felt how heavy my legs were I remembered I still had to pull my eleven-to-seven shift, had to get urine samples from all the diabetics on the ward and help with old Sipperly's tube-feeding, I started feeling very old, like *I* should be joining the Seniors', not Evelyn.

Then in the eighth frame Janey laid one right on the nose of the head-pin, first time she hit the pocket square all night, and there it stood. The 7–10 split. Sort of taunting, like a gap-toothed grin staring at her. It was real quiet in the lanes then, the way it goes sometimes, like a break in the storm. Janey stood looking at it with her hands on her hips while her ball came back in slow motion. She picked it up and got her feet set and then held still for the longest time, concentrating. She was going for it, we could tell she was going to try to make it and we all held our breaths.

Janey stepped to the line with a little bounce and rolled the ball smooth and light, rolled it on the very edge of the right-hand gutter with just the slightest bit of reverse English on it and it teetered on the edge all the way down, then faded at the end just barely nipping the 10, sliding it across to tip the 7–pin as it went down, tilting that 7 on its edge and if we'd had the breath we'd of blown it over but then the bastard righted itself, *righted* and began to wobble, wobbled a little Charlie Chaplin walk across the wood and plopped flat on its back into the gutter.

Well, we all set up a whoop and Janey turned to us with this little hopeful smile on her face, cheeks all glowing again like a little girl who just done her First Communion coming back down the aisle looking to her folks for approval and even Bobbi, who was up next, even Bobbi give her a big hug while little Scooter drew X's all over the score sheet.

Responding to What You Read

1. This selection presents a "slice of life"—a brief, realistic account that focuses on the hopes and frustrations of ordinary people engaged in ordinary daily activities. What details can you find in the selection that help bring to life this "slice of life"?

2. When Janey converts the 7–10 split at the end of the story, it clearly is a special moment. Based on what you learn about these women in the course of the story, why is this moment a special one?

Writer's Workshop

This story is told from the point of view of a **first-person narrator.** Everything we learn in the story we learn from Mae. We know what she knows about the other characters and what she thinks about the other characters, but nothing more. We do not know what the other characters know or think.

Write a brief story using a first-person narrator. Develop your story around a simple social situation: a bowling date, a pizza party, a movie outing, a picnic, a trip to an amusement park, or the like. Select one character from your story and tell the events from that character's point of view, in the first person. Remember to relate only what that character knows and thinks.

PERSPECTIVES

A Rare Bird Sighted Again

Vic Ziegel

Mark Fidrych

Tom Clark

This "rare bird" soared to fame for only a couple of seasons and then moved on— but what a flight!

Vic Ziegel is a sports columnist for the New York Daily News *known for his humorous, heart-warming, and—when necessary—hard-hitting observations on the world of sports. He also writes feature stories profiling interesting New Yorkers, stories that capture the life, spirit, and energy of New York City. Regarding his work in general and this article on Mark Fidrych in particular, he says, "I have been writing about sports and interesting people in sports since 1964. I became a sportswriter because I thought it was the one section in a newspaper that allowed you to write in an entertaining way. I still feel that way. So Fidrych was a perfect subject. He's an open, delightful man."*

A Rare Bird Sighted Again

His professional career lasted 10 seasons, but only four came in the big leagues. A great year, a tough year, and two absolutely lousy years. He tried to come back, more than once, and couldn't.

He lives on a farm now, and drives a truck. His farm, his truck, his still-terrific smile.

"I go back to Detroit when they invite me," says Mark (The Bird) Fidrych, "and the guys at the airport who handle the bags, they say, 'How you doing, Mr. Fidrych?' It makes you feel great. I'm lucky that people still remember me."

No, no, that must be wrong. There is no Mr. Fidrych. The blond curly hair is still sticking out from under his baseball cap. The little-boy grin still on his face. If The Bird has grown up and become Mr. Fidrych, where does that leave the rest of us?

Don't they call you Bird, I asked. "They're young guys," he answered.

And he's 38, a few weeks away from 39, with a wife and a 6-year-old daughter and a telephone answering machine for people who need him and his 10-wheel truck to pick up and haul asphalt or gunk from septic systems.

When he comes home at night, he lets his daughter, Jessica, help him with the mail. People write and ask for his autograph. They enclose the

Sports Illustrated cover that shows him on the mound, in his Detroit uniform, with Big Bird standing behind him.

He became The Bird on a Rookie League club in Bristol, Tenn., because a teammate, Jeff Hogan, made the connection after watching "Sesame Street." Hogan, he said, told him, "You walk goofy, and you're here, there, everywhere. Between the white lines you're serious, but outside them you don't know what's going on."

He was 19 and living away from home for the first time. "I had an apartment," he said, "and I found out what a phone bill was. What rent was." Rent, it turned out, was what he never had. So he'd call the real Mr. Fidrych, and say, "The rent's due, Dad."

A couple of years later, he was in the big leagues. And for one sweet season, he managed to make the very serious business of throwing a baseball seem like great fun. Out there on the mound, with everybody staring at him, he talked to the ball, and talked to himself. He puttered around the mound. He talked to his fielders, congratulated them after putouts.

Silly stuff, maybe, but there was nothing silly about the results. His rookie season, 1976, he was 19–9. A 2.34 earned-run average, 24 complete games. He started the All-Star Game—the excuse to have him here yesterday for the Heroes of Baseball Old-Timers' Game—and still remembers meeting President Gerald Ford that day. It wasn't his idea.

Somebody was lining up the players to shake hands with the President, and Fidrych said, probably hopping up and down, "I'll meet him after the game. I got a game to play now."

They held him down long enough to introduce the pitcher to the President, both of whom walked goofy. Yesterday, standing behind the batting cage, Fidrych remembered the conversation. "I said, 'OK. Mr. Ford, how you doing? I got a game to play. I hope you understand.'"

A year later he was invited back for the All-Star Game in Yankee Stadium, "but I told them to get somebody else, my arm was blown out." First his knee, then his arm. He was in spring training, running back to the clubhouse. There was a small fence, three feet, maybe a little higher. There was a gate, too. But Bird decided to jump the fence. He twisted a knee.

Surgery kept him out until June. Tendinitis, and a bad elbow, kept him from matching his rookie numbers. He hung on, a wounded Bird, until 1980.

The farm, about 45 minutes from Boston, came next. He keeps sheep and cattle and calls it "a gentleman's farm, nonprofit. It feeds me, that's about it. It's 121 acres, mostly woods. Someday I'll clear it."

Not long ago, when he took his daughter to the supermarket, a woman asked if he was Mark Fidrych. "You want his autograph?" Jessica said. "He'll give you his autograph."

He loves getting mail and goes wherever he's invited, and there's an occasional card show. There could be more shows, but this is Fidrych, who's a different sort of bird. The first one he did, the kids in line for his autograph handed him tickets. "I said, 'Whoa, time out. What are these tickets?'"

Somebody explained that each of the kids was paying a few extra bucks for his signature. "I said, 'Forget that.' If they want me at the show, they pay me, but they can't charge extra for tickets. It's my say, so I say it. If they won't do it that way, I say, 'Fine, you don't want me then.'"

"I don't mind," says Mark Fidrych, who's got a farm, and a truck, and a still-terrific smile. "I got other things to do with my life."

ABOUT THE AUTHOR•ABOUT THE AUTHOR•ABOUT THE AUTHOR•ABOUT THE AUTHOR

T*om Clark is the author of* When Things Get Tough on Easy Street *and* Champagne and Baloney: The Rise and Fall of Finley's A's. *He teaches poetry at New College of California.*

Mark Fidrych

Nobody ever rode a higher wave or gave us more
back of what it taught
Or thought less of it,
Shrugging off the fame it
5   brought, calling it "no big deal"
And, once it was taken
away, refusing bitterness with such
Amazing grace.
Absence of damage limits one's perception
10   of existence.
Suffering, while not to be pursued,
Yields at least what Mark
termed "trains of thoughts,"
Those late, sad milk runs to Evansville
15   and Pawtucket
Which he viewed
not simply as pilgrimages
Of loss, but as interesting trips
In themselves—tickets to ride
20   that long dark tunnel through
Which everybody—even those less gifted—must sooner
Or later pass
Because, "hey, that's what you call life."

Responding to What You Read

What impression do you get of Mark Fidrych from reading both of these pieces of writing? Support your opinion with examples from the selections.

Writer's Workshop

Using research resources (the internet and your local library, for example), find two different articles written about Mark Fidrych during the time he was playing baseball in the major leagues. Write a short paper in which you summarize what the writers of these two articles said about Fidrych when he was at his peak. Attach copies of the articles to your report.

From *The Chosen*

Chaim Potok

Winning takes on a new meaning in this intense softball game.

ABOUT THE AUTHOR•ABOUT THE AUTHOR•ABOUT THE AUTHOR•ABOUT THE AUTHOR

Chaim Potok, who was born in 1929, is the author of a number of acclaimed novels, including My Name is Asher Lev, The Chosen, *from which this excerpt was taken, and a sequel,* The Promise. *Potok began to write fiction when he was sixteen. He earned a Ph.D. in philosophy from the University of Pennsylvania. Potok was trained and ordained as a rabbi and served as U.S. Army Chaplain in Korea.*

Life *magazine said of* The Chosen, *"His remarkable book will give universality to a tiny section of Williamsburg in Brooklyn, as [James] Joyce gave an eternity of urbane meaning to one day in Dublin's Fair City." Elie Weisel called* The Chosen *"profoundly moving and beautifully told."*

From *The Chosen*

Danny and I probably would never have met—or we would have met under altogether different circumstances—had it not been for America's entry into the Second World War and the desire this bred on the part of some English teachers in the Jewish parochial schools to show the gentile world that yeshiva[1] students were as physically fit, despite their long hours of study, as any other American student. They went about proving this by organizing the Jewish parochial schools in and around our area into competitive

---

1. yeshiva: a Jewish day school.

leagues, and once every two weeks the schools would compete against one another in a variety of sports. I became a member of my school's varsity softball team.

On a Sunday afternoon in early June, the fifteen members of my team met with our gym instructor in the play yard of our school. It was a warm day, and the sun was bright on the asphalt floor of the yard. The gym instructor was a short, chunky man in his early thirties who taught in the mornings in a nearby public high school and supplemented his income by teaching in our yeshiva during the afternoons. He wore a white polo shirt, white pants, and white sweater, and from the awkward way the little black skullcap sat perched on his round, balding head, it was clearly apparent that he was not accustomed to wearing it with any sort of regularity. When he talked he frequently thumped his right fist into his left palm to empha-size a point. He walked on the balls of his feet, almost in imitation of a boxer's ring stance, and he was fanatically addicted to professional baseball. He had nursed our softball team along for two years, and by a mixture of patience, luck, shrewd manipulations during some tight ball games, and hard, fist-thumping harangues[2] calculated to shove us into a patriotic awareness of the importance of athletics and physical fitness for the war effort, he was able to mold our original team of fifteen awkward fumblers into the top team of our league. His name was Mr. Galanter, and all of us wondered why he was not off somewhere fighting in the war.

During my two years with the team, I had become quite adept at sec-ond base and also developed a swift underhand pitch that would tempt a batter into a swing but would drop into a curve at the last moment and slide just below the flaying bat for a strike. Mr. Galanter always began a ball game by putting me at second base and would use me as a pitcher only in very tight moments, because, as he put it once, "My baseball philosophy is grounded on the defensive solidarity of the infield."

That afternoon we were scheduled to play the winning team of another neighborhood league, a team with a reputation for wild, offensive slugging and poor fielding. Mr. Galanter said he was counting upon our infield to act as a solid defensive front. Throughout the warm-up period, with only our team in the yard, he kept thumping his right fist into his left palm and shouting at us to be a solid defensive front.

---

2. harangues: ranting lectures.

"No holes," he shouted from near home plate. "No holes, you hear? Goldberg, what kind of solid defensive front is that? Close in. A battleship could get between you and Malter. That's it. Schwartz, what are you doing, looking for paratroops? This is a ball game. The enemy's on the ground. That throw was wide, Goldberg. Throw it like a sharpshooter. Give him the ball again. Throw it. Good. Like a sharpshooter. Very good. Keep the infield solid. No defensive holes in this war."

We batted and threw the ball around, and it was warm and sunny, and there was the smooth, happy feeling of the summer soon to come, and the tight excitement of the ball game. We wanted very much to win, both for ourselves and, more especially, for Mr. Galanter, for we had all come to like his fist-thumping sincerity. To the rabbis[3] who taught in the Jewish parochial schools, baseball was an evil waste of time, a spawn of the potentially assimilationist[4] English portion of the yeshiva day. But to the students of most of the parochial schools, an inter-league baseball victory had come to take on only a shade less significance than a top grade in Talmud,[5] for it was an unquestioned mark of one's Americanism, and to be counted a loyal American had become increasingly important to us during these last years of the war.

So Mr. Galanter stood near home plate, shouting instructions and words of encouragement, and we batted and tossed the ball around. I walked off the field for a moment to set up my eyeglasses for the game. I wore shell-rimmed glasses, and before every game I would bend the earpieces in so the glasses would stay tight on my head and not slip down the bridge of my nose when I began to sweat. I always waited until just before a game to bend down the earpieces, because, bent, they would cut into the skin over my ears, and I did not want to feel the pain a moment longer than I had to. The tops of my ears would be sore for days after every game, but better that, I thought, than the need to keep pushing my glasses up the bridge of my nose or the possibility of having them fall off suddenly during an important play.

Davey Cantor, one of the boys who acted as a replacement if a first-stringer had to leave the game, was standing near the wire screen behind

---

3. rabbis: spiritual leaders of the Jewish community.
4. assimilationist: a person who advocates absorbing the culture of another population or group.
5. Talmud: the body of knowledge and tradition upon which the Jewish faith is based.

home plate. He was a short boy, with a round face, dark hair, owlish glasses, and a very Semitic[6] nose. He watched me fix my glasses.

"You're looking good out there, Reuven," he told me.

"Thanks," I said.

"Everyone is looking real good."

"It'll be a good game."

He stared at me through his glasses. "You think so?" he asked.

"Sure, why not?"

"You ever seen them play, Reuven?"

"No."

"They're murderers."

"Sure," I said.

"No, really. They're wild."

"You saw them play?"

"Twice. They're murderers."

"Everyone plays to win, Davey."

"They don't only play to win. They play like it's the first of the Ten Commandments."

I laughed. "That yeshiva?" I said. "Oh, come on, Davey."

"It's the truth."

"Sure," I said.

"Reb Saunders ordered them never to lose because it would shame their yeshiva or something. I don't know. You'll see."

"Hey, Malter!" Mr. Galanter shouted. "What are you doing, sitting this one out?"

"You'll see," Davey Cantor said.

"Sure." I grinned at him. "A holy war."

He looked at me.

"Are you playing?" I asked him.

"Mr. Galanter said I might take second base if you have to pitch."

"Well, good luck."

"Hey, Malter!" Mr. Galanter shouted. "There's a war on, remember?"

"Yes, sir!" I said, and ran back out to my position at second base.

We threw the ball around a few more minutes, and then I went up to home plate for some batting practice. I hit a long one out to left field, and

---

6. **Semitic:** Jewish

then a fast one to the shortstop, who fielded it neatly and whipped it to first. I had the bat ready for another swing when someone said, "Here they are," and I rested the bat on my shoulder and saw the team we were going to play turn up our block and come into the yard. I saw Davey Cantor kick nervously at the wire screen behind home plate, then put his hands into the pockets of his dungarees.[7] His eyes were wide and gloomy behind his owlish glasses.

I watched them come into the yard.

There were fifteen of them, and they were dressed alike in white shirts, dark pants, white sweaters, and small black skullcaps. In the fashion of the very Orthodox,[8] their hair was closely cropped, except for the area near their ears from which mushroomed the untouched hair that tumbled down into the long side curls. Some of them had the beginnings of beards, straggly tufts of hair that stood in isolated clumps on their chins, jawbones, and upper lips. They all wore the traditional undergarment beneath their shirts, and the tzitzit, the long fringes appended to the four corners of the garment, came out above their belts and swung against their pants as they walked. These were the very Orthodox, and they obeyed literally the Biblical commandment *And ye shall look upon it,* which pertains to the fringes.

In contrast, our team had no particular uniform, and each of us wore whatever he wished: dungarees, shorts, pants, polo shirts, sweat shirts, even undershirts. Some of us wore the garment, others did not. None of us wore the fringes outside his trousers. The only element of uniform that we had in common was the small, black skullcap which we, too, wore.

They came up to the first-base side of the wire screen behind home plate and stood there in a silent black-and-white mass, holding bats and balls and gloves in their hands. I looked at them. They did not seem to me to present any picture of ferocity. I saw Davey Cantor kick again at the wire screen, then walk away from them to the third-base line, his hands moving nervously against his dungarees.

Mr. Galanter smiled and started toward them, moving quickly on the balls of his feet, his skullcap perched precariously on the top of his balding head.

A man disentangled himself from the black-and-white mass of players and took a step forward. He looked to be in his late twenties and wore a

---

7. dungarees: denim pants, jeans.
8. Orthodox: a reference to those Jews who adhere strictly to Jewish law and apply it to everyday life.

black suit, black shoes, and a black hat. He had a black beard, and he carried a book under one arm. He was obviously a rabbi, and I marveled that the yeshiva had placed a rabbi instead of an athletic coach over its team.

Mr. Galanter came up to him and offered his hand.

"We are ready to play," the rabbi said in Yiddish,[9] shaking Mr. Galanter's hand with obvious uninterest.

"Fine," Mr. Galanter said in English, smiling.

The rabbi looked out at the field. "You played already?" he asked.

"How's that?" Mr. Galanter said.

"You had practice?"

"Well, sure—"

"We want to practice."

"How's that?" Mr. Galanter said again, looking surprised.

"You practiced, now we practice."

"You didn't practice in your own yard?"

"We practiced."

"Well, then—"

"But we have never played in your yard before. We want a few minutes."

"Well, now," Mr. Galanter said, "there isn't much time. The rules are each team practices in its own yard."

"We want five minutes," the rabbi insisted.

"Well—" Mr. Galanter said. He was no longer smiling. He always liked to go right into a game when we played in our own yard. It kept us from cooling off, he said.

"Five minutes," the rabbi said. "Tell your people to leave the field."

"How's that?" Mr. Galanter said.

"We cannot practice with your people on the field. Tell them to leave the field."

"Well, now," Mr. Galanter said, then stopped. He thought for a long moment. The black-and-white mass of players behind the rabbi stood very still, waiting. I saw Davey Cantor kick at the asphalt floor of the yard. "Well, all right. Five minutes. Just five minutes, now."

"Tell your people to leave the field," the rabbi said.

---

9. Yiddish: a Jewish language derived from the German, Hebrew, and Slavic languages that originated in Middle and Eastern Europe.

Mr. Galanter stared gloomily out at the field, looking a little deflated. "Everybody off!" he shouted, not very loudly. "They want a five-minute warm-up. Hustle, hustle. Keep those arms going. Keep it hot. Toss some balls around behind home. Let's go!"

The players scrambled off the field.

The black-and-white mass near the wire screen remained intact. The young rabbi turned and faced his team.

He talked in Yiddish. "We have the field for five minutes," he said. "Remember why and for whom we play."

Then he stepped aside, and the black-and-white mass dissolved into fifteen individual players who came quickly onto the field. One of them, a tall boy with sand-colored hair and long arms and legs that seemed all bones and angles, stood at home plate and commenced hitting balls out to the players. He hit a few easy grounders and pop-ups, and the fielders shouted encouragement to one another in Yiddish. They handled themselves awkwardly, dropping easy grounders, throwing wild, fumbling fly balls. I looked over at the young rabbi. He had sat down on the bench near the wire screen and was reading his book.

Behind the wire screen was a wide area, and Mr. Galanter kept us busy there throwing balls around.

"Keep those balls going!" he fist-thumped at us. "No one sits out this fire fight! Never underestimate the enemy!"

But there was a broad smile on his face. Now that he was actually seeing the other team, he seemed not at all concerned about the outcome of the game. In the interim between throwing a ball and having it thrown back to me, I told myself that I liked Mr. Galanter, and I wondered about his constant use of war expressions and why he wasn't in the army.

Davey Cantor came past me, chasing a ball that had gone between his legs.

"Some murderers," I grinned at him.

"You'll see," he said as he bent to retrieve the ball.

"Sure," I said.

"Especially the one batting. You'll see."

The ball was coming back to me, and I caught it neatly and flipped it back.

"Who's the one batting?" I asked.

"Danny Saunders."

"Pardon my ignorance, but who is Danny Saunders?"

"Reb Saunder's son," Davey Cantor said, blinking his eyes.

"I'm impressed."

"You'll see," Davey Cantor said, and ran off with his ball.

My father, who had no love at all for Hasidic[10] communities and their rabbinical overlords, had told me about Rabbi Isaac Saunders and the zealousness with which he ruled his people and settled questions of Jewish law.

I saw Mr. Galanter look at his wristwatch, then stare out at the team on the field. The five minutes were apparently over, but the players were making no move to abandon the field. Danny Saunders was now at first base, and I noticed that his long arms and legs were being used to good advantage, for by stretching and jumping he was able to catch most of the wild throws that came his way.

Mr. Galanter went over to the young rabbi who was still sitting on the bench and reading.

"It's five minutes," he said.

The rabbi looked up from his book. "Ah?" he said.

"The five minutes are up," Mr. Galanter said.

The rabbi stared out at the field. "Enough!" he shouted in Yiddish. "It's time to play!" Then he looked down at the book and resumed his reading.

The players threw the ball around for another minute or two, and then slowly came off the field. Danny Saunders walked past me, still wearing his first baseman's glove. He was a good deal taller than I, and in contrast to my somewhat ordinary but decently proportioned features and dark hair, his face seemed to have been cut from stone. His chin, jaw and cheekbones were made up of jutting hard lines, his nose was straight and pointed, his lips full, rising to a steep angle from the center point beneath his nose and then slanting off to form a too-wide mouth. His eyes were deep blue, and the sparse tufts of hair on his chin, jawbones, and upper lip, the close-cropped hair on his head, and the flow of side curls along his ears were the color of sand. He moved in a loose-jointed, disheveled sort of way, all arms and legs, talking in Yiddish to one of his teammates and ignoring me completely as he passed by. I told myself that I did not like his Hasidic-bred sense of superiority and that it would be a great pleasure to defeat him and his team in this afternoon's game.

The umpire, a gym instructor from a parochial school two blocks away, called the teams together to determine who would bat first. I saw him

---

10. **Hasidic:** a reference to those Jews who are Hasidim, members of a sect that originated in Poland and demands strict obedience of religious law.

throw a bat into the air. It was caught and almost dropped by a member of the other team.

During the brief hand-over-hand choosing, Davey Cantor came over and stood next to me.

"What do you think?" he asked.

"They're a snooty bunch," I told him.

"What do you think about their playing?"

"They're lousy."

"They're murderers."

"Oh, come on, Davey."

"You'll see," Davey Cantor said, looking at me gloomily.

"I just did see."

"You didn't see anything."

"Sure," I said. "Elijah the prophet comes in to pitch for them in tight spots."

"I'm not being funny," he said, looking hurt.

"Some murderers," I told him, and laughed.

The teams began to disperse. We had lost the choosing, and they had decided to bat first. We scampered onto the field. I took up my position at second base. I saw the young rabbi sitting on the bench near the wire fence and reading. We threw a ball around for a minute. Mr. Galanter stood alongside third base, shouting his words of encouragement at us. It was warm, and I was sweating a little and feeling very good. Then the umpire, who had taken up his position behind the pitcher, called for the ball and someone tossed it to him. He handed it to the pitcher and shouted, "Here we go! Play ball!" We settled into our positions.

Mr. Galanter shouted, "Goldberg, move in!" and Sidney Goldberg, our shortstop, took two steps forward and moved a little closer to third base. "Okay, fine," Mr. Galanter said. "Keep that infield solid!"

A short, thin boy came up to the plate and stood there with his feet together, holding the bat awkwardly over his head. He wore steel-rimmed glasses that gave his face a pinched, old man's look. He swung wildly at the first pitch, and the force of the swing spun him completely around. His earlocks lifted off the sides of his head and followed him around in an almost horizontal circle. Then he steadied himself and resumed his position near the plate, short, thin, his feet together, holding his bat over his head in an awkward grip.

The umpire called the strike in a loud, clear voice, and I saw Sidney Goldberg look over at me and grin broadly.

"If he studies Talmud like that, he's dead," Sidney Goldberg said.

I grinned back at him.

"Keep that infield solid!" Mr. Galanter shouted from third base. "Malter, a little to your left! Good!"

The next pitch was too high, and the boy chopped at it, lost his bat and fell forward on his hands. Sidney Goldberg and I looked at each other again. Sidney was in my class. We were similar in build, tall and lithe, with some-what spindly arms and legs. He was not a very good student, but he was an excellent shortstop. We lived on the same block and were good but not close friends. He was dressed in an undershirt and dungarees and was not wearing the four-cornered garment. I had on a light-blue shirt and dark-blue work pants, and I wore the four-cornered garment under the shirt.

The short, thin boy was back at the plate, standing with his feet together and holding the bat in his awkward grip. He let the next pitch go by, and the umpire called it a strike. I saw the young rabbi look up a moment from his book, then resume reading.

"Two more just like that!" I shouted encouragingly to the pitcher. "Two more, Schwartzie!" And I thought to myself, Some murderers.

I saw Danny Saunders go over to the boy who had just struck out and talk to him. The boy looked down and seemed to shrivel with hurt. He hung his head and walked away behind the wire screen. Another short, thin boy took his place at the plate. I looked around for Davey Cantor but could not see him.

The boy at bat swung wildly at the first two pitches and missed them both. He swung again at the third pitch, and I heard the loud thwack of the bat as it connected with the ball, and saw the ball move in a swift, straight line toward Sidney Goldberg, who caught it, bobbled it for a moment, and finally got it into his glove. He tossed the ball to me, and we threw it around. I saw him take off his glove and shake his left hand.

"That hurt," he said, grinning at me.

"Good catch," I told him.

"That hurt like hell," he said, and put his glove back on his hand.

The batter who stood now at the plate was broad-shouldered and built like a bear. He swung at the first pitch, missed, then swung again at the sec-ond pitch and sent the ball in a straight line over the head of the third baseman into left field. I scrambled to second, stood on the base and shouted for the ball. I saw the left fielder pick it up on the second bounce and relay it to me. It was coming in a little high, and I had my glove raised for it. I felt more than saw the batter charging toward second, and as I was getting my glove on the ball he smashed into me like a truck. The ball went over my head, and I fell forward heavily onto the asphalt floor of the yard, and he passed me, going toward third, his fringes flying out behind him, holding his skullcap to his head with his right hand so it would not fall off. Abe Goodstein, our first baseman, retrieved the ball and whipped it home, and the batter stood at third, a wide grin on his face.

The yeshiva team exploded into wild cheers and shouted loud words of congratulations in Yiddish to the batter.

Sidney Goldberg helped me get to my feet.

"That momzer!"[11] he said. "You weren't in his way!"

"Wow!" I said, taking a few deep breaths. I had scraped the palm of my right hand.

"What a momzer!" Sidney Goldberg said.

I saw Mr. Galanter come storming onto the field to talk to the umpire. "What kind of play was that?" he asked heatedly. "How are you going to rule that?"

"Safe at third," the umpire said. "Your boy was in the way."

Mr. Galanter's mouth fell open. "How's that again?"

"Safe at third," the umpire repeated.

Mr. Galanter looked ready to argue, thought better of it, then stared over at me. "Are you all right, Malter?"

"I'm okay," I said, taking another deep breath.

Mr. Galanter walked angrily off the field.

"Play ball!" the umpire shouted.

The yeshiva team quieted down. I saw that the young rabbi was now looking up from his book and smiling faintly.

A tall, thin player came up to the plate, set his feet in correct position, swung his bat a few times, then crouched into a waiting stance. I saw it was Danny Saunders. I opened and closed my right hand, which was still sore from the fall.

---

11. momzer: a Yiddish term of abuse, usually directed to one who is nasty or devious.

"Move back! Move back!" Mr. Galanter was shouting from alongside third base, and I took two steps back.

I crouched, waiting.

The first pitch was wild, and the yeshiva team burst into loud laughter. The young rabbi was sitting on the bench, watching Danny Saunders intently.

"Take it easy, Schwartzie!" I shouted encouragingly to the pitcher. "There's only one more to go!"

The next pitch was about a foot over Danny Saunders' head, and the yeshiva team howled with laughter. Sidney Goldberg and I looked at each other. I saw Mr. Galanter standing very still alongside third, staring at the pitcher. The rabbi was still watching Danny Saunders.

The next pitch left Schwartzie's hand in a long, slow line, and before it was halfway to the plate I knew Danny Saunders would try for it. I knew it from the way his left foot came forward and the bat snapped back and his long, thin body began its swift pivot. I tensed, waiting for the sound of the bat against the ball, and when it came it sounded like a gunshot. For a wild fraction of a second I lost sight of the ball. Then I saw Schwartzie dive to the ground, and there was the ball coming through the air where his head had been, and I tried for it but it was moving too fast, and I barely had my glove raised before it was in center field. It was caught on a bounce and thrown to Sidney Goldberg, but by that time Danny Saunders was standing solidly on my base and the yeshiva team was screaming with joy.

Mr. Galanter called for time and walked over to talk to Schwartzie. Sidney Goldberg nodded to me, and the two of us went over to them.

"That ball could've killed me!" Schwartzie was saying. He was of medium size, with a long face and a bad case of acne. He wiped sweat from his face. "My God, did you see that ball?"

"I saw it," Mr. Galanter said grimly.

"That was too fast to stop, Mr. Galanter," I said in Schwartzie's defense.

"I heard about that Danny Saunders," Sidney Goldberg said. "He always hits the pitcher."

"You could've told me," Schwartzie lamented. "I could've been ready."

"I only *heard* about it," Sidney Goldberg said. "You always believe everything you hear?"

"God, that ball could've killed me!" Schwartzie said again.

"You want to go on pitching?" Mr. Galanter said. A thin sheen of sweat covered his forehead, and he looked very grim.

"Sure, Mr. Galanter," Schwartzie said, "I'm okay."

"You're sure?"

"Sure I'm sure."

"No heroes in this war, now," Mr. Galanter said. "I want live soldiers, not dead heroes."

"I'm no hero," Schwartzie muttered lamely. "I can still get it over, Mr. Galanter. God, it's only the first inning."

"Okay, soldier," Mr. Galanter said, not very enthusiastically. "Just keep our side of this war fighting."

"I'm trying my best, Mr. Galanter," Schwartzie said.

Mr. Galanter nodded, still looking grim, and started off the field. I saw him take a handkerchief out of his pocket and wipe his forehead.

●　　●　　●　　●

The umpire came over to us. "You boys planning to chat here all afternoon?" he asked. He was a squat man in his late forties, and he looked impatient.

"No, sir," I said very politely, and Sidney and I ran back to our places.

Danny Saunders was standing on my base. His white shirt was pasted to his arms and back with sweat.

"That was a nice shot," I offered.

He looked at me curiously and said nothing.

"You always hit it like that to the pitcher?" I asked.

He smiled faintly. "You're Reuven Malter," he said in perfect English. He had a low, nasal voice.

"That's right," I said, wondering where he had heard my name.

"You're father is David Malter, the one who writes articles on the Talmud?"

"Yes."

"I told my team we're going to kill you apikorsim[12] this afternoon." He said it flatly, without a trace of expression in his voice.

I stared at him and hoped the sudden tight coldness I felt wasn't showing on my face. "Sure," I said. "Rub your tzitzit for good luck."

---

12. apikorsim: Gr., those who lack religious conviction.

I walked away from him and took up my position near the base. I looked toward the wire screen and saw Davey Cantor standing there, staring out at the field, his hands in his pockets. I crouched down quickly, because Schwartzie was going into his pitch.

The batter swung wildly at the first two pitches and missed each time. The next one was low, and he let it go by, then hit a grounder to the first baseman, who dropped it, flailed about for it wildly, and recovered it in time to see Danny Saunders cross the plate. The first baseman stood there for a moment, drenched in shame, then tossed the ball to Schwartzie. I saw Mr. Galanter standing near third base, wiping his forehead. The yeshiva team had gone wild again, and they were all trying to get to Danny Saunders and shake his hand. I saw the rabbi smile broadly, then look down at his book and resume reading.

Sidney Goldberg came over to me. "What did Saunders tell you?" he asked.

"He said they were going to kill us apikorsim this afternoon."

He stared at me. "Those are nice people, those yeshiva people," he said, and walked slowly back to his position.

The next batter hit a long fly ball to right field. It was caught on the run.

"Hooray for us," Sidney Goldberg said grimly as we headed off the field. "Any longer and they'd ask us to join them for the Mincha Service.[13]

"Not us," I said. "We're not holy enough."

"Where did they learn to hit like that?"

"Who knows?" I said.

We were standing near the wire screen, forming a tight circle around Mr. Galanter.

"Only two runs," Mr. Galanter said, smashing his right fist into his left hand. "And they hit us with all they had. Now we give them *our* heavy artillery. Now *we* barrage *them!*" I saw that he looked relieved but that he was still sweating. His skullcap seemed pasted to his head with sweat. "Okay!" he said. "Fire away!"

The circle broke up, and Sidney Goldberg walked to the plate, carrying a bat. I saw the rabbi was still sitting on the bench, reading. I started to walk around behind him to see what book it was, when Davey Cantor came over, his hands in his pockets, his eyes still gloomy.

---

13. **Mincha Service:** an afternoon prayer service held daily in a synagogue.

"Well?" he asked.

"Well what?" I said.

"I told you they could hit."

"So you told me. So what?" I was in no mood for his feelings of doom, and I let my voice show it.

He sensed my annoyance. "I wasn't bragging or anything," he said, looking hurt. "I just wanted to know what you thought."

"They can hit," I said.

"They're murderers," he said.

I watched Sidney Goldberg let a strike go by and said nothing.

"How's your hand?" Davey Cantor asked.

"I scraped it."

"He ran into you real hard."

"Who is he?"

"Dov Shlomowitz," Davey Cantor said. "Like his name, that's what he is," he added in Hebrew. "Dov" is the Hebrew word for bear.

"Was I blocking him?"

Davey Cantor shrugged. "You were and you weren't. The ump could've called it either way."

"He felt like a truck," I said, watching Sidney Goldberg step back from a close pitch.

"You should see his father. He's one of Reb Saunders' shamashim. Some bodyguard he makes."

"Reb Saunders has bodyguards?"

"Sure he has bodyguards," Davey Cantor said. "They protect him from his own popularity. Where've you been living all these years?"

"I don't have anything to do with them."

"You're not missing a thing, Reuven."

"How do you know so much about Reb Saunders?"

"My father gives him contributions."

"Well, good for your father," I said.

"He doesn't pray there or anything. He just gives him contributions."

"You're on the wrong team."

"No, I'm not, Reuven. Don't be like that." He was looking very hurt. "My father isn't a Hasid or anything. He just gives them some money a couple times a year."

"I was only kidding, Davey." I grinned at him. "Don't be so serious about everything."

I saw his face break into a happy smile, and just then Sidney Goldberg hit a fast, low grounder and raced off to first. The ball went right through the legs of the shortstop and into center field.

"Hold it at first!" Mr. Galanter screamed at him, and Sidney stopped at first and stood on the base.

The ball had been tossed quickly to second base. The second baseman looked over toward first, then threw the ball to the pitcher. The rabbi glanced up from the book for a moment, then went back to his reading.

"Malter, coach him at first!" Mr. Galanter shouted, and I ran up the base line.

"They can hit, but they can't field," Sidney Goldberg said, grinning at me as I came to a stop alongside the base.

"Davey Cantor says they're murderers," I said.

"Old gloom-and-gloom Davey," Sidney Goldberg said, grinning.

Danny Saunders was standing away from the base, making a point of ignoring us both.

The next batter hit a high fly to the second baseman, who caught it, dropped it, retrieved it, and made a wild attempt at tagging Sidney Goldberg as he raced past him to second.

"Safe all around!" the umpire called, and our team burst out with shouts of joy. Mr. Galanter was smiling. The rabbi continued reading, and I saw that he was now slowly moving the upper part of his body back and forth.

"Keep your eyes open, Sidney!" I shouted from alongside first base. I saw Danny Saunders look at me, then look away. Some murderers, I thought. Shleppers[14] is more like it.

"If it's on the ground run like hell," I said to the batter who had just come onto first base, and he nodded at me. He was our third baseman, and he was about my size.

"If they keep fielding like that we'll be here till tomorrow," he said, and I grinned at him.

I saw Mr. Galanter talking to the next batter, who was nodding his head vigorously. He stepped to the plate, hit a hard grounder to the pitcher, who

---

14. **shleppers:** a Yiddish term denoting those who move slowly or awkwardly.

fumbled it for a moment then threw it to first. I saw Danny Saunders stretch for it and stop it.

"Out!" the umpire called. "Safe on second and third!"

As I ran up to the plate, I almost laughed aloud at the pitcher's stupidity. He had thrown it to first rather than third, and now we had Sidney Goldberg on third, and a man on second. I hit a grounder to the shortstop and instead of throwing it to second he threw it to first, wildly, and again Danny Saunders stretched and stopped the ball. But I beat the throw and heard the umpire call out, "Safe all around! One in!" And everyone on our team was patting Sidney Goldberg on the back. Mr. Galanter smiled broadly.

"Hello again," I said to Danny Saunders, who was standing near me, guarding his base. "Been rubbing your tzitzit lately?"

He looked at me, then looked slowly away, his face expressionless.

Schwartzie was at the plate, swinging his bat.

"Keep your eyes open!" I shouted to the runner on third. He looked too eager to head for home. "It's only one out!"

He waved a hand at me.

Schwartzie took two balls and a strike, then I saw him begin to pivot on the fourth pitch. The runner on third started for home. He was almost halfway down the base line when the bat sent the ball in a hard line drive straight at the third baseman, the short, thin boy with the spectacles and the old man's face, who had stood hugging the base and who now caught the ball more with his stomach than with his glove, managed somehow to hold on to it, and stood there, looking bewildered and astonished.

I returned to first and saw our player who had been on third and who was now halfway to home plate turn sharply and start a panicky race back.

"Step on the base!" Danny Saunders screamed in Yiddish across the field, and more out of obedience than awareness the third baseman put a foot on the base.

The yeshiva team howled its happiness and raced off the field. Danny Saunders looked at me, started to say something, stopped, then walked quickly away.

I saw Mr. Galanter going back up the third-base line, his face grim. The rabbi was looking up from his book and smiling.

I took up my position near second base, and Sidney Goldberg came over to me.

"Why'd he have to take off like that?" he asked.

I glared at our third baseman, who was standing near Mr. Galanter and looking very dejected.

"He was in a hurry to win the war," I said bitterly.

"What a jerk," Sidney Goldberg said.

"Goldberg, get over to your place!" Mr. Galanter called out. There was an angry edge to his voice. "Let's keep that infield solid!"

Sidney Goldberg went quickly to his position. I stood still and waited.

It was hot, and I was sweating beneath my clothes. I felt the earpieces of my glasses cutting into the skin over my ears, and I took the glasses off for a moment and ran a finger over the pinched ridges of skin, then put them back on quickly because Schwartzie was going into a windup. I crouched down, waiting, remembering Danny Saunders' promise to his team that they would kill us apikorsim. The word had meant, originally, a Jew educated in Judaism who denied basic tenets of his faith, like the existence of God, the revelation, the resurrection of the dead. To people like Reb Saunders, it also meant any educated Jew who might be reading, say, Darwin,[15] and who was not wearing side curls and fringes outside his trousers. I was an apikoros to Danny Saunders, despite my belief in God and Torah,[16] because I did not have side curls and was attending a parochial school where too many English subjects were offered and where Jewish subjects were taught in Hebrew instead of Yiddish, both unheard-of-sins, the former because it took time away from the study of Torah, the latter because Hebrew was the Holy Tongue and to use it in ordinary classroom discourse was a desecration of God's Name. I had never really had any personal contact with this kind of Jew before. My father had told me he didn't mind their beliefs. What annoyed him was their fanatic sense of righteousness, their absolute certainty that they and they alone had God's ear, and every other Jew was wrong, totally wrong, a sinner, a hypocrite, an apikoros, and doomed, therefore, to burn in hell. I found myself wondering again how they had learned to hit a ball like that if time for the study of Torah was so precious to them and why they had sent a rabbi along to waste his time sitting on a bench during a ball game.

Standing on the field and watching the boy at the plate swing at a high ball and miss, I felt myself suddenly very angry, and it was at that point for me the game stopped being merely a game and became a war. The fun and

---

15. Darwin: Charles Darwin, the scientist who originated the theory of evolution in 1860.
16. Torah: The law of the Jewish religion.

excitement was out of it now. Somehow the yeshiva team had translated this afternoon's baseball game into a conflict between what they regarded as their righteousness and our sinfulness. I found myself growing more and more angry, and I felt the anger begin to focus itself upon Danny Saunders, and suddenly it was not at all difficult for me to hate him.

Schwartzie let five of their men come up to the plate that half inning and let one of those five score. Sometime during that half inning, one of the members of the yeshiva team had shouted at us in Yiddish, "Burn in hell, you apikorsim!" and by the time that half inning was over and we were standing around Mr. Galanter near the wire screen, all of us knew that this was not just another ball game.

Mr. Galanter was sweating heavily, and his face was grim. All he said was, "We fight it careful from now on. No more mistakes." He said it very quietly, and we were all quiet, too, as the batter stepped up to the plate.

We proceeded to play a slow, careful game, bunting whenever we had to, sacrificing to move runners forward, obeying Mr. Galanter's instructions. I noticed that no matter where the runners were on the bases, the yeshiva team always threw to Danny Saunders, and I realized that they did this because he was the only infielder who could be relied upon to stop their wild throws. Sometime during the inning, I walked over behind the rabbi and looked over his shoulder at the book he was reading. I saw the words were Yiddish. I walked back to the wire screen. Davey Cantor came over and stood next to me, but he remained silent.

We scored only one run that inning, and we walked onto the field for the first half of the third inning with a sense of doom.

Dov Shlomowitz came up to the plate. He stood there like a bear, the bat looking like a matchstick in his beefy hands. Schwartzie pitched, and he sliced one neatly over the head of the third baseman for a single. The yeshiva team howled, and again one of them called out to us in Yiddish, "Burn, you apikorsim!" and Sidney Goldberg and I looked at each other without saying a word.

Mr. Galanter was standing alongside third base, wiping his forehead. The rabbi was sitting quietly, reading his book.

I took off my glasses and rubbed the tops of my ears. I felt a sudden momentary sense of unreality, as if the play yard, with its black asphalt and its white base lines, were my entire world now, as if all the previous years of my life had led me somehow to this one ball game, and all the future years of my life would depend upon its outcome. I stood there for a moment, holding the glasses in my hand and feeling frightened. Then I took a deep breath, and the feeling passed. It's only a ball game, I told myself. What's a ball game?

Mr. Galanter was shouting at us to move back. I was standing a few feet to the left of second, and I took two steps back. I saw Danny Saunders walk up to the plate, swinging a bat. The yeshiva team was shouting at him in Yiddish to kill us apikorsim.

Schwartzie turned around to check the field. He looked nervous and was taking his time. Sidney Goldberg was standing up straight, waiting. We looked at each other, then looked away. Mr. Galanter stood very still alongside third base, looking at Schwartzie.

The first pitch was low, and Danny Saunders ignored it. The second one started to come in shoulder-high, and before it was two thirds of the way to the plate, I was already standing on second base. My glove was going up as the bat cracked against the ball, and I saw the ball move in a straight line directly over Schwartzie's head, high over his head, moving so fast he hadn't even had time to regain his balance from the pitch before it went past him. I saw Dov Shlomowitz heading toward me and Danny Saunders racing to first, and I heard the yeshiva team shouting and Sidney Goldberg screaming, and I jumped, pushing myself upward off the ground with all the strength I had in my legs and stretching my glove hand till I thought it would pull out of my shoulder. The ball hit the pocket of my glove with an impact that numbed my hand and went through me like an electric shock, and I felt the force pull me backward and throw me off balance, and I came down hard on my left hip and elbow. I saw Dov Shlomowitz whirl and start back to first, and I pushed myself up into a sitting position and threw the ball awkwardly to Sidney Goldberg, who caught it and shipped it to first. I heard the umpire scream "Out!" and Sidney Goldberg ran over to help me to my feet, a look of disbelief and ecstatic joy on his face. Mr. Galanter shouted "Time!" and came racing onto the field. Schwartzie was standing in his pitcher's position with his mouth open. Danny Saunders stood on the base line a few feet from first, where he had stopped after I had caught the ball, staring out at me, his face frozen to stone. The rabbi was staring at me, too, and the yeshiva team was deathly silent.

"That was a great catch, Reuven!" Sidney Goldberg said, thumping my back. "That was sensational!"

I saw the rest of our team had suddenly come back to life and was throwing the ball around and talking up the game.

Mr. Galanter came over. "You all right, Malter?" he asked. "Let me see that elbow."

I showed him the elbow. I had scraped it, but the skin had not been broken.

"That was a good play," Mr. Galanter said, beaming at me. I saw his face was still covered with sweat, but he was smiling broadly now.

"Thanks, Mr. Galanter."

"How's that hand?"

"It hurts a little."

"Let me see it."

I took off the glove, and Mr. Galanter poked and bent the wrist and fingers of the hand.

"Does that hurt?" he asked.

"No," I lied.

"You want to go on playing?"

"Sure, Mr. Galanter."

"Okay," he said, smiling at me and patting my back. "We'll put you in for a Purple Heart on that one, Malter."

I grinned at him.

"Okay," Mr. Galanter said. "Let's keep this infield solid!"

He walked away, smiling.

"I can't get over that catch," Sidney Goldberg said.

"You threw it real good to first," I told him.

"Yeah," he said. "While you were sitting on your tail."

We grinned at each other and went to our positions.

Two more of the yeshiva team got to bat that inning. The first one hit a single, and the second one sent a high fly to short, which Sidney Goldberg caught without having to move a step. We scored two runs that inning and one run the next, and by the top half of the fifth inning we were leading five to three. Four of their men had stood up to bat during the top half of the fourth inning, and they had got only a single on an error to first. When we took to the field in the top half of the fifth inning, Mr. Galanter was walking back and forth alongside third on the balls of his feet, sweating, smiling, grinning, wiping his head nervously; the rabbi was no longer reading; the yeshiva team was silent as death. Davey Cantor was playing second, and I stood in the pitcher's position. Schwartzie had pleaded exhaustion and since this was the final inning—our parochial school schedules only permitted us time for five-inning games—and the yeshiva team's last chance at bat, Mr. Galanter was taking no chances and told me to pitch. Davey Cantor was a poor fielder, but Mr. Galanter was counting on my pitching to finish off the game. My left hand was still sore from the catch, and the wrist hurt whenever I caught a ball, but the right hand was fine, and the pitches went in fast and dropped into the curve just when I wanted them to. Dov Shlomowitz stood at the plate, swung three times at what looked to him to be perfect pitches, and hit nothing but air. He stood there looking bewildered after the third swing, then slowly walked away. We threw the ball around the infield, and Danny Saunders came up to the plate.

The members of the yeshiva team stood near the wire fence, watching Danny Saunders. They were very quiet. The rabbi was sitting on the bench, his book closed. Mr. Galanter was shouting at everyone to move back. Danny Saunders swung his bat a few times, then fixed himself into position and looked out at me.

Here's a present from an apikoros, I thought, and let go the ball. It went in fast and straight, and I saw Danny Saunders' left foot move out and his bat go up and his body begin to pivot. He swung just as the ball slid into its curve, and the bat cut savagely through empty air, twisting him around and sending him off balance. His black skullcap fell off his head, and he regained his balance and bent quickly to retrieve it. He stood there for a moment, very still, staring out at me. Then he resumed his position at the plate. The ball came back to me from the catcher, and my wrist hurt as I caught it.

The yeshiva team was very quiet, and the rabbi had begun to chew his lip.

I lost control of the next pitch, and it went wide. On the third pitch, I went into a long, elaborate windup and sent him a slow, curving blooper, the kind a batter always wants to hit and always misses. He ignored it completely, and the umpire called it a ball.

I felt my left wrist begin to throb as I caught the throw from the catcher. I was hot and sweaty, and the earpieces of my glasses were cutting deeply into the flesh above my ears as a result of the head movements that went with my pitching.

Danny Saunders stood very still at the plate, waiting.

Okay, I thought, hating him bitterly. Here's another present.

The ball went to the plate fast and straight, and dropped just below his swing. He checked himself with difficulty so as not to spin around, but he went off his balance again and took two or three staggering steps forward before he was able to stand up straight.

The catcher threw the ball back, and I winced at the pain in my wrist. I took the ball out of the glove, held it in my right hand and turned around for a moment to look out at the field and let the pain in my wrist subside. When I turned back I saw that Danny Saunders hadn't moved. He was holding his bat in his left hand, standing very still and staring at me. His eyes were dark, and his lips were parted in a crazy, idiot grin. I heard the umpire yell "Play ball!" but Danny Saunders stood there, staring at me and grinning. I turned and looked out at the field again, and when I turned back he was still standing there, staring at me and grinning. I could see his teeth between his parted lips. I took a deep breath and felt myself wet with sweat. I wiped my right hand on my pants and saw Danny Saunders step slowly to the plate and set his legs in position. He was no longer grinning. He stood looking at me over his left shoulder, waiting.

I wanted to finish it quickly because of the pain in my wrist, and I sent in another fast ball. I watched it head straight for the plate. I saw him go into a sudden crouch, and in the fraction of a second before he hit the ball I realized that he had anticipated the curve and was deliberately swinging low. I was still a little off balance from the pitch, but I managed to bring my glove hand up in front of my face just as he hit the ball. I saw it coming at me, and there was nothing I could do. It hit the finger section of my glove, deflected off, smashed into the upper rim of the left lens of my glasses, glanced off my forehead, and knocked me down. I scrambled around for it wildly, but by the time I got my hand on it Danny Saunders was standing safely on first.

I heard Mr. Galanter call time, and everyone on the field came racing over to me. My glasses lay shattered on the asphalt floor, and I felt a sharp pain in my left eye when I blinked. My wrist throbbed, and I could feel the bump coming up on my forehead. I looked over at first, but without my glasses Danny Saunders was only a blur. I imagined I could still see him grinning.

I saw Mr. Galanter put his face next to mine. It was sweaty and full of concern. I wondered what all the fuss was about. I had only lost a pair of glasses, and we had at least two more good pitchers on the team.

"Are you all right, boy?" Mr. Galanter was saying. He looked at my face and forehead. "Somebody wet a handkerchief with cold water!" he shouted. I wondered why he was shouting. His voice hurt my head and rang in my ears. I saw Davey Cantor run off, looking frightened. I heard Sidney Goldberg say something, but I couldn't make out his words. Mr. Galanter put his arm around my shoulders and walked me off the field. He sat me down on the bench next to the rabbi. Without my glasses everything more than about ten feet away from me was blurred. I blinked and wondered about the pain in my left eye. I heard voices and shouts, and then Mr. Galanter was putting a wet handkerchief on my head.

"You feel dizzy, boy?" he said.

I shook my head.

"You're sure now?"

"I'm all right," I said, and wondered why my voice sounded husky and why talking hurt my head.

"You sit quiet now," Mr. Galanter said. "You begin to feel dizzy, you let me know right away."

"Yes, sir," I said.

He went away. I sat on the bench next to the rabbi, who looked at me once, then looked away. I heard shouts in Yiddish. The pain in my left eye was so intense I could feel it in the base of my spine. I sat on the bench a long time, long enough to see us lose the game by a score of eight to seven, long enough to hear the yeshiva team shout with joy, long enough to begin to cry at the pain in my left eye, long enough for Mr. Galanter to come over to me at the end of the game, take one look at my face and go running out of the yard to call a cab.

Responding to What You Read

1. In this story, why did some teachers in the Jewish schools arrange sports competition among the schools?

2. Why are Reuven and his teammates scorned by Danny Saunders and his father, a rabbi?

3. Mr. Galanter speaks to his team in the language of war. Why is the image of war appropriate for this story? Consider both the story's setting and what happens in the story.

Writer's Workshop

This excerpt from the first chapter of *The Chosen* features a lot of fast-moving dialogue, which contributes to the excitement and pace of the action. Write a scene involving a critical moment in a sports contest. Use fast-moving dialogue to help tell your story. In addition to writing paragraphs that describe the action, include lively conversations that move the action along. The use of dialogue will help you *show* what happens, rather than *tell* what happens.

Alternate Media Response

Choose one of the conversations from this selection. Videotape two students playing the characters. Choose something short—about two to three minutes in length. Study it before taping, so that you can capture the sense of the conversation, as well as the emotional intensity of it.

PERSPECTIVES

Van Arsdale's Pond

Peter LaSalle

Flying

Stan Rogers

A boy's dream collides with the realities of adult life in two selections that pay tribute to the pure joy of dribbling a puck on clear ice.

ABOUT THE AUTHOR•ABOUT THE AUTHOR•ABOUT THE AUTHOR•ABOUT THE AUTHOR

Peter LaSalle *is the author of a novel,* Strange Sunlight, *and a short story collection,* The Graves of Famous Writers, *as well as the collection* Hockey Sur Glace, *in which this story appears. LaSalle's fiction has appeared in* Paris Review, Best American Short Stories, *and* Prize Stories: The O. Henry Awards. *He graduated from Harvard and has taught in America and in France.*

Van Arsdale's Pond

The boys said they didn't care if the ice wasn't good on Whittaker's Pond, because there was the other pond they had heard about. No, they had never been there, but that didn't matter—they had heard.

Maybe the ice had come suddenly in December, before Christmas the way it sometimes could, altogether unexpected. Somebody's older brother inevitably had a tale about skating on Thanksgiving Day, when the cut-out turkeys were still scotch-taped to the windows of Nausauket Elementary School, but nobody really believed that. Though by early December it might take only two or three truly cold nights of the red alcohol in the thermometer outside a frosted window cringing low in the clear, frigid darkness, and then lower. And to see Whittaker's Pond then was to come upon it the next afternoon after the last buzzing school bell had finally sounded at three, to hike the half-mile or so off the state two-lane and over the dun-colored knolls, then into the shadowy woods proper with the crunching leaves and the minty pines and the bunches of white birches, to finally spot it below, Whittaker's Pond. Before a snowfall, the ice might be glaringly black, not frozen much up by the end with the earthen dam that the Eagle Scouts had rebuilt who knows how many years before (had any kid actually *known* an Eagle Scout?), and surely more than the rule-of-thumb six inches thick down by the shallow end where the squat hoarfrosted bushes grew right through the surface and would at least give you something to grab onto if you were the first kid gingerly inching out to test if it was safe (one flimsy shoe or boot placed soft, like a floating dandelion puff, then the other). But it probably wasn't December, and the issue now was not really whether the ice was safe, but whether it was smooth enough and reasonably skatable after a midseason thaw. And, again, even if the ice wasn't good, they knew about the other pond.

One thing that was certain was that the boys' mothers, young, did what they always did on winter afternoons. They took time away from their sitting in front of a rattling Singer[1] machine, or baking pies in the cramped kitchens heady with the aromas of shortening and cinnamon, and they got everything ready for the boys. One mother liked to place her son's long wool skating socks, the gray ones, on the radiator in the hallway; she would have them warmed when he came through the back storm door, in such a hurry because "There's ice, Mom!" and the others were waiting for him and he was already late. Another mother might simply gather together what she knew her son would need, have the scuffed skates and the taped stick ready, the puck on which she noticed what she had never noticed before: the boy had carved his initials into the hard black rubber, probably with a carpenter's nail, and how lovely was his attempt at scrolling the letters for the job that must have taken him hours, making each period after each letter an ornate asterisk.

A moment like that could render a mother, standing in her housewife's dress and apron, staring at the puck, very sad.

And the boys were not in the classroom any longer. They were not gazing at the clock above the coatroom, and they were not banging past each other in their crazed charge to flee through the big battered green doors and out of the place at last. At this point they had already been home, already enjoyed the snack of Hydrox cookies and milk that waited for them, let's say, on a chrome-trimmed kitchen table, and the pack of them, six all told, were trudging up a knoll, there beside the two-lane. They wore galoshes, heavy coats, and peaked leather caps or knit toques.[2] They carried their skates by putting them onto the blade end of the stick, either slung by the loop of the tied-together dirty laces or the stick poked through the handy space below the sole on the skates' bottoms; they jutted the sticks over their shoulders, and the effect was that of what could be seen in old fairy-tale books, telling the story of any meandering tramp with his long pole and full sack of belongings toted that way, exactly the same for all of them.

---

1. Singer: a brand of sewing machine.
2. toques: soft, close-fitting hats.

One could watch them from a distance, going down the snow-covered slope of another knoll now; they were a moving line, a queue, each with the stick over the shoulder, the skates dangling. They appeared to be on a real journey, not just a long walk to a pond. They entered into the woods.

There was the sharp, clean smell of the snow itself that slapped your nostrils when you inhaled. A fat jay on a bare tree limb screeched away at them, then nearly detonated off in a swoosh of fluttering blue, the branch still shaking.

Of course, the boys talked:

"I wonder about it," a tall one for his age said, "and who knows what Whittaker's will be like after so much melting."

"You could be right." A rosy-cheeked boy said that, optimistic. "But I have a feeling it's going to be OK, and it will be good ice, I'm sure, even if we haven't had ice for a week."

"More than a week," the taller boy said.

"It warmed up over the weekend," one of the twins said.

"It did, you're right about that," the other one of the twins said. "It warmed up a lot over the weekend."

"But last night was cold, and that's all that counts," the rosy-cheeked boy told them.

"I suppose," one of the twins said.

"Yeah," the other said.

Because this wasn't like the first freeze of a season whatsoever. As already said, with a first freeze, be it the reputed Thanksgiving surprise or late ice, not coming until a week after New Year's, the situation was basically simple. First the fragile skin of a surface, then the huge extended star patterns in it when it turned solid, and finally the thick, lenslike covering, sturdier and sturdier, as hopefully the subsequent days brought nothing more in the sky than the welcome gray dimness, no sun and only cold. But once a surface had formed for the year, usually intact until March, any number of variations could occur.

If it stayed cold, there eventually came the snow, sometimes a howling blizzard, and the cover of accumulated white posed the source of the complication. In the most frigid of winters, when the weather lady on the one television station that came in clear in this part of the state sang of storms flopping down from Canada one after another, in that kind of cold the boys could shovel a rectangle for play. And while that surface could quickly be gouged to ruts from the wear of consecutive afternoons of games, and while there was always the nuisance of losing a puck into the downy dust of the pile when somebody missed a pass along the edge, that meant, nevertheless, they had ice, and ice didn't have to be perfect: nobody ever expected perfect ice after the first freeze of the year, that famous black ice. The boys sometimes talked of how they almost had it in them to rig up long plywood slabs with the stems of old broken hockey sticks for handles nailed to the boards, for the variety of ready plows that teenage guys on the high-school team heartily manned, four of them to a slab, pushing hard to clean a whole pond for practice sessions. But, understandably, these boys were too young and not that organized; just lugging a couple of heavy snow shovels through the woods and to Whittaker's Pond was work enough, a feat to challenge Hannibal with his bell-jangling elephants transporting war supplies across the towering Alps, as far as they were concerned. The real problems began with a midseason melt. The snow could turn to slush, refreezing when the next cold front arrived in uneven lumps like a cake that hadn't risen right, or, much worse, porous, crusted, and flimsy with no surface gloss to speak of, everywhere a pinto patterning of giant air bubbles each a few feet wide to be crunched into by blades, what their skates could barely stumble across, never mind glide over. In short, the boys had no idea what they would find at Whittaker's Pond after this midseason warming and the return to the cold. They could be lucky, certainly, and sometimes a melt was thorough enough to mean a flood of water atop the surface all over again, and then a fine glaze indeed with the subsequent refreezing.

They walked on through the woods. The twins bounced lines off one another like echoes, their talk never saying much of anything. The rosy-cheeked boy kept telling everybody that he knew the ice would be good, and the taller boy wasn't sure of that or much else lately, but he was willing to try to believe that all would prove OK. The group of them probably talked about how tough the cattle-drive master, Gil Favor, was on *Rawhide,* how funny the show with Dobie Gillis could be. They probably talked as well about the faraway territory called "girls," somebody claiming that in his classroom that very morning there was a prime example of a girl's bossiness, then playing up to the teacher, from a certain Cheryl Beaupre, a performance nobody would *believe*. . . . But mostly they talked about the ice, what they might find at Whittaker's Pond. There was a measure of bullying, sad to say, from the boy who was noticeably wiry, gruff too; he picked on a boy with a soft voice who always found himself last in the queue.

"It could have melted a lot, it might not even be safe," the bullying boy said, and turning to the boy with the soft voice, he told him, "What if you fell through?"

The soft-voiced boy didn't answer him.

"You don't drown, you know, you just go into shock, like somebody plugged one of your fingers into a hungry hundred-and-twenty-volt socket. Freezing shock, worse than electric shock, and just like that."

He snapped his fingers, leered at the other boy. He was delighting in scaring him.

"Shut up," one of the twins told the bully.

"Yeah, shut up," the other one said.

At home the mothers maybe returned to the sewing machine, or started on what had to be done at the ironing board, the electric flat fragrant of heat and scorched cotton, and one of those dime-store plastic daisies stuck into the top of a soda bottle used for sprinkling water during the task. Maybe one of them walked to a window, put fingers to the cold pane, and whispered aloud but to nobody in particular: "My son is in the woods now, going to the pond. All I can do is hope that all is well and safe for him." And the fathers? The fathers worked jobs like that of auto mechanic or assistant records clerk somewhere in the steamheated basement of the town hall, and occasionally one of them, weary at this stage in the long afternoon, would just sigh to think, "How, oh how, did I ever get this old?"

Until, as soon as the boys could see through the trees to the lopsided oval of Whittaker's Pond, they knew that the worst thing imaginable—the ultimate destruction of midseason ice—had happened. And any good luck with the days of melt producing a sizable water coating that in turn pristinely refroze, those hopes were gone when they saw what they saw: yes, there had been snow that melted to slush, but somewhere in the process, kids, probably not even in grade school, had committed the transgression of transgressions, stomping indiscriminately and savagely on the pond with their rubber boots in a maddened patterning of indented dance steps, which had eventually frozen solid and ruined any chance of decent skating, any chance of pond hockey completely.

The bullying boy seemed to take satisfaction in this disaster, saying:

"Just as I figured, a total mess." He turned again to the boy he had been picking on, adding, "And now you won't even be able to freeze to death, or drown."

"It must have been real little kids," that other boy said blankly in reply, "kids who nobody ever told that you aren't supposed to ruin ice. They must have come from those new houses in the plat in back."

The boys stared in disbelief. (Years later the bullying boy, Jimmy Arsenault, was killed in a foreign war that nobody supported, as his valiantly attempting to save a wounded pal brought him close to an enemy sniper. The timid boy, Wayne Wright, might have gone on to a position of great success if the rule worked that the world eventually found a balance in such opposites, like the bullying boy becoming a selfless battle hero of sorts. But that didn't happen. The timid boy didn't turn out to be a known movie star, or even a mayor; he would never marry, would in time end up in a meaningless town office job himself, living alone with a tiger-striped cat in a local apartment house, where the neighbors considered him strange. Concerning what became of somebody in life, as with what kind of ice you might find, there often seemed little more than sheer chance.) Meanwhile, the twins were now starting to growl their disappointment. . . .

(Who knew what became of them, because wasn't it true that nobody ever knew or heard what became of twins later on? It seemed that being twins in itself was a full-time justification, a defining task, in life; they were the Ericksons.)

"There's the other pond," the optimistic boy said. "The kids from over on Long Street were talking about it at school. They say it's better than Whittaker's, anyway, and with it sitting on a chicken farm like that, nobody much knows about it except for them and the farmer. Nobody will have wrecked that ice, and they're all probably out there already, those Long Street kids, they're probably playing and having a ball. Who cares about this?" He tipped his head toward the pond, Whittaker's, which all of them had been anticipating skating on since they had woken that morning, when they realized exactly how cold it had been during the night and that the thaw was finally over; they had been thinking about it the entire day in the blur of the several hours of school. "Who *cares*?"

But the twins announced they were tired. They didn't feel like tramping through the snow anymore, would just as well head home and watch late-afternoon TV cartoons in their basement rumpus room. And the bullying boy, possibly out of inherent perversity, argued that in his opinion you couldn't even get to Van Arsdale's chicken farm this way, through these woods, and the soft-voiced, bullied boy needed no more persuasion than that and completely agreed with him.

"But what about what we've been saying the whole way here," the rosy-cheeked boy said, "how we kept telling each other that if the ice was no good on Whittaker's, we can still go to the other pond, a *better* pond, I tell you."

"That was way back then," one of the twins said.

"Way back when," the other said, liking the rhyme of it, chuckling.

"That's funny," the first twin said.

"Yeah," the other said.

The entire contingent was about to abandon the plan of going on, but the boy who was tall for his age spoke up:

"I'll go with you," he said to the optimistic boy.

"Well, here's somebody who wants good ice," that boy replied to him.

The others were soon gone, and the two remaining boys crossed the pond's ruined ice, waded slow through the deep drifts along the other side, and headed on through the pillars of the tall trees. The day was still now, losing light. They walked for a half-hour.

"I think they might have been right," was the only thing the rosy-cheeked boy said.

And with that he pivoted, and also was gone.

So, the boy who was taller kept going without the rosy-cheeked boy. (Here there was predictability: the rosy-cheeked boy, cheerful by nature, eventually attended a good college, then worked to establish his own successful real estate agency; he would have a wonderful wife and five children. His name was Alan Lelaidier.) The taller boy marched through the trees, and he wondered why he was determined to go on, to be frank. Was it to prove a point? Or did he, in fact, expect to find good ice at the pond at Van Arsdale's chicken farm, a crew of boys playing hockey there and welcoming him into their game? He didn't know. To be frank again, he wasn't as much as sure if he had *actually* gone into the woods with skates and hockey stick along with the bunch of his pals that afternoon, or if this too were but another imagining, the way so much felt to him like but another imagining lately. And in the imagining, the insubstantiality[3] of it, smoke wafted from chimneys in the frozen late afternoon of a forgotten Rhode Island town, where mothers kept so lovingly busy in warm, wooden bungalows, and fathers, weary, wrestled through jobs that seemed to matter little, to lead nowhere. The boy was cold, and when he got to the top of another knoll, into a clearing with some tumbledown snow-fencing, he could see that the sky had lifted; a band of the palest of blue was widening above the hills black with their blanketing of winter trees, and he could see the buttery wedge of a moon. Without the cloud cover, the night would be very, very cold.

His toes were numb in the galoshes, he flipped the fuzzy gray earflaps down on his peaked leather cap, which felt good. (But was this really him? Was this Larry Gaudette? Or was this the shadow of somebody he often suspected he was, alone, the way he would always be alone in the course of an early marriage that didn't work out, then separated from his children in later years with carpentry jobs in Connecticut and upstate New York, places that were continents away from who he was, where he was from—more alone than ever. He *was* almost watching a boy trudge along.) Still, he didn't care about the cold. He could picture the pond at Van Arsdale's. He could envision it protected in a little bowl of hills, the farmer's white clapboard chicken sheds on a rise beyond that, the lights in the house's windows yellow at dusk.

He saw himself skating on a beautifully glassy surface, good ice, all right, dribbling a puck, telling himself how he had never liked anything in the world, loved anything, as much as to hear his blades cutting over the ice, to be skating.

He trudged on, suspecting that possibly it—*everything, always*—could turn out OK, even if somebody like the overoptimistic boy, who had left, ultimately saw folly in it. There *might* be good ice, and trying to think only of that, he, like so many of us, continued deeper and deeper into the woods.

---

3. insubstantiality: flimsiness; lacking firmness or substance.

ABOUT THE AUTHOR•ABOUT THE AUTHOR•ABOUT THE AUTHOR•ABOUT THE AUTHOR

Stan Rogers, born in 1949 in Hamilton, Ontario, Canada, was a folk singer and songwriter. His friend Emily Friedman and his wife Ariel Rogers describe him as "a big man—six feet four—built like a fire truck, and possessed of a voice that rumbled from his toes." They add, "Stan was a passionate Canadian partisan, and much of his short creative life was taken up with song cycles that chronicled the East, the Plains, the West, and finally the Great Lakes and Ontario. It was a natural progression for a wanderer . . . to scan a continent and finally return to write of the wonders of home." Tragically, Stan Rogers died in a fire aboard an airplane in 1983.

"Flying," which appears on Rogers' From Fresh Water CD (Fogarty's Cove Music), is described in the liner notes this way: "Hockey invades every household in Canada on some level. It is our National sport. Real aficionados play all year long. This is probably why first-time visitors to this country turn up with their skates in July! Competition is severe in the Junior leagues. Once every several years we get one like [Wayne] Gretzky. 'Flying' is an allegory—it is also the very real story of a third-round hopeful who once coached Gretzky and now coaches little leaguers and sells saunas."

Flying

It was just like strapping 'em on and starting again.
Coaching these kids to the top and calling them men
I was a third round pick in the NHL
And that's three years of living in hell
5   And going up flying, and going home dying.

My life was over the boards and playing the game.
And every day checking the papers and finding my name.
And Dad would go crazy when the scouts would call;
He'd tell me that I'd have it all
10   Ninety-nine of us trying, only one of us flying.

And every kid over the boards listens for the sound.
The roar of the crowd is their ticket for finally leaving this town
To be just one more hopeful in the Junior A,
Dreaming of that miracle play.
15   And going up flying, going home dying.

I tell them to think of the play and not of the fame.
If they got any future at all, it's not in the game
'Cause they'll be crippled and starting all over again
Selling on commission and remembering
20   When they were flying, remembering dying.

And every kid over the boards listens for the sound;
The roar of the crowd is their ticket for finally leaving this town
To be just one more hopeful in the Junior A,
Dreaming of that miracle play.
25   And going up flying, and going home dying.

Responding to What You Read

1. What is the universal experience that "Van Arsdale's Pond" is about, beyond that of boys looking for ice to play hockey on?

2. Is "Flying" an optimistic song or a pessimistic one? Justify your answer with evidence from the song itself.

Writer's Workshop

These selections offer another opportunity for writing a comparison and contrast essay. Look for similarities and differences between LaSalle's short story and Rogers's song about hockey. Start with the attitude, or tone, of each piece. Look at the diction—the word choice—employed by each author, and look at the images—the word pictures—created. What feeling are you left with after reading each selection?

Alternate Media Response

1. Draw the scene of the boys walking through the woods looking for the perfect skating pond. Try to capture the joy and tranquility of that scene.

2. Locate a recording of "Flying" and listen to the way Stan Rogers interprets his song. Do you agree with his interpretation? Try your hand at creating music for "Flying." Think of an existing melody that you believe would be appropriate and substitute the words from "Flying." Perform "your song" for the class.

PERSPECTIVES

Ballad of a Ballgame

Christine Lavin

Baseball

Bill Zavatsky

Don't give up hope. Sometimes even "losers" have their moment in the sun.

ABOUT THE AUTHOR•ABOUT THE AUTHOR•ABOUT THE AUTHOR•ABOUT THE AUTHOR

Christine Lavin is a diminutive (she tells you that in her song) song-writer/performer who travels the country and entertains with her biting comments about different aspects of contemporary life. "Ballad of a Ballgame" can be found on her Beau Woes CD (Philo 1107).

Ballad of a Ballgame

Do you remember that song by Janis Ian?
The one where she complains about not getting chosen
    for the basketball team?
Remember "For those whose names were never called
5   when choosing sides for basketball"?
I would've written about that
    except she'd done it first.
'Cause when you're five foot two—
    okay, five one-and-a-half—
10   And everybody else in the whole gym class is five foot three
        and even taller,
it hurts.

Truth is, I hadn't thought about that for years,
    and then a recent phone call rekindled all those fears.
15   "A softball game," Robin said. "And you're invited."

Softball, great, that's my game,
    why, softball's practically my middle name.
"I'll be right over," I said, sounding excited.
    Even though I can't throw, I can't hit,
20   I can't run, I admit.
      I can't catch, I can't pitch;
In softball I haven't found my niche.

But I don't let details get in my way.
    Team sports, that's what I love to play.
25   So I got dressed.
    I got my sneakers tied.
Made it to the park in time for choosing sides.

"Pick me, pick me, pick me, pick me."

"Pick me, pick me, pick me, pick me."

30   Glove? Yeah, I own a glove, but I didn't bring it because
    it's being repaired.
But I could always borrow from the other team.

"Pick me, pick me, pick me, pick me."

This part goes on for quite awhile
35   because twenty people showed up to play,
They picked ten to a side.
    So the ranks of the unchosen were depleted
And the ranks of the chosen swelled, and I was still standing there.
    I tried to act really casual
40   You know, I looked down at the ground,
    looked up at the sky.
I noticed clouds were rolling in,
    and a wind had kicked up off the river, a bad sign.
Well, déjà vu, I was the last one chosen,
45   even after her highness Felicity Rosen.
They put me in a field so far out and to the right,
    I was practically out of sight.
But everybody said I had a
    real good day.
50   I didn't make any errors.
    I didn't make any plays.

You see, the ball never actually came out my way, and I figured,
    the afternoon is gonna end this way.

Now, coming up to bat was a whole different
55   kind of humbling experience.
I took one swing and missed, which was no surprise.
    I took another swing and missed; that was no surprise.
But I practiced strategy.
I let one go by; it was called a ball.
60   And I had a proud moment which didn't last long,
'cause then the pitcher threw one,
    I just couldn't resist,
I swung and I actually hit it.
    But it was a pathetic little dribbler
65 right back to the mound,
    and the pitcher threw it over to first base
    and I was out.
Which again is no surprise.
But as I was walking to the bench to pick up my glove,
70   the captain of the other team
Said to the captain of my team,
    "Hey, it's okay,
She doesn't know how to play,
    so we won't count her outs."
75 And I turned to her and I said,
    "No, wait a minute!"
I want my outs to count, I want you to count my outs,"
    which made me instantly unpopular with my whole team.
So I said, "Oh, I get it,
80   don't count my outs,
That's good strategy, too; it makes me feel so special.
    Thank you very much, thank you, thank you."

Well, eventually I resumed my place in the outfield
 and continued watching the dandelions grow
85 And blossom and turn into puffs and blow away
  in the chilly wind.
Watch the clouds above me spelling doom in the sky.
 And it wasn't long before I began to question
My worth as a human being.
90 And my reason for living.

And then top of the seventh,
  two on, two out.
A crack of the bat, a mighty clout.
 My whole team turned and cringed to see
95 That speeding ball heading vaguely toward me.
  I ran as fast as I could.
I said a prayer.
  I stuck out my glove. The ball landed in there.
No one could believe it on either team.
100 They hooted and hollered. They stomped and screamed.
And even total strangers watching clapped and cheered,
  aware that God had performed a miracle here.

I was carried to the bench.

I was handed a beer.

105 And then the clouds broke apart and the sun reappeared.
I'm exaggerating about the sun coming out
  but it feels like it did in my heart
Because I wanted to live again.
Oh, by the way, we lost that game 17 to 3,
110 but I considered it a moral victory.
And Janis Ian, wherever you might be,
  take heart:
There's hope for you 'cause there's hope for me.

Oh, take me out to the ballgame.
115 Take me out to the crowd.
Buy me some peanuts, I'll buy you Crackerjacks
As long as you count my outs when I come up to bat
Root, root, root, root, root, root, for both teams
We don't want to lose; we're all the same.
120 Oh, won't you please take me out
To the old ballgame?

ABOUT THE AUTHOR•ABOUT THE AUTHOR•ABOUT THE AUTHOR•ABOUT THE AUTHOR

Bill Zavatsky, *who was born in 1943, says of his sports experiences, "To tell the truth, I was an erratic athlete at best, and baseball (not to mention other sports) plunged me into moments of the deepest shame and grief that I experienced as a child. Some days I could hit anything anywhere; my glove was foolproof, immense. Then during one game I charged a little infield dribbler and, instead of scooping it up, I kicked it across the diamond into the opposing team's dugout.*

"The end-of-season 'grudge match' [in "Baseball"] took place pretty much as described. And even though I felt a tremendous sense of relief when I was old enough to bury my hat and glove in my closet forever, the sport did give me the gift of a poem that I'm proud of."

Zavatsky has published a collection of poetry, Theories of Rain and Other Poems. *He teaches English at the Trinity School in New York City.*

Baseball

We were only farm team
not "good enough" to
make big Little League
with its classic uniforms
5 deep lettered hats.

But our coach said
we *were* just as good
maybe better
so we played
10   the Little League champs
in our stenciled tee shirts
and soft purple caps
when the season was over.

What happened that afternoon
15   I can't remember—
whether we won or tied.
But in my mind I lean back
to a pop-up hanging
in sunny sky
20   stopped
nailed to the blue
losing itself in a cloud
over second base
where I stood waiting.

25   Ray Michaud who knew
my up-and-down career
as a local player
my moments of graceful genius
my unpredictable ineptness
30   screamed arrows at me
from the dugout
where he waited to bat:
"He's gonna drop it! He
don't know how to catch,
35   you watch it drop!"

The ball kept climbing
higher, a black dot
no rules of gravity, no
brakes, a period searching

40   for a sentence, and the sentence read:
     "You're no good, Bill
     you won't catch this one now
     you know you never will."

     I watched myself looking up
45   and felt my body rust, falling
     in pieces to the ground
     a baby trying to stand up
     an ant in the shadow of a house

     I wasn't there
50   had never been born
     would stand there forever
     a statue squinting upward
     pointed out laughed at
     for a thousand years
55   teammates dead, forgotten
     bones of anyone who played baseball
     forgotten
     baseball forgotten, played no more
     played by robots on electric fields
60   who never missed
     or cried in their own sweat

     I'm thirty-four years old.
     The game was over twenty years ago.
     All I remember of that afternoon
65   when the ball came down

     is that
     I caught it.

Responding to What You Read

1. Both of these poems are **narrative poems**; they tell stories. What similarities are there in the narrative voices (the people who tell the story) in both of these poems?

2. An **allusion** is a reference to a person, a place, an event, or an idea. For a writer, using allusions can be an effective way of packing a good deal of meaning into a few words. Christine Lavin alludes to two other songs in "Ballad of a Ballgame," and even quotes from them. What are they? What do they add to her song? If they were removed, what would the effect be?

Writer's Workshop

1. A **ballad** is a song that tells a story. Most ballads are divided into stanzas of four lines with the last word in every other line rhyming. Early ballads often dealt with violent events. Later ballads, particularly in America, dealt with legendary heroes, such as Casey Jones or John Henry. The language of a ballad is plain and direct. In what respects is "Ballad of a Ballgame" a true ballad? In what respects is it different? Discuss these questions with your classmates.

2. Writing humor is no joke. It doesn't come easily. See if you can capture in verse a moment in sports that contains failure and, finally, some kind of triumph. Write a ballad of at least three stanzas. Take a fresh, humorous approach to your subject. Try to include one or more allusions. Pattern your ballad after the characteristics described in the first activity of this Writer's Workshop.

CHAPTER 4

Sports and
the Family

Involvement in sports can have a profound impact on relationships between fathers and sons, mothers and daughters, and sisters and brothers. In this chapter, you will meet

- *a girl who discovers a connection between her love for winning and the needs of her younger brother*

- *fathers and sons who reflect on the bonds that are forged through baseball, tennis, mountain climbing, and sailing*

- *mothers who watch with pride as their daughters compete—and succeed*

- *families who cope with the sacrifices that seem inevitable in the pursuit of athletic excellence*

The selections in this chapter explore relationships between sports and the family. *As you read about the families profiled here, concentrate not only on the choices that are made and goals that are achieved but also on the insights gained and lessons learned.*

Raymond's Run

Toni Cade Bambara

A girl loves to run, and win, but then discovers a new goal—
something beyond herself.

ABOUT THE AUTHOR•ABOUT THE AUTHOR•ABOUT THE AUTHOR•ABOUT THE AUTHOR

*T*oni Cade Bambara was born in 1939 in New York City. She was educated at Queens College and studied at the University of Florence in Italy and also in Paris. Her works include The Sea Birds Are Still Alive; The Salt Eaters; If Blessing Comes; and Gorilla, My Love, a collection of short stories. She also wrote screenplays, including "Raymond's Run," produced by PBS in 1985, and "The Bombing of Osage," for which she won the Best Documentary of 1986 award from the Pennsylvania Association of Broadcasters, as well as the Documentary Award from the National Black Programming Consortium.

Bambara, who was praised for her ability to capture street talk realistically in her prose and for her depiction of the love that exists in African-American families and communities, died in 1995.

Raymond's Run

I don't have much work to do around the house like some girls. My mother does that. And I don't have to earn my pocket money by hustling; George runs errands for the big boys and sells Christmas cards. And anything else that's got to get done, my father does. All I have to do in life is mind my brother Raymond, which is enough.

Sometimes I slip and say my little brother Raymond. But as any fool can see he's much bigger and he's older too. But a lot of people call him my little brother cause he needs looking after cause he's not quite right. And a lot of smart mouths got lots to say about that too, especially when George was minding him. But now, if anybody has anything to say to Raymond, anything to say about his big head, they have to come by me. And I don't play the dozens[1] or believe in standing around with somebody in my face doing a lot of talking. I much rather just knock you down and take my chances even if I am a little girl with skinny arms and a squeaky voice, which is how I got the name Squeaky. And if things get too rough, I run. And as anybody can tell you, I'm the fastest thing on two feet.

There is no track meet that I don't win the first place medal. I use to win the twenty-yard dash when I was a little kid in kindergarten. Nowadays it's the fifty-yard dash. And tomorrow I'm subject to run the quarter-meter relay all by myself and come in first, second, and third. The big kids call me Mercury cause I'm the swiftest thing in the neighborhood. Everybody knows that—except two people who know better, my father and me.

He can beat me to Amsterdam Avenue with me having a two fire-hydrant headstart and him running with his hands in his pockets and whistling. But that's private information. Cause can you imagine some thirty-five-year-old man stuffing himself into PAL shorts to race little kids? So far as everyone's concerned, I'm the fastest and that goes for Gretchen, too, who has put out the tale that she is going to win the first place medal this year. Ridiculous. In the second place, she's got short legs. In the third place, she's got freckles. In the first place, no one can beat me and that's all there is to it.

I'm standing on the corner admiring the weather and about to take a stroll down Broadway so I can practice my breathing exercises, and I've got Raymond walking on the inside close to the buildings cause he's subject to fits of fantasy and starts thinking he's a circus performer and that the curb is a tightrope strung high in the air. And sometimes after a rain, he likes to step down off his tightrope right into the gutter and slosh around getting his shoes and cuffs wet. Then I get hit when I get home. Or sometimes if you don't watch him, he'll dash across traffic to the island in the middle of

---

1. play the dozens: a ritualized word game in which opponents try to outdo each other in insults.

Broadway and give the pigeons a fit. Then I have to go behind him apologizing to all the old people sitting around trying to get some sun and getting all upset with the pigeons fluttering around them, scattering their newspapers and upsetting the wax-paper lunches in their laps. So I keep Raymond on the inside of me, and he plays like he's driving a stage coach which is O.K. by me so long as he doesn't run me over or interrupt my breathing exercises, which I have to do on account of I'm serious about my running and don't care who knows it.

Now some people like to act like things come easy to them, won't let on that they practice. Not me. I'll high prance down 34th Street like a rodeo pony to keep my knees strong even if it does get my mother uptight so that she walks ahead like she's not with me, don't know me, is all by herself on a shopping trip, and I am somebody else's crazy child.

Now you take Cynthia Procter for instance. She's just the opposite. If there's a test tomorrow, she'll say something like, "Oh I guess I'll play handball this afternoon and watch television tonight," just to let you know she ain't thinking about the test. Or like last week when she won the spelling bee for the millionth time, "A good thing you got 'receive,' Squeaky, cause I would have got it wrong. I completely forgot about the spelling bee." And she'll clutch the lace on her blouse like it was a narrow escape. Oh, brother.

But of course when I pass her house on my early morning trots around the block, she is practicing the scales on the piano over and over and over and over. Then in music class, she always lets herself get bumped around so she falls accidently on purpose onto the piano stool and is so surprised to find herself sitting there, and so decides just for fun to try out the ole keys and what do you know—Chopin's waltzes just spring out of her fingertips and she's the most surprised thing in the world. A regular prodigy. I could kill people like that.

I stay up all night studying the words for the spelling bee. And you can see me anytime of day practicing running. I never walk if I can trot and shame on Raymond if he can't keep up. But of course he does, cause if he hangs back someone's liable to walk up to him and get smart, or take his allowance from him, or ask him where he got that great big pumpkin head. People are so stupid sometimes.

So I'm strolling down Broadway breathing out and breathing in on counts of seven, which is my lucky number, and here comes Gretchen and her sidekicks—Mary Louise who used to be a friend of mine when she first moved to

Harlem from Baltimore and got beat up by everybody till I took up for her on account of her mother and my mother used to sing in the same choir when they were young girls, but people ain't grateful, so now she hangs out with the new girl Gretchen and talks about me like a dog; and Rosie who is as fat as I am skinny and has a big mouth where Raymond is concerned and is too stupid to know that there is not a big deal of difference between herself and Raymond and that she can't afford to throw stones. So they are steady coming up Broadway and I see right away that it's going to be one of those Dodge City scenes cause the street ain't that big and they're close to the buildings just as we are. First I think I'll step into the candy store and look over the new comics and let them pass. But that's chicken and I've got a reputation to consider. So then I think I'll just walk straight on through them or over them if necessary. But as they get to me, they slow down. I'm ready to fight, cause like I said I don't feature a whole lot of chitchat, I much prefer to just knock you down right from the jump and save everybody a lotta precious time.

"You signing up for the May Day races?" smiles Mary Louise, only it's not a smile at all.

A dumb question like that doesn't deserve an answer. Besides, there's just me and Gretchen standing there really, so no use wasting my breath talking to shadows.

"I don't think you're going to win this time," says Rosie, trying to signify with her hands on her hips all salty, completely forgetting that I have whupped her behind many times for less salt than that.

"I always win cause I'm the best," I say straight at Gretchen who is, as far as I'm concerned, the only one talking in this ventriloquist-dummy routine.

Gretchen smiles but it's not a smile and I'm thinking that girls never really smile at each other because they don't know how and don't want to know how and there's probably no one to teach us how cause grown-up girls don't know either. Then they all look at Raymond who has just brought his mule team to a standstill. And they're about to see what trouble they can get into through him.

"What grade you in now, Raymond?"

"You got anything to say to my brother, you say it to me, Mary Louise Williams of Raggedy Town, Baltimore."

"What are you, his mother?" sasses Rosie.

"That's right, Fatso. And the next word out of anybody and I'll be their mother too." So they just stand there and Gretchen shifts from one leg to the other and so do they. Then Gretchen puts her hands on her hips and is about to say something with her freckle-face self but doesn't. Then she walks around me looking me up and down but keeps walking up Broadway, and her sidekicks follow her. So me and Raymond smile at each other and he says "Gidyap" to his team and I continue with my breathing exercises, strolling down Broadway toward the icey man on 145th with not a care in the world cause I am Miss Quicksilver herself.

I take my time getting to the park on May Day because the track meet is the last thing on the program. The biggest thing on the program is the May Pole dancing which I can do without, thank you, even if my mother thinks it's a shame I don't take part and act like a girl for a change. You'd think my mother'd be grateful not to have to make me a white organdy dress with a big satin sash and buy me new white baby-doll shoes that can't be taken out of the box till the big day. You'd think she'd be glad her daughter ain't out there prancing around a May Pole getting the new clothes all dirty and sweaty and trying to act like a fairy or a flower or whatever you're supposed to be when you should be trying to be yourself, whatever that is, which is, as far as I am concerned, a poor Black girl who really can't afford to buy shoes and a new dress you only wear once a lifetime cause it won't fit next year.

I was once a strawberry in a Hansel and Gretel pageant when I was in nursery school and didn't have no better sense than to dance on tiptoe with my arms in a circle over my head doing umbrella steps and being a perfect fool just so my mother and father could come dressed up and clap. You'd think they'd know better than to encourage that kind of nonsense. I am not a strawberry. I do not dance on my toes. I run. That is what I am all about. So I always come late to the May Day program, just in time to get my number pinned on and lay in the grass till they announce the fifty-yard dash.

I put Raymond in the little swings, which is a tight squeeze this year and will be impossible next year. Then I look around for Mr. Pearson who pins the numbers on. I'm really looking for Gretchen if you want to know the truth, but she's not around. The park is jam-packed. Parents in hats and corsages and breast-pocket handkerchiefs peeking up. Kids in white dresses and light blue suits. The parkees unfolding chairs and chasing the rowdy kids from Lenox as if they had no right to be there. The big guys with their caps on backwards, leaning against the fence swirling the basketballs on the tips of their fingers waiting for all these crazy people to clear out the park so they can play. Most of the kids in my class are carrying bass drums and glockenspiels and flutes. You'd think they'd put in a few bongos or something for real like that.

Then here comes Mr. Pearson with his clipboard and his cards and pencils and whistles and safety pins and fifty million other things he's always dropping all over the place with his clumsy self. He sticks out in a crowd cause he's on stilts. We used to call him Jack and the Beanstalk to get him mad. But I'm the only one that can outrun him and get away, and I'm too grown for that silliness now.

"Well, Squeaky," he says checking my name off the list and handing me number seven and two pins. And I'm thinking he's got no right to call me Squeaky, if I can't call him Beanstalk.

"Hazel Elizabeth Deborah Parker," I correct him and tell him to write it down on his board.

"Well, Hazel Elizabeth Deborah Parker, going to give someone else a break this year?" I squint at him real hard to see if he is seriously thinking I should lose the race on purpose just to give someone else a break.

"Only six girls running this time," he continues, shaking his head sadly like it's my fault all of New York didn't turn out in sneakers. "That new girl should give you a run for your money." He looks around the park for Gretchen like a periscope in a submarine movie. "Wouldn't it be a nice gesture if you were . . . to ahhh . . ."

I give him such a look he couldn't finish putting that idea into words. Grownups got a lot of nerve sometimes. I pin number seven to myself and stomp away—I'm so burnt. And I go straight for the track and stretch out on the grass while the band winds up with "Oh the Monkey Wrapped His Tail Around the Flag Pole," which my teacher calls by some other name. The man on the loudspeaker is calling everyone over to the track and I'm on my back looking at the sky trying to pretend I'm in the country, but I can't, because even grass in the city feels hard as sidewalk and there's just no pretending you are anywhere but in a "concrete jungle" as my grandfather says.

The twenty-yard dash takes all of the two minutes cause most of the little kids don't know no better than to run off the track or run the wrong way or run smack into the fence and fall down and cry. One little kid though has got the good sense to run straight for the white ribbon up ahead so he wins. Then the second graders line up for the thirty-yard dash and I don't even bother to turn my head to watch cause Raphael Perez always wins. He wins before he even begins by psyching the runners, telling them they're going to trip on their shoelaces and fall on their faces or lose their shorts or something, which he doesn't really have to do since he is very fast, almost as fast as I am. After that is the forty-yard dash which I use to run when I was in first grade. Raymond is hollering from the swings cause he knows I'm about to do my thing cause the man on the loudspeaker has just announced the fifty-yard dash, although he might just as well be giving a recipe for Angel Food cake cause you can hardly make out what he's saying for the static. I get up and slip off my sweat pants and then I see Gretchen standing at the starting line kicking her legs out like a pro. Then as I get into place I see that ole Raymond is in line on the other side of the fence, bending down with his fingers on the ground just like he knew what he was doing. I was going to yell at him but then I didn't. It burns up your energy to holler.

Every time, just before I take off in a race, I always feel like I'm in a dream, the kind of dream you have when you're sick with fever and feel all hot and weightless. I dream I'm flying over a sandy beach in the early morning sun, kissing the leaves of the trees as I fly by. And there's always the smell of apples, just like in the country when I was little and use to think I was a choo-choo train, running through the field of corn and chugging up the hill to the orchard. And all the time I'm dreaming this, I get lighter and lighter until I'm flying over the beach again, getting blown through the sky like a feather that weighs nothing at all. But once I spread my fingers in the dirt and crouch over for the Get on Your Mark, the dream goes and I am solid again and am telling myself, Squeaky you must win, you must win, you are the fastest thing in the world, you can even beat your father up Amsterdam if you really try. And then I feel my weight coming back just behind my knees then down to my feet then into the earth and the pistol shot explodes in my blood and I am off and weightless again, flying past the other runners, my arms pumping up and down and the whole world is quiet except for the crunch as I zoom over the gravel in the track. I glance to my left and there is no one. To the right a blurred Gretchen who's got her chin jutting out as if it would win the race all by itself. And on the other side of the fence is Raymond with his arms down to his side and the palms tucked up behind him, running, in his very own style and it's the first time I ever saw that and I almost stop to watch my brother Raymond on his first run. But the white ribbon is bouncing toward me and I tear past it racing into the distance till my feet with a mind of their own start digging up footfuls of dirt and brake me short. Then all the kids standing on the side pile on me, banging me on the back and slapping my head with their May Day programs, for I have won again and everybody on 151st Street can walk tall for another year.

"In first place . . ." the man on the loudspeaker is clear as a bell now. But then he pauses and the loudspeaker starts to whine. Then static. And I lean down to catch my breath and here comes Gretchen walking back for she's overshot the finish line too, huffing and puffing with her hands on her hips taking it slow, breathing in steady time like a real pro and I sort of like her a little for the first time. "In first place . . ." and then three or four voices get all mixed up on the loudspeaker and I dig my sneaker into the grass and stare at Gretchen who's staring back, we both wondering just who did win. I can hear old Beanstalk arguing with the man on the loudspeaker and then a few others running their mouths about what the stop watches say.

Then I hear Raymond yanking at the fence to call me and I wave to shush him, but he keeps rattling the fence like a gorilla in a cage like in them gorilla movies, but then like a dancer or something he starts climbing up nice and easy but very fast. And it occurs to me, watching how smoothly he climbs hand over hand and remembering how he looked running with his arms down to his side and with the wind pulling his mouth back and his teeth showing and all, it occurred to me that Raymond would make a very fine runner. Doesn't he always keep up with me on my trots? And he surely knows how to breathe in counts of seven cause he's always doing it at the dinner table, which drives my brother George up the wall. And I'm smiling to beat the band cause if I've lost this race, or if me and Gretchen tied, or even if I've won, I can always retire as a runner and begin a whole new career as a coach with Raymond as my champion. After all, with a little more study I can beat Cynthia and her phony self at the spelling bee. And if I bugged my mother, I could get piano lessons and become a star. And I have a big rep as the baddest thing around. And I've got a roomful of ribbons and medals and awards. But what has Raymond got to call his own?

So I stand there with my new plan, laughing out loud by this time as Raymond jumps down from the fence and runs over with his teeth showing and his arms down to the side which no one before him has quite mastered as a running style. And by the time he comes over I'm jumping up and down so glad to see him—my brother Raymond, a great runner in the family tradition. But of course everyone thinks I'm jumping up and down because the men on the loudspeaker have finally gotten themselves together and compared notes and are announcing "In first place—Miss Hazel Elizabeth Deborah Parker." (Dig that.) "In second place—Miss Gretchen P. Lewis." And I look over at Gretchen wondering what the P stands for. And I smile. Cause she's good, no doubt about it. Maybe she'd like to help me coach Raymond; she obviously is serious about running, as any fool can see. And she nods to congratulate me and then she smiles. And I smile. We stand there with this big smile of respect between us. It's about as real a smile as girls can do for each other, considering we don't practice real smiling every day you know, cause maybe we too busy being flowers or fairies or strawberries instead of something honest and worthy of respect . . . you know . . . like being people.

Responding to What You Read

1. What aspects of sport does "Raymond's Run" capture?

2. Do you think the author was able to create a believable first-person female voice? Explain. How would this story have been different if the main character were a boy?

Writer's Workshop

Create a fictional first-person voice and have that voice narrate an experience in a sports event, as Squeaky does in "Raymond's Run." Write about something you know well. Make your narrative lively with colorful descriptions and sharp-witted observations. Try to create a voice as confident and cocky as Squeaky's.

Alternate Media Response

Tape a short video version of this story. Have a first-person narrator tell the events, as Squeaky does in "Raymond's Run." You will need to decide what to leave in from the story and what to take out. These are crucial questions for every person who adapts material from one medium to another. After completing your video, you might enjoy viewing the professional video of "Raymond's Run" (mentioned in About the Author) to learn how it was adapted and to compare it to your version.

PERSPECTIVES

Fathers Playing Catch with Sons

Donald Hall

That Dark Other Mountain

Robert Francis

Fathers and sons find meaning in playing catch and running down a mountain—tossing the ball from one generation to another.

Donald Hall was born in 1928. He is a poet and essayist, and the author of many collections of poetry, as well as books about poetry. In addition, he has written Dock Ellis in the Country of Baseball, Fathers Playing Catch With Sons: Essays on Sport (Mostly Baseball), *and* The Farm Summer 1942, *a children's book based on his childhood experiences growing up in New Hampshire.*

Fathers Playing Catch with Sons

My father and I played catch as I grew up. Like so much else between fathers and sons, playing catch was tender and tense at the same time. He wanted to play with me. He wanted me to be good. He seemed to *demand* that I be good. I threw the ball into his catcher's mitt. Attaboy. Put her right there. I threw straight. Then I tried to put something on it; it flew twenty feet over his head. Or it banged into the sidewalk in front of him breaking stitches and ricocheting off a pebble into the gutter of Greenway Street. Or it went wide to his right and lost itself in Mrs. Davis's bushes. Or it went wide to his left and rolled across the street while drivers swerved their cars.

I was wild, I was *wild*. I had to be wild for my father. What else could I be? Would you have wanted me to have *control*?

But I was, myself, the control on him. He had wanted to teach school, to coach and teach history at Cushing Academy in Ashburnham, Massachusetts, and he had done it for two years before he was married. The salary was minuscule and in the twenties people didn't get married until they had the money to live on. Since he wanted to marry my mother, he made the only decision he could make: he quit Cushing and went into the family business, and he hated business, and he wept when he fired people, and he wept when he was criticized, and his head shook at night, and he coughed from all the cigarettes, and he couldn't sleep, and he almost died when an ulcer hemorrhaged when he was forty-two, and ten years later, at fifty-two, he died of lung cancer.

But the scene I remember—at night in the restaurant, after a happy, foolish day in the uniform of a Pittsburgh Pirate—happened when he was twenty-five and I was almost one year old. So I do not "remember" it at all. It simply rolls itself before my eyes with the intensity of a lost memory suddenly found again, more intense than the moment itself ever is.

It is 1929, July, a hot Saturday afternoon. At the ballpark near East Rock, in New Haven, Connecticut, just over the Hamden line, my father is playing semipro baseball. I don't know the names of the teams. My mother has brought me in a basket, and she sits under a tree, in the shade, and lets me crawl when I wake up.

My father is very young, very skinny. When he takes off his cap—the uniform is gray, the bill of the cap blue—his fine hair is parted in the middle. His face is very smooth. Though he is twenty-five, he could pass for twenty. He plays shortstop, and he is paid twenty-five dollars a game. I don't know where the money comes from. Do they pass the hat? They would never raise so much money. Do they charge admission? They must charge admission, or I am wrong that it was semipro and that he was paid. Or the whole thing is wrong, a memory I concocted. But of course the reality of 1929—and my mother and the basket and the shade and the heat—does not matter, not to the memory of the living nor to the bones of the dead nor even to the fragmentary images of broken light from that day which wander light-years away in unrecoverable space. What matters is the clear and fine knowledge of this day as it happens now, permanently and repeatedly, on a deep layer of the personal Troy.[1]

There, where this Saturday afternoon of July in 1929 rehearses itself, my slim father performs brilliantly at shortstop. He dives for a low line drive and catches it backhand, somersaults, and stands up holding the ball. Sprinting into left field with his back to the plate, he catches a fly ball that almost drops for a Texas leaguer. He knocks down a ground ball, deep in the hole and nearly to third base, picks it up, and throws the man out at first with a peg as flat as the tape a runner breaks. When he comes up to bat, he feels lucky. The opposing pitcher is a side-armer. He always hits side-armers. So he hits two doubles and a triple, drives in two runs and scores two runs, and his team wins 4 to 3. After the game a man approaches him,

---

1. **Troy:** ancient city of Homeric epic, discovered in 1873 by Heinrich Schliemann under the layers of later cities.

while he stands, sweating and tired, with my mother and me in the shade of the elm tree at the rising side of the field. The man is a baseball scout. He offers my father a contract to play baseball with the Baltimore Orioles, at that time a double-A minor league team. My father is grateful and gratified; he is proud to be offered the job, but he must refuse. After all, he has just started working at the dairy for his father. It wouldn't be possible to leave the job that had been such a decision to take. And besides, he adds, there is the baby.

My father didn't tell me he turned it down because of me. All he told me, or that I think he told me: he was playing semipro at twenty-five dollars a game; he had a good day in the field, catching a ball over his shoulder running away from the plate; had a good day hitting, too, because he could always hit a side-armer. But he turned down the Baltimore Oriole offer. He couldn't leave the dairy then, and besides, he knew that he had just been lucky that day. He wasn't really that good.

But maybe he didn't even tell me that. My mother remembers nothing of this. Or rather she remembers that he played on the team for the dairy, against other businesses, and that she took me to the games when I was a baby. But she remembers nothing of semipro, of the afternoon with the side-armer, of the offered contract. Did I make it up? Did my father exaggerate? Men tell stories to their sons, loving and being loved.

I don't care.

Baseball is fathers and sons. Football is brothers beating each other up in the backyard, violent and superficial. Baseball is the generations, looping backward forever with a million apparitions of sticks and balls, cricket and rounders, and the games the Iroquois played in Connecticut before the English came. Baseball is fathers and sons playing catch, lazy and murderous, wild and controlled, the profound archaic song of birth, growth, age, and death. This diamond encloses what we are.

This afternoon—March 4, 1973—when I played ball and was not frightened, I walked with the ghost of my father, dead seventeen years. The ballplayers would not kill me, nor I them. This is the motion, and the line that connects me now to the rest of the world, the motion past fear and separation.

ABOUT THE AUTHOR•ABOUT THE AUTHOR•ABOUT THE AUTHOR•ABOUT THE AUTHOR

S*ee the biography of Robert Francis on page 19.*

That Dark Other Mountain

My father could go down a mountain faster than I
Though I was first one up.
Legs braced or with quick steps he slid the gravel slopes
Where I picked cautious footholds.

5   Black, Iron, Eagle, Doublehead, Chocorua
Wildcat and Carter Dome—
He beat me down them all. And that last other mountain
And that dark other mountain.

Responding to What You Read

1. What do you think Donald Hall means when he says that "like so much else between fathers and sons, playing catch was tender and tense at the same time"?

2. In what way does Robert Francis use mountain climbing to illustrate both a young person's and an older person's characteristics?

3. What is "that dark other mountain"? What clues in the poem tell you?

Writer's Workshop

In a short essay discuss the ways in which father-and-son relationships are remembered in these two selections. To organize your thoughts, consider these questions: What tone of voice is used in each selection? What mood is conveyed? What point does each author make?

Alternate Media Response

Illustrate these selections. Draw pictures or collect photos from newspapers and magazines that convey the subject and mood of "Fathers Playing Catch with Sons" or "That Dark Other Mountain."

Playing to Win

Margaret A. Whitney

Marveling at the intensity in her athlete daughter, a mother watches and thinks, "Drive, Ann, drive."

ABOUT THE AUTHOR•ABOUT THE AUTHOR•ABOUT THE AUTHOR•ABOUT THE AUTHOR

Margaret A. Whitney wrote this essay when she was a doctoral candidate in technical communications at Rensselaer Polytechnic Institute in Troy, New York. It was first published in the New York Times Magazine.

Playing to Win

My daughter is an athlete. Nowadays, this statement won't strike many parents as unusual, but it does me. Until her freshman year in high school, Ann was only marginally interested in sport of any kind. When she played, she didn't swing hard, often dropped the ball, and had an annoying habit of tittering on field or court.

Indifference combined with another factor that did not bode well for a sports career. Ann was growing up to be beautiful. By the eighth grade, nature and orthodontics had produced a 5-foot 8-inch 125-pound, brown-eyed beauty with a wonderful smile. People told her, too. And, as many young women know, it is considered a satisfactory accomplishment to be pretty and stay pretty. Then you can simply sit still and enjoy the unconditional positive regard. Ann loved the attention too, and didn't consider it demeaning when she was awarded "Best Hair," female category, in the eighth-grade yearbook.

So it came as a surprise when she became a jock. The first indication that athletic indifference had ended came when she joined the high school cross-country team. She signed up in early September and ran third for the team within three days. Not only that. After one of those 3.1-mile races up hill and down dale on a rainy November afternoon, Ann came home muddy and bedraggled. Her hair was plastered to her head, and the mascara she had applied so carefully that morning ran in dark circles under her eyes. This is it, I thought. Wait until Lady Astor sees herself. But the kid with the best eighth grade hair went on to finish the season and subsequently letter in cross-country, soccer, basketball, and softball.

I love sports, she tells anyone who will listen. So do I, though my midlife quest for a doctorate leaves me little time for either playing or watching. My love of sports is bound up with the goals in my life and my hopes for my three daughters. I have begun to hear the message of sports. It is very different from many messages that women receive about living, and I think it is good.

My husband, for example, talked to Ann differently when he realized that she was a serious competitor and not just someone who wanted to get in shape so she'd look good in a prom dress. Be aggressive, he'd advise. Go for the ball. Be intense.

Be intense. She came in for some of the most scathing criticism from her dad, when, during basketball season, her intensity waned. You're pretending to play hard, he said. You like it on the bench? Do you like to watch while your teammates play?

I would think, how is this kid reacting to such advice? For years, she'd been told at home, at school, by countless advertisements, "Be quiet, Be good, Be still." When teachers reported that Ann was too talkative, not obedient enough, too flighty. When I dressed her up in frilly dresses and admonished her not to get dirty. When ideals of femininity are still, quiet, cool females in ads whose vacantness passes for sophistication. How can any adolescent girl know what she's up against? Have you ever really noticed intensity? It is neither quiet nor good. And it's definitely not pretty.

In the end, her intensity revived. At half time, she'd look for her father, and he would come out of the bleachers to discuss tough defense, finding the open player, squaring up on her jump shot. I'd watch them at the edge of the court, a tall man and a tall girl, talking about how to play.

Of course, I'm particularly sensitive at this point in my life to messages about trying hard, being active, getting better through individual and team effort. Ann, you could barely handle a basketball two years ago. Now you're bringing the ball up against the press. Two defenders are after you. You must dribble, stop, pass. We're depending on you. We need you to help us. I wonder if my own paroxysms[1] of uncertainty would be eased had more people urged me—be active, go for it!

Not that dangers don't lurk for the females of her generation. I occasionally run this horror show in my own mental movie theater: an unctuous[2] but handsome lawyerlike drone of a young man spies my Ann. Hmmm, he says, unconsciously to himself, good gene pool, and wouldn't she go well with my BMW and condo? Then I see Ann with a great new hairdo kissing the drone goodby-honey and setting off to the nearest mall with splendid-looking children to spend money.

But the other night she came home from softball tryouts at 6 in the evening. The dark circles under her eyes were from exhaustion, not makeup. I tried too hard today, she says. I feel like I'm going to puke.

After she has revived, she explains. She wants to play a particular position. There is competition for it. I can't let anybody else get my spot, she says, I've got to prove that I can do it. Later we find out that she has not gotten the much-wanted third-base position, but she will start with the varsity team. My husband talks about the machinations[3] of coaches and tells her to keep trying. You're doing fine, he says. She gets that I-am-going-to-keep-trying look on her face. The horror-show vision of Ann-as-Stepford-Wife[4] fades.

Of course, Ann doesn't realize the changes she has wrought, the power of her self-definition. I'm an athlete, Ma, she tells me when I suggest participation in the school play or the yearbook. But she has really caused us all to rethink our views of existence: her younger sisters who consider sports a natural activity for females, her father whose

---

1. paroxysms: sudden or violent emotions.
2. unctuous: smug and falsely earnest.
3. machinations: crafty actions and schemes
4. Stepford Wife: reference to *The Stepford Wives*, a 1975 movie about a woman who grows paranoid when she discovers that the housewives in the suburban community she has moved to are all impossibly docile and submissive.

advocacy of women has increased, and me. Because when I doubt my own abilities, I say to myself, Get intense, Margaret. Do you like to sit on the bench?

And my intensity revives.

I am not suggesting that participation in sports is the answer for all young women. It is not easy—the losing, jealousy, raw competition and intense personal criticism of performance.

And I don't wish to imply that the sports scene is a morality play either. Girls' sports can be funny. You can't forget that out on that field are a bunch of people who know the meaning of the word cute. During one game, I noticed that Ann had a blue ribbon tied on her ponytail, and it dawned on me that every girl on the team had an identical bow. Somehow I can't picture the Celtics gathered in the locker room of the Boston Garden agreeing to wear the same color sweatbands.

No, what has struck me, amazed me and made me hold my breath in wonder and in hope is both the ideal of sport and the reality of a young girl not afraid to do her best.

I watch her bringing the ball up the court. We yell encouragement from the stands, though I know she doesn't hear us. Her face is red with exertion, and her body is concentrated on the task. She dribbles, draws the defense to her, passes, runs. A teammate passes the ball back to her. They've beaten the press. She heads toward the hoop. Her father watches her, her sisters watch her, I watch her. And I think, drive, Ann, drive.

Responding to What You Read

1. How did the way Ann grew up conflict with her need to be "intense" on the athletic field in order to succeed there?

2. In the "horror show in my own mental movie theater" that the narrator describes, what is it that she fears for her daughter's future? Be specific.

3. After this essay was published, the following letter-to-the-editor from Malvine Cole of Jamaica, Vermont, was printed:

> As a competitive swimmer when I was a girl, I lived for those moments when, body poised, toes tingling, I would hear the official intone: "Judges and timers ready? On your mark, get set . . ." I would crack-splash into the pool and go for it, to the piercing cries of my mother, at the pool's edge: "C'mon Mal!" Between events, my father would boast, in my presence, "You should see that kid swim!"
>
> I had to swim, I had to win because I was loved for doing—for winning—and not for being who I was otherwise. This feeling has shadowed me since.
>
> So I must caution Mrs. Whitney to relax about her daughter the athlete, and make it clear that she loves her on the court and off, when she wins or loses.

What is the letter-writer's point? Do you think that her point is valid? Explain.

Writer's Workshop

Reread the last paragraph of this selection. Then think about an intense moment you have had in sports—a moment when you were giving your all, totally caught up in the action and needs of the moment. Write at least two paragraphs in which you describe what is going through your mind—what you are thinking about—at that moment.

PERSPECTIVES

Basketball Season

Donna Tartt

Three Cheers for My Daughter

Kathleen Cushman

"She has seen the face of the god, drunk the wine of female power and known its rites . . ."

ABOUT THE AUTHOR•ABOUT THE AUTHOR•ABOUT THE AUTHOR•ABOUT THE AUTHOR

Donna Tartt was born in 1964 in Mississippi. She was educated at the University of Mississippi and Bennington College in Vermont. Her novel, The Secret History, is set at a college similar to Bennington.

Basketball Season

The year I was a freshman cheerleader, I was reading *1984*. I was fourteen years old then and failing algebra and the fact that I was failing it worried me as I would worry now if the Mafia was after me, or if I had shot somebody and the police were coming to get me. But I did not have an awful lot of time to brood about this. It was basketball season then, and there was a game nearly every night. In Mississippi the schools are far apart, and sometimes we would have to drive two hundred miles to get to Panola Academy, Sharkey-Issaquena, funny how those old names come back to me; we'd leave sometimes before school was out, not get home till twelve or one in the morning. I was not an energetic teenager and this was hard on me. Too much exposure to the high-decibel world of teen sports—shrieking buzzers; roaring stomping mobs; thunderous feet of players charging up the court— kept me in a kind of perpetual stunned condition; the tin roof echo of rural gymnasiums rang through all my silences, and frequently at night I woke in a panic, because I thought a player was crashing through my bedroom window or a basketball was flying at me and about to knock my teeth out.

I read *1984* in the back seats of Cadillacs, Buicks, Lincoln Town Cars, riding through the flat wintry Delta with my saddle oxfords off and my school-books piled beneath my feet. Our fathers—professional men, mostly, lawyers and optometrists, prosperous local plumbers—took turns driving us back and forth from the games; the other cheerleaders griped about this but though I griped along with them, I was secretly appalled at the rowdy team bus, full of boys who shouted things when you walked by their table in the cafeteria and always wanted to copy your homework. The cars, on the other hand, were wide, spacious, quiet. Somebody's mother would usually have made cookies; there were always potato chips and old issues of *Seventeen*. The girls punched listlessly at the radio; applied Bonne Bell lip gloss; did their home-work or their hair. Sometimes a paperback book would make the rounds. I remember reading one book about a girl whose orphaned cousin came to live with her, gradually usurping the girl's own position in the household and becoming homecoming queen and family favorite. ("'Why can't *you* be more like Stephanie!' yelled Mom, exasperated.") It turned out that Stephanie was not the girl's real cousin at all, but a witch: a total surprise to the nincompoop parents, who had not noticed such key signs as Stephanie failing to show up in photographs, or the family dog ("Lady") and the girl's horse ("Wildfire") going crazy every time Stephanie came within fifty feet.

Now that I think about it, I believe I read *Animal Farm* before *1984*. I read it in the car, too, riding through monotonous cottonfields in the weak winter afternoon, on the way to a tournament at Yalobusha Academy. It upset me a little, especially the end, but the statement "All Animals are Equal, but Some Animals are more Equal than Others" echoed sentiments which I recognized as prevalent in the upper echelons[1] of the cheerleading squad. Our captain was a mean senior girl named Cindy Clark. She talked a lot about spirit and pep, and how important it was we work as a team, but she and her cronies ostracized[2] the younger girls and were horrible to us off the court. Cindy was approximately my height and was forced to be my partner in some of the cheers, a circumstance which displeased her as much as it did myself. I remember a song that was popular around that time—it had lyrics that went:

We are family
I've got all my sisters with me

This had for some reason been incorporated into one of the chants and Cindy and I were frequently forced to sing it together: arms around each other, leaning on each other like drunks, beaming with joy and behaving in every way like the sisters which we, in fact, were most certainly not.

Though there was a sharp distinction between the older girls and the younger ones, we were also divided, throughout our ranks and regardless of age, into two distinct categories: those of snob and slut. The snobs had flat

---

1. echelons: levels or grades within an organization.
2. ostracized: excluded.

chests, pretty clothes, and were skittish and shrill. Though they were always sugar-sweet to one's face, in reality they were a nasty, back-biting lot, always doing things like stealing each other's boyfriends and trying to rig the elections for the Beauty Revue. The sluts were from poorer families, and much better liked in general. They drank beer, made out with boys in the hallways, and had horrible black hickeys all over their necks. Our squad was divided pretty much half and half. Physically and economically, I fell into the category of snob, but I did poorly in school and was not gung-ho or clubbish enough to fit in very well with the rest of them. (To be a proper snob, one had always to be making floats for some damn parade or other, or organizing pot-luck dinners for the Booster Club.) The sluts, I thought, took a more sensible view of such foolishness; they smoked and drank; I found them, as a rule, much nicer. Being big girls generally, they were the backbones of the stances, the foundations from which the pyramids rose and, occasionally, fell; I, being the smallest on the squad, had to work with them rather closely, in special sessions after the regular cheerleading practices, since they were the ones who lifted me into the air, who spotted me in gymnastics, upon whose shoulders I had to stand to form the obligatory pyramid. They all had pet names for me, and—though vigorously heterosexual—babied me in what I am sure none of them realized was a faintly lecherous way: tickles and pinches, slaps on the rump, pulling me into their laps in crowded cars and crooning stupid songs from the radio into my ear. Most of this went on in the after-school practices. At the games they completely ignored me, as every fiber of their attention was devoted to flirting with—and contriving to make out with—various boys. As I was both too young to be much interested in boys, and lacking in the fullness of bosom and broadness of beam which would have made them much interested in me, I was excluded from this activity. But still they felt sorry for me, and gave me tips on how to make myself attractive (pierced ears, longer hair, tissue paper in the bra)—and, when we were loitering around after practices, often regaled me with worldly tales of various sexual, obstetric, and gynecological horrors, some of which still make my eyes pop to think about.

   The gymnasiums were high-ceilinged, barnlike, drafty, usually in the middle of some desolate field. We were always freezing in our skimpy plaid skirts, our legs all goose pimples as we clapped and stamped on the yellowed wooden floor. (Our legs, being so much exposed, were frequently chapped from cold, yet we were forbidden to put lotion on them, Cindy and the older girls having derived a pathological horror of "grease" from—

as best as I could figure—the Clearasil ads in *Tiger Beat* and *Seventeen*—this despite the fact that grease was the primary element of all our diets.) Referee's whistle; sneakers squealing on the varnish. "Knees together," Cindy would hiss down the line, or "Spit out that gum," before she hollered "Ready!" and we clapped our hands down to our sides in unison and yelled the response: "O-Kay!" At halftime there were the detested stances, out in the middle of the court, which involved perilous leaps, and complex timing, and—more likely than not—tears and remonstrations in the changing rooms. These were a source of unremitting dread, and as soon as they were over and the buzzer went off for the third quarter the younger girls rushed in a greedy flock to the snack bar for Cokes and French fries, Hershey bars, scattering to devour them in privacy while Cindy and her crew slunk out to the parking lot to rendezvous with their boyfriends. We were all of us, all the time, constantly sick—coughing, blowing our noses, faces flushed with fever—a combination of cold, bad food, cramped conditions, and yelling ourselves hoarse every night. Hoarseness was, in fact, a matter of pride: we were accused of shirking if our voices weren't cracked by the end of the evening, the state to which we aspired being a rasping, laryngitic croak. I remember the only time the basketball coach—a gigantic, stone-faced, terrifying man who was also the principal of the school and who, to my way of thinking, held powers virtually of life or death (there were stories of his punching kids out, beating them till they had bruises, stories which perhaps were not apocryphal in a private school like my own, which prided itself on what it called "old-fashioned discipline" and where corporal punishment was a matter of routine)—the only time this coach ever spoke to me was to compliment me on my burnt-out voice, which he overheard in the hall the morning after a game. "Good job," he said. My companions and I were struck speechless with terror. After he was gone they stared at me with awestruck apprehension and then, one by one, drifted gently away, not wishing to be seen in the company of anyone who had attracted the attention—even momentarily—of this dangerous lunatic.

There were pep squads, of a sort, in George Orwell's Oceania. I read about them with interest. Banners, procession, slogans, games were as popular there as they were at Kirk Academy. Realizing that there were certain correspondences between this totalitarian[3] nightmare and my own high

---

3. totalitarian: authoritarian; dictatorial.

school gave me at first a feeling of smug superiority, but after a time I began to have an acute sense of the meaninglessness of my words and gestures. Did I really care if we won or lost? No matter how enthusiastically I jumped and shouted, the answer to this was unquestionably No. This epiphany[4] both confused and depressed me. And yet I continued—outwardly at least—to display as much pep as ever. "I always look cheerful and I never shirk anything," says Winston Smith's girlfriend, Julia. "Always yell with the crowd, that's what I say. It's the only way to be safe." Our rival team was called the Patriots. I remember one rally, the night before a big game, when a dummy Patriot was hanged from the gymnasium rafters, then taken outside and burned amid the frenzied screams and stomps of the mob. I yelled as loud as anybody even though I was suffused by an airy, perilous sense of unreality, a conviction—despite the apparently desperate nature of this occasion—that none of it meant anything at all. In my diary that night—a document which was as secretive and, to my mind at least, as subversive as Winston's own—I noted tersely: "Hell's own Pep Rally. Freshmen won the spirit stick. Rah, rah."

It was on the rides home—especially on the nights we'd won—that the inequity of not being allowed on the team bus was most keenly felt by the cheerleaders. Moodily, they stared out the windows, dreaming of back seats, and letter jackets, and smooching with their repulsive boyfriends. The cars smelled like talcum powder and Tickle deodorant and—if we were with one of the nicer dads, who had allowed us to stop at a drive-in—cheeseburgers and French fries. It was too dark to read. Everyone was tired, but for some reason we were all too paranoid to go to sleep in front of each other; afraid we might drool, perhaps, or inadvertently scratch an armpit.

Whispers, giggles, sighs. We rode four to a car and all four of us would be crammed in the back seat; bare arms touching, goosebumped knees pressed together, our silences punctuated by long ardent slurps of Tab. The console lights of the Cadillac dashboards were phosphorescent, eerie. The radio was mostly static that time of night but sometimes you could get a late-night station coming out of Greenwood or Memphis; slow songs, that's what everyone wanted, sloppy stuff by Olivia Newton-John

---

4. epiphany: an illuminating discovery.

or Dan Fogelberg. (The cheerleaders had a virtual cult of Olivia Newton-John; they tried to do their hair like her, emulate her in every possible way, and were fond of speculating what Olivia would or would not do in certain situations. She was like the ninth, ghost member of the squad. I was secretly gratified when she plummeted—with alarming swiftness—from favor because someone heard a rumor that she was gay.)

Olivia or not, the favorite song that winter hands down was "You Light Up My Life" by Debby Boone. It must have been number one for months; at least, it seemed to come on the radio just about every other song, which was fine with everybody. When it came on the girls would all start singing it quietly to themselves, staring out the window, each in their own little world; touching the fogged window-glass gently with their fingertips and each thinking no one could hear them, but all their voices combined in a kind of low, humming harmony that blended with the radio:

So many nights
I sit by my window
Waiting for someone
To sing me his song . . .

Full moon; hard frost on the stubbled cottonfields. They opened up on either side of the car in long, gray spokes, like a fan.

Kathleen Cushman, born in 1950, first published this piece in the New York Times Magazine *in 1989. Since then, she has published essays, criticism, articles, and fiction in the* Atlantic Monthly, New Woman, *and many other publications and anthologies. She has taught writing at Harvard University and now writes for a national audience about education reform. Cushman and her cheerleader-daughter Montana co-authored* Circus Dreams: The Making of a Circus Artist, *which describes Montana's experiences at 18, studying flying trapeze in France.*

Montana, who is the subject of "Three Cheers for My Daughter," followed her four years in the circus with four years at Harvard. She is currently studying for her doctorate in folklore at U.C.L.A. and frequently performs her solo trapeze act in schools.

Three Cheers for My Daughter

I screamed when my daughter told me at 16 that she was trying out to be a cheerleader; I remember the moment precisely. My daughter—strong-willed and strong-armed, critical and deep and smart—approached me with a trace of hesitation in her step. Mom, she said, I have something to tell you, and I don't think you're going to like it.

In that instant I saw her at six months, at six years, as a young teenager and in all the years before and after, her promise and prowess and the way she marched against hunger and held placards on highway bridges for Mondale and Ferraro. How could this child born of the Summer of Love, this darling of my countercultured eye, catapult so squarely into the conventional as to become a cheerleader! I *knew* this would happen, I wailed in wanton shame, forgetting everything I ever learned about what good mothers are supposed to say and do. I knew it 16 years ago—I knew, I knew.

Of course, she made the team. Of course, in fact, by the next year, through sheer will and desire, she became the captain of that motley squad of girls who braved ignominy[1] before the crowds with their pom-poms and their perms. I would not go to the games; I could picture them all too clearly. She would leave in her little blue skirt, her sturdy legs exposed from the tops of her panty hose down to the little white socks—sox—above the borrowed black-and-white saddle shoes. Her handed-down sweater pulled across her chest. When she opened her mouth to yell in those first games, my husband told me—for he would go to watch, out of loyalty and fascination and an attraction for basketball in any form—barely a whisper came out. My daughter was not one to shout out loud before a crowd.

Reports trickled in. They had attempted a pyramid and she had fallen off. They had made up a dance in practice, to an old song by the Supremes. One girl, in the terrible face of the crowd, had turned and fled; others sulked in the girls locker room, offended by imagined slights. She came home from one game, her face distended with tears, and would not speak at all. An acquaintance remarked on her amazing pluck—she had done a back flip on the gym floor for an individual cheer routine. I cringed. The girls were athletes, I pointed out to her one night, just as much as the basketball players were. I know that, Mom, she said. That's why I do it, so everyone else will know it, too.

Finally one evening, fortified by wine at dinner, disguised in a voluminous down coat left by a house guest, carrying the baby so I might leave at the half, I showed up at the gym on a game night. From the bench, her face registered disbelief, along with an ambiguous rictus[2] that could have been effort, pain, or even pleasure. I imagine my smile looked about the same. I perched precariously on an upper bleacher's edge and held the baby's bottle with white knuckles, waiting to watch them cheer.

It wasn't so bad. The gymnasium steamed with sweat and wet wool, surged with the continuous tidal roar of hormones, adrenalin and the public address system. The crowd leaned forward on their seats, shifted and turned and revealed themselves as only teachers, only parents, only kids. When our team would make a point, the kid who scored was cheered by name, by one of the girls in blue and white; and when there was a break, for time out or for the end of the quarter, the girls would all get up and bounce. It passed swiftly like some unfamiliar ritual, the maidens paying

---

1. ignominy: embarrassment.
2. rictus: a gaping grin or grimace.

homage to the warriors. Its very familiarity was alarming and comforting in like degree. No one winced but me, and I only inside, I think.

The next spring, when two full seasons had passed and my daughter was still a cheerleader, I found myself in another, large gym, an hour's drive away, speechless again in the face of these cheerleaders together. I had grown resigned and even equable[3] with time, and she more confident.

These days her cheers were audible and her smiles less forced, and I would show up at games recognizable in my own coat. The pyramids worked; the chants showed the mark of her wit. The audiences had grown to expect the girls' skills; they bellowed approval and stayed in their seats at the half. Now the squad was competing for a regional cheerleading crown, and I was there, waving a little blue flag and feeling like a person from another planet and wishing her luck.

All through the long day in the echoing gym, the teams pranced forth and did their drills. Little girls from Catholic schools, silky Spandex reflecting every prepubescent curve, ground their baby hips to sexy music in front of beaming parents and nuns. Squads of young women in flouncing pleats paraded like stiff-armed robots, their girlish voices disguised and gruff, grunting drill-sergeant monosyllables that exhorted us—ordered us—to score, fight, win. At the break, rock-and-roll poured out from giant speakers and all the girls danced on the wide wooden floor, a swirling kaleidoscope of school colors. The whole event was Dionysian,[4] ritualistic, bizarre—a wild concatenation of female passions, a screaming, ritualized celebration of sex and power, under the sanction of the state.

Our girls did fine. They were awarded a trophy for "most spirit," which meant that they had cheered loud and visibly for all the other teams that won. The dance they had prepared for weeks was perfectly executed, very tight; no one knew why they were not judged the best. At the end of the day, exhausted and drooping, they took their brave blue banner and went home.

The cheerleading season was over. The girls scattered to their summer jobs before college; their trophy gathers dust on the principal's shelf. I don't see a lot of those manic smiles these days; my daughter's face has relaxed into its usual weary lines; she shouts only when the phone is for me. But

---

3. equable: marked by lack of extremes or of sudden sharp changes.

4. Dionysian: being of a frenzied nature; derived from Dionysus, the god of wine in Roman mythology.

once in a while some gesture or some look will flicker like summer lightning through her limbs, across her face, and I am reminded that she has
seen the face of the god, drunk the wine of female power and known its
rites—and I tell myself with humble awe that strange as it may seem, it was
cheerleading that made it so.

Responding to What You Read

1. In what ways did Donna Tartt think her cheerleading squad had elements
   of the world of the novel *1984* in it?

2. What common elements do Tartt and Cushman see in cheerleading?

3. What did Kathleen Cushman become "resigned to" about her daughter?
   Did Cushman's daughter benefit from her participation in cheerleading?
   Support your answer with evidence from the selection.

Writer's Workshop

You know the world you live in very well. Perhaps it is similar to the one
Donna Tartt describes in her account. As a student, your world includes bus
rides or car-pooling to school, lunch with friends in the cafeteria, cramming
for a test in study hall, road trips to football and basketball games, pizza parties, hanging out at the mall, and part-time jobs at the drive-in or mini mart.

   Choose an activity that is part of the world you live in and describe it
in a short essay. Using Donna Tartt's account for inspiration, fill your essay
with the sights and sounds and flavors of your world.

Alternate Media Response

Videotape at least two different squads of cheerleaders in action. Analyze
the performance of each team. Discuss with your classmates the qualities
that make a cheerleading squad good. What values can be learned from
cheerleading that can be applied to other endeavors?

PERSPECTIVES

Tracee

Robert Lipsyte

This Skater Chooses to Come Home, of All Things

George Vecsey

How much would you sacrifice to become the best athlete in the world? A gymnast and a figure skater offer very different answers in the following selections.

ABOUT THE AUTHOR•ABOUT THE AUTHOR•ABOUT THE AUTHOR•ABOUT THE AUTHOR

R*obert Lipsyte is well known for his young adult novel about boxing,* The Contender. *He is a sports and city columnist for the* New York Times, *and in 1992 he was a finalist for the Pulitzer Prize for commentary. He has been a correspondent for CBS's "Sunday Morning" and for NBC News, and won an Emmy for on-camera achievement as host of "The Eleventh Hour," a nightly public affairs program on New York City's Public Broadcasting station.*

Tracee

Dawn breaks chilly and damp, and Tracee Talavera feels crummy. Her muscles ache, her throat is sore, she has a slight headache. She would like to stay burrowed in this warm bed in this cozy room crowded with five other girls and dozens of cuddly stuffed animals. From the muffled groans around her, she can tell that the others feel the same way.

She sits up. There are no days off on the road to the Olympics. Besides, she thinks, a crummy day may be just what she needs. She's been feeling too good lately. Maybe she needs the experience of working out while she feels bad.

That way, if she goes to a championship meet with a sore throat and a headache she'll be prepared. The difference between winning and losing in gymnastics is sometimes just a sneeze, a twitch, a frown. Maybe this lousy day will pay off.

The difference between Tracee Talavera and the millions of other teenaged girls who do gymnastics is more than muscle strength and balance and coordination. It is the willingness to get up at 4:45 A.M., no matter how she feels, and, perhaps even more important, the motivation to find a golden glimmer in a gray funk.

By 6 A.M. Tracee and the other young Elite (top competitive level) gymnasts who live together are limbering up for their daily workout in a chilly, chalk-dusty gym in Eugene, Oregon. If Tracee is still feeling crummy, she isn't showing it. Once warmed up, she races across the gym, somersaults over a leather vaulting horse, and plunges into a pond of foam rubber.

She bounds to her feet and glances at coach Dick Mulvihill for approval. He turns away from Tracee to watch another girl.

Tracee's expression hardens, her eyes narrow. She jogs back to her starting position, waits until Mulvihill is looking at her, then starts again, charging down the narrow runway, leaping into the air, flipping over the horse. This time, as she rises from the foam, Mulvihill is nodding at her. Tracee smiles. She hurries away to try it again.

"She's hungry," says Mulvihill, a few minutes later. We are standing together in the gym as the camera crew shoots Tracee making an entry in the precise workout journal that every serious gymnast keeps. "She's the first one on the apparatus and just about the last to leave. She sets the pace for all the kids and she hustles all the time."

"Hunger, is that what you look for in a beginning gymnast?" I ask Mulvihill.

"I like to look at their eyes," he says. "If they're looking around and they sort of have a hungry, steely, squinty look, like they're sizing up the other girls."

"You sound like a prizefight manager," I say.

"I used to box myself," he says.

Six hundred miles away, Tracee's parents, Nancy and Rip Talavera, are just getting up. They think about Tracee every day, and their thoughts are mixed with pride and sorrow.

"Tracee went up to Eugene when she was eleven," says Nancy. "She's now sixteen. We've lost five years of her youth that we can never regain. It's a situation where you've given your child to someone else to raise and it's a loss."

Tracee calls home once a week from Eugene, and chitchats with her mother about grandma, the pets, neighbors. Nancy always felt it was important to keep Tracee up to date on family trivia so she wouldn't feel like a stranger when she came home. But Rip rarely talks to Tracee when she calls. He says it's too painful, he misses her so much. And Rip seems to be protecting himself from further hurt when he says, "In fact, when she does come back, it really is disappointing, because she's not the kid who left here." When I ask him about the eleven-year-old Tracee who left, his voice cracks. "That's like a dream."

Allowing Tracee to leave home was an emotionally painful decision, and an expensive one. It cost almost $10,000 a year in tuition and living expenses for Tracee to attend Mulvihill's National Academy of Artistic Gymnastics. And the decision was a gamble—balanced against the hope that Tracee would become a champion was the fear that she could be physically hurt or become psychologically stunted, a gym rat instead of a well-rounded person.

But the Talaveras had been heading toward that decision since Tracee was an infant, a non-stop crib bouncer, living-room rug flipper, a trampoline tumbler. She was pure energy looking for an outlet.

She found that outlet when she was five. Like millions of others around the world, she was captivated by Olga Korbut, the tiny gymnast from the Soviet Union who won a gold medal in the 1972 Olympics. Watching the Games on television, Tracee, and her sister, Coral, who was eight, determined to become gymnasts, too.

This wasn't as easy in 1972 as it would become a few years later when children's gymnastics classes sprang up like fast-food franchises. The Talaveras found no lessons available in San Francisco. They enrolled their daughters in acrobatics classes (after a year, the girls complained that the classes weren't "hard enough"), in ballet ("too slow"), and trampoline, before they eventually found a gymnastics club south of the city.

In the next few years, gymnastics came to dominate the Talaveras' family life. The girls moved up the levels of competition and their parents became their cheerleaders, chauffeurs, trainers. They searched for better coaching. They found a good coach in Walnut Creek, a suburb within driving distance of their San Francisco home. After a while, they moved to Walnut Creek.

During summer vacations, they traveled to Eugene so the girls could work out with Mulvihill and his wife, Linda Metheny, a gymnast in three Olympics.

Both sisters were strong and light for their body size, graceful, energetic, and talented. But Tracee had the kid sister advantage of growing up with an older, more advanced gymnast; whatever Coral learned, Tracee learned, too. She also had what one Japanese coach called "konjo," an inner drive, a fighter's fire to keep going, to never quit.

In 1976, Nadia Comaneci of Rumania replaced Olga Korbut as the Olympic gymnastic darling and all over the world strong little girls fantasized about replacing Nadia. Tracee's potential was recognized. She was a California champion at nine, she was on track to the Olympic trials.

Excitement grew in the Talavera household. If Tracee continued to develop, she might be the darling of the 1980 Olympics in Moscow. When the girls' Walnut Creek coach left California for a better job, Tracee and Coral went to live at the Academy in Eugene, to train full time with Mulvihill.

"She was the imp," remembers Mulvihill. "The vivacious little teeny-bopper that darted around and really didn't know what was going on but was having a good time."

Coral was injured and became discouraged. She left after a year. The Talaveras thought that Tracee would come home, too, but she stayed. She began winning local, state, and regional titles. She won two United States championships and a bronze medal at the World Games in Moscow. She won a place on the 1980 Olympic team.

She also seemed to flourish in the cloistered life at the Academy, a carefully regulated existence that allows no dating and hardly any activities beyond gymnastics and regular public school. Even school was bent around gymnastics. Tracee attended only three or four classes a day, mostly math, English, and foreign languages. She got credit for gym, music, art, and social studies because of gymnastics and the international travel—she got to China, Japan, and Europe even if she never got to the school cafeteria.

"Sometimes you wish you could go to dances and football games and people's parties and stuff," says Tracee, "but then you sort of think, well, I'm getting more out of life right now than they are and I can always go to parties later. So it's sort of . . . it's worth it, I think."

The girls of the Academy work out six days a week, three on the compulsory exercises that every gymnast must perform in competition, three days for the optional exercises that each performs to show off her own particular strength. Six hours a day of the vaulting horse and the tumbling mat and the uneven parallel bars and the balance beams, the endless floor routines practiced until each muscle has a memory of its own, pushing through the pain and boredom and the low days when the coach scowls or, worse, ignores her, coming back after sprained ankles and pulled muscles and torn tendons and broken toes, ignoring the clouds of chalk dust and the chilly dawns and the constant "rips," the little skin tears in the palm that plague most gymnasts.

Many girls drop out of high-level competitive gymnastics, particularly those who have been pushed by their parents after their own interest waned. Some of those girls, afraid to confront their parents, will "eat their way out" of competition, or purposely get hurt.

Tracee's conflict was different. Her passion for gymnastics was growing, even as her parents began to doubt that her life was taking the right course.

In the summer of 1980, Tracee's world came apart. First, President Carter canceled United States participation in the Olympics; there would be no trip to Moscow, no chance to become the first American female gymnast to win an Olympic medal, no shot at becoming the imp of the world.

Then, her father demanded that she leave the Academy and come home to stay.

"She was hooked on gymnastics, she wanted to do gymnastics at all costs," explains Rip now. He wanted her to concentrate on her studies so she could attend a good college. "Tracee has to be prepared for life, and gymnastics isn't going to prepare her for life. It's a good experience in life, but it's not what's essential. Nobody is going to ask her how her double back was when she's looking for a job."

Tracee came home to Walnut Creek in the fall of 1980. She was fourteen. She never stopped nagging her mother and father to send her back to Eugene.

"She made it sufficiently tough," says Nancy, "that my husband and I let her go back. We wanted it to work so bad, but she didn't want it to work. She'd go to a local gym and she'd complain about everything."

Nancy's eyes fill with tears when she remembers the four months that Tracee was home. "She made us feel guilty that she wasn't doing her gymnastics in what she felt was the best place. Anytime there was a little problem, she'd say, 'Well, in Eugene we did it like this.'"

Nancy and Rip wanted Tracee to lead a "normal" life. But Walnut Creek wasn't "normal" for Tracee anymore.

"My gymnastics wasn't going anywhere," remembers Tracee. "I wanted to come back the whole time."

"She made it real impossible," says Rip. The final incident was a meet in Oakland, California. Coach Mulvihill was there, and Rip couldn't help noticing their easy rapport, how Tracee brightened up. After four months, Rip gave up and let Tracee return to Eugene.

"My dad just got sick of my nagging," says Tracee.

When she said that, she gave a little laugh. It sounded cold. I wondered how much guilt might be behind that little laugh. Tracee wanted to become the best that she could be, she obviously burned to be great. Her parents were ambitious for her, too. And yet, the pride they all felt was mixed with so much pain. They had all made sacrifices so Tracee could go for the gold.

When I interviewed Rip in the fall of 1982, he said that he no longer pays any money to the Academy. Coach Mulvihill would not discuss his financial arrangements. But there was no doubt that Tracee was a prime attraction at the Academy. Her picture was on the cover of Academy publications, her poster was on sale in the office. The Academy has a local booster club of people who donate money.

I wondered how many Eugene girls attended classes at the Academy because Tracee was there. How many girls from other cities came to live at the Academy because they dreamed of becoming Olympians, too.

But staying there may be harder than getting there.

"It's not for everyone," says Tracee. We're sitting in the upstairs living room of the Mulvihill house rather than the downstairs lounge area of the dormitory, because one of the girls is sick and we don't want to disturb her. The interview, one of an increasing number that Tracee undergoes, is just an interruption in this day that broke chill and damp and crummy. After her workout, she lifted weights, jogged, and went to school.

Meanwhile, six hundred miles to the south, Rip and Nancy are thinking about her, wishing they were there to monitor her studies, wondering if the Mulvihills care as much about her life outside gymnastics as they do.

Rip thinks about the addiction to glory, and what will happen to her psyche and her body as she pounds away toward the next Olympics. Nancy thinks about what will happen to her when her gymnastics career is over.

"I've seen a lot of kids who haven't had the same success they had as a gymnast feel they're a failure," she says. "A couple of kids have gone anorexic[1] because they're still striving to be that cute little gymnast that they were at eleven and twelve and thirteen and now they're seventeen and they're not getting that attention."

The family is still deeply involved in gymnastics. Coral coaches at her college, Nancy judges meets, and Rip teaches at a small local club. He says he is more relaxed with other people's daughters than he ever was with his own.

"So I lose Tracee," he says, glancing around the gym, "but I got about thirty other kids here that I work with. So these are like my, you know, almost like my family."

---

1. **anorexic:** affected with anorexia nervosa, a psychological disorder, primarily among young women, characterized by fear of gaining weight, and often leading to malnutrition and excessive weight loss.

Nancy nods when I ask her if she ever thinks about that decision they made years ago to let their daughters become gymnasts, and the decisions that followed to let Tracee devote her life to it. "She had a talent and we were lucky enough to be able to let her pursue it. I don't think what we've done would be much different than what most parents would do. Most parents want to do what's best for their kids. And I feel that's what we've done."

Back in Eugene, Tracee does her homework, has supper with the other girls, then watches some television, "General Hospital" or another soap opera taped earlier in the day. She will go to sleep early. She has to get up tomorrow morning at 4:45.

"Some girls just can't take it," said Tracee when I saw her. "First of all, they're used to their own rooms. They're used to, like, having the whole room, everything of theirs and they get this little space."

She talked about the trouble she has readjusting when she returns to her parents' house a few times a year on brief vacations.

"It's really weird going back home," she says. "You know, here, all fourteen of us go here, then all fourteen go there. It's done in such large groups and like at home I'm sort of by myself a lot. And you know, there's only four people in my family so it's just like, gosh it's so empty you know, there's no one there."

But in June of 1983, Tracee responded to her parents' wishes and came home again. Her grandmother was dying and her father, Rip, was more upset than ever by Tracee's absence.

Tracee settled into the life of the family. She spent the summer working out in the gym where Rip volunteered. She still planned to try out for the Olympic team.

Was Tracee going to stay home this time? The last time I called, her mother's voice sounded uncertain as she said, "I'm keeping my fingers crossed."

George Vecsey, who was born on July 4, 1939, writes a sports column for the New York Times, *and has published books on a variety of subjects, including a history of the New York Mets,* Joy in Mudville; *and two biographies,* Loretta Lynn, Coal Miner's Daughter *and* Get to the Heart, *the story of singer Barbara Mandrell.*

Regarding the selection that follows, Vecsey says, "I became aware of Sarah Hughes through a mutual friend. . . .I found Sarah to be very well grounded and was particularly touched that she was not the center of attention in the home." Vecsey adds, "There is a lot of pressure to be at 'big' games and write 'result' columns, but I work hard at keeping my options for the personal column about interesting people, about money and politics and race and gender. . . . I try to write for a Times *reader who may indeed be a woman, educated, not particularly a hard-core sports fan."*

This Skater Chooses to Come Home, of All Things

Her mom was wearing the silver medal. Her two younger sisters were doing their homework in the den. And Sarah Hughes was bubbling about being back in school yesterday after a week's absence.

"It was great to see my friends," Sarah said. "Everybody's the same. I took a little detour, I went to Croatia, and nothing's changed."

One little thing has changed. Last Saturday in the city of Zagreb, 13-year-old Sarah Hughes jumped and glided to a silver medal in the world junior figure skating championships, putting herself in a career glide path behind Americans like Kristi Yamaguchi, Nancy Kerrigan, Michelle Kwan and Tara Lipinski.

To this bubbly girl with braces, Yamaguchi is an esteemed face on a souvenir Wheaties box, perched in Sarah's bedroom. Kwan is such an idol that Sara lost the power of speech upon spotting her in a restaurant, leaving Sarah's older sister, Rebecca, to do the talking.

For all her youthful reverence, Sarah Hughes is not a total outsider, having won the national juniors last January.

However, she is triple-lutzing her way toward the top in a highly unusual manner—living at home, with her parents, her two brothers, her three sisters and the family dog.

She is a homebody. Imagine that.

For some female prodigies, the family becomes stifling, even dangerous, as it did for the Pierce and Lucic families in tennis and the Moceanu family in gymnastics.

At Sarah's age, junior tennis players learn their trade in so-called academies, gymnasts cast their fate with driven coaches who take over the father role, and figure skaters move across the globe to work with a celebrity coach or dominant national center.

"We were at the banquet in Zagreb and Sarah noticed that none of the Russian skaters had a parent with her," said John Hughes, the father.

John and Amy Hughes are dedicated to staying close to Sarah, now a distinct contender for a medal at the nationals in Salt Lake City in February.

Sarah still returns to her home and the family dog and a stash of Beanie Babies thrown to the ice by fans.

Yesterday, Sarah took out her violin and was so dissatisfied by the rust that she had to run through it again.

"That is the way Sarah is," said her mother.

Until recently, Sarah even played in the orchestra at Great Neck North Middle School, but she had to make a concession to her skating routine.

Sarah says she prefers to "work the smartest, not the hardest," and is confident she can pursue an Olympic gold medal with Robin Wagner, who coaches her at Iceland in nearby New Hyde Park, not a full practice facility.

"Robin is really great," Sarah said yesterday. "She keeps preparing me for things. But it's really up to me. I have to push myself."

Wagner, who competed on a national level, was a choreographer for four years while Sarah worked with Patti Johnson. "You don't have to pull a child from the family," Wagner said. "The socialization is very important to Sarah."

Sarah also travels to Newark, Del., to work with Jeff DiGregorio, who once coached Tara Lipinski. Sarah gave credit to DiGregorio for putting in the triple lutz that helped her win the national juniors in Philadelphia.

"Yes, I would like to see her more," DiGregorio said yesterday, "but it's been hard for her to get down here. She is a natural, very cat-like, with a great sense of where she is in the air. But I would not encourage her to leave her family because she needs the normal chaos, and I mean that in a positive sense, of being around her family."

It is a vibrant and talented family. John Hughes, a prominent tax lawyer, was the all-America captain of the undefeated Cornell hockey team in 1969–70 and was the last cut of the Toronto Maple Leafs (in favor of Darryl Sittler, he notes). Amy Hughes, a Cornell graduate and certified public accountant, is now recovering after a grueling series of treatments for breast cancer a year ago.

The parents understand that the children will leave the nest. Rebecca, 21, is a senior at Harvard and editor of the weekly *Independent*. David, 17, is spending the winter in Chicago, playing for a Junior A hockey team. The other three are home. Matthew, age 15, plays hockey in high school. Emily, 9, is also a promising figure skater. And Taylor, 7, is still exploring her skills.

"At home, Sarah is just one of six," the father said. "She has to fight with everybody else for her TV shows. I wouldn't want her going away and just hanging around a rink when she wasn't skating. She'll do fine with her skating. It's after her skating that I'm thinking about."

Success in the juniors does not automatically mean a road to a medal. Yamaguchi was the last former American junior champion to win an Olympic gold medal, back in 1992.

"This is a very important championship," Sarah said yesterday. "But you don't know what will happen later. This doesn't mean I'm definitely going to make it."

Right now she has her family and her friends—and her homework. Her social studies teacher told her to prepare a report on Croatia, turning her silver-medal journey into a school field trip. Sarah Hughes is determined to make it work both ways.

Responding to What You Read

Are the attitudes of the parents in these two selections similar or different? Explain your answer and support it with evidence from the selections.

Writer's Workshop

In an **argumentative** essay the writer takes one point of view on an issue and supports that point of view with strong evidence and logical reasoning.

Write an argumentative essay on the following topic: Which is more important—a child's chance at national or even international acclaim in amateur athletics or keeping a family together and possibly sacrificing that fame?

PERSPECTIVES

Tennis

Roger Angell

Rough Passage: A Family's Voyage of Discovery

Tom Wicker

Fathers and sons—whether fighting it out on the tennis court or fighting for survival at sea, the tensions and the bonds remain the same.

ABOUT THE AUTHOR•ABOUT THE AUTHOR•ABOUT THE AUTHOR•ABOUT THE AUTHOR

R*oger Angell, who has been called "the best baseball writer America has ever produced," became a fiction editor at* The New Yorker *magazine in 1956. He is now an editor and staff writer at the magazine. Since 1982, he has written over ninety "Sporting Scene" pieces, mostly about baseball, but also including pieces on tennis, hockey, football, rowing, and horse racing. His book* Once More Around the Park *(1991) brings together some of the baseball articles he has written over the past thirty years.*

Regarding the following selection, Angell says, "The story is based loosely on my own struggles to defeat my energetic and still youthful father at tennis, when I was in my early thirties. Almost everything else is made up, except the moment when the narrator remembers an afternoon in his teens when his father was playing in a small local tournament and the narrator wants *him to lose. Remembering that painful wish may have been the impetus for writing the story. . . . Seven or eight years after the story appeared, my father did have a heart attack, just after we'd been playing tennis together. He didn't collapse, or anything, but while we were waiting for the doctor and ambulance, he and I mentioned the coincidence, and I said, 'If you die now, I'll never forgive you.' He laughed, warily, and* didn't *die—lived on, I'm happy to say, for many more years."*

Tennis

The thing you ought to know about my father is that he plays a lovely game of tennis. Or rather, he used to, up to last year, when all of a sudden he had to give the game up for good. But even last summer, when he was fifty-five years of age, his game was something to see. He wasn't playing any of your middle-aged tennis, even then. None of that cute stuff, with lots of cuts and drop shots and getting everything back, that most older men play when they're beginning to carry a little fat and don't like to run so much. That wasn't for him. He still played all or nothing—the big game with a hard serve and coming right in behind it to the net. Lots of running in that kind of game, but he could still do it. Of course, he'd begun to make more errors in the last few years and that would annoy the hell out of him. But still he wouldn't change—not him. At that, his game was something to see when he was on. Everybody talked about it. There was always quite a little crowd around his court on the weekends, and when he and the other men would come off the court after a set of doubles, the wives would see their husbands all red and puffing. And then they'd look at my old man and see him grinning and not even breathing hard after *he'd* been doing all the running back after the lobs and putting away those overheads, and they'd say to him, "Honestly, Hugh, I just don't see how you do it, not at your age. It's *amazing*! I'm going to take my Steve [or Bill or Tom] off cigarettes and put him on a diet. He's ten years younger and just look at him." Then my old man would light up a cigarette and smile and shake his head and say, "Well, you know how it is. I just play a lot." And then a minute later he'd look around at everybody lying on the lawn there in the sun and pick out me or one of the other younger fellows and say, "Feel like a set of singles?"

If you know north Jersey at all, chances are you know my father. He's Hugh Minot—the Montclair one, not the fellow out in New Brunswick. Just about the biggest realty man in the whole section, I guess. He and my mother have this place in Montclair, thirty-five acres, with a swimming pool and a big vegetable garden and this En-Tout-Cas[1] court. A lovely home. My father got a little name for himself playing football at Rutgers, and that helped him when he went into business, I guess. He never played tennis in college, but after getting out he wanted something to sort of fill in for the football—something he could do well, or do better than the next man. You know how people are. So he took the game up. Of course, I was too little to remember his tennis game when he was still young, but friends of his have told me that it was really hot. He picked the game up like nothing at all, and a couple of pros told him if he'd only started earlier he might have gotten up there in the big time—maybe even with a national ranking, like No. 18 or so. Anyhow, he kept playing and I guess in the last twenty years there hasn't been a season where he missed more than a couple of weekends of tennis in the summertime. A few years back, he even joined one of these fancy clubs in New York with indoor courts, and he'd take a couple of days

---

1. En-Tout-Cas: Fr., in any event.

off from work and go in there just so he could play in the wintertime. Once, I remember, he played doubles in there with Alice Marble and I think Sidney Wood.[2] He told my mother about that game lots of times, but it didn't mean much to her. She used to play tennis years ago, just for fun, but she wasn't too good and gave it up. Now the garden is the big thing with her, and she hardly ever comes out to their court, even to watch.

I play a game of tennis just like my father's. Oh, not as good. Not nearly as good, because I haven't had the experience. But it's the same game, really. I've had people tell me that when they saw us playing together—that we both made the same shot the same way. Maybe my backhand was a little better (when it was on), and I used to think that my old man didn't get down low enough on a soft return to his forehand. But mostly we played the same game. Which isn't surprising, seeing that he taught me the game. He started way back when I was about nine or ten. He used to spend whole mornings with me, teaching me a single shot. I guess it was good for me and he did teach me a good, all-round game, but even now I can remember that those morning lessons would somehow discourage both of us. I couldn't seem to learn fast enough to suit him, and he'd get upset and shout across at me, "Straight arm! Straight arm!" and then *I'd* get jumpy and do the shot even worse. We'd both be glad when the lesson ended.

I don't mean to say that he was so *much* better than I was. We got so we played pretty close a lot of the time. I can still remember the day I first beat him at singles. It was in June of 1937. I'd been playing quite a lot at school and this was my first weekend home after school ended. We went out in the morning, no one else there, and as usual, he walked right through me the first set—about 6–1 or so. I played much worse than my regular game then, just like I always did against him for some reason. But the next set I aced him in the second game and that set me up and I went on and took him, 7–5. It was a wonderful set of tennis and I was right on top of the world when it ended. I remember running all the way back to the house to tell Mother about it. The old man came in and sort of smiled at her and said something like, "Well, I guess I'm old now, Amy."

But don't get the idea I started beating him then. That was the whole trouble. There I was, fifteen, sixteen years old and getting my size, and I

---

2. **Alice Marble . . . Sidney Wood:** two famous American tennis champions of the 1940s.

began to think, Well, it's about time you took him. He wasn't a young man any more. But he went right on beating me. Somehow I never played well against him and I knew it, and I'd start pressing and getting sore and of course my game would go blooey.

I remember one weekend when I was in college, a whole bunch of us drove down to Montclair in May for a weekend—my two roommates and three girls we knew. It was going to be a lot of fun. But then we went out for some tennis and of course my father was there. We all played some mixed doubles, just fooling around, and then he asked me if I wanted some singles. In that casual way of his. And of course it was 6–2, 6–3, or some such thing. The second set we were really hitting out against each other and the kids watching got real quiet, just as if it was Forest Hills. And then when we came off, Alice, my date, said something to me. About him, I mean. "I think your father is a remarkable man," she said. "Simply remarkable. Don't you think so?" Maybe she wanted to make me feel better about losing, but it was a dumb question. What could I say except yes?

It was while I was in college that I began to play golf a little. I liked the game and I even bought clubs and took a couple of lessons. I broke ninety one day and wrote home to my father about it. He'd never played golf and he wrote back with some little gag about its being an old man's game. Just kidding, you know, and I guess I should have expected it, but I was embarrassed to talk about golf at home after that. I wasn't really very good at it, anyway.

I played some squash in college, too, and even made the B team, but I didn't try out for the tennis team. That disappointed my father, I think, because I wasn't any good at football, and I think he wanted to see me make some team. So he could come and see me play and tell his friends about it, I guess. Still, we did play squash a few times and I could beat him, though I saw that with time he probably would have caught up with me.

I don't want you to get the idea from this that I didn't have a good time playing tennis with him. I can remember the good days very well—lots of days where we'd played some doubles with friends or even a set of singles where my game was holding up or maybe even where I'd taken one set. Afterward we'd walk back together through the orchard, with my father knocking the green apples off the path with his racket the way he always did and the two of us hot and sweaty while we smoked cigarettes and talked about lots of things. Then we'd sit on the veranda and drink a can of beer before taking a dip in the pool. We'd be very close then, I felt.

And I keep remembering a funny thing that happened years ago—oh, away back when I was thirteen or fourteen. We'd gone away, the three of us, for a month in New Hampshire in the summer. We played a lot of tennis that month and my game was coming along pretty fast, but of course my father would beat me every single time we played. Then he and I both entered the little town championship there the last week in August. Of course, I was put out in the first round (I was only a kid), but my old man went on into the finals. There was quite a big crowd that came to watch that day, and they had a referee and everything. My father was playing a young fellow—about twenty or twenty-one, I guess he was. I remember that I sat by myself, right down beside the court, to watch, and while they were warming up I looked at this man playing my father and whispered to myself, but almost out loud, "Take him! Take him!" I don't know why, but I just wanted him to beat my father in those finals, and it sort of scared me when I found that out. I wanted him to give him a real shellacking. Then they began to play and it was a very close match for a few games. But this young fellow was good, really good. He played a very controlled game, waiting for errors and only hitting out for winners when it was a sure thing. And he went on and won the first set, and in the next my father began to hit into the net and it was pretty plain that it wasn't even going to be close in the second set. I kept watching and pretty soon I felt very funny sitting there. Then the man won a love game off my father and I began to shake. I jumped up and ran all the way up the road to our cabin and into my room and lay down on my bed and cried hard. I kept thinking how I'd wanted to have the man win, and I knew it was about the first time I'd ever seen my father lose a love game. I never felt so ashamed. Of course, that was years and years ago.

I don't think any of this would have bothered me except for one thing—I've always *liked* my father. Except for this game, we've always gotten along fine. He's never wanted a junior-partner son, either in his office or at home. No Judge Hardy stuff or "Let me light your cigar, sir." And no backslapping, either. There have been times where I didn't see much of him for a year or so, but when we got together (at a ball game, say, or during a long trip in a car), we've always found we could talk and argue and have a lot of laughs, too. When I came back on my last furlough[3] before I went

---

3. furlough: leave from duty given to a soldier.

overseas during the war, I found that he'd chartered a sloop.[4] The two of us went off for a week's cruise along the Maine coast, and it was swell. Early-morning swims and trying to cook over charcoal and the wonderful quiet that comes over those little coves after you've anchored for the night and the wind has dropped and perhaps you're getting ready to shake up some cocktails. One night there, when we were sitting on deck and smoking cigarettes in the dark, he told me something that he never even told my mother—that he'd tried to get into the Army and had been turned down. He just said it and we let it drop, but I've always been glad he told me. Somehow it made me feel better about going overseas.

Naturally, during the war I didn't play any tennis at all. And when I came back I got married and all, and I was older, so of course the game didn't mean as much to me. But still, the first weekend we played at my father's—the very first time I'd played him in four years—it was the same as ever. And I'd have sworn I had outgrown the damn thing. But Janet, my wife, had never seen me play the old man before and *she* spotted something. She came up to our room when I was changing afterward. "What's the matter with you?" she asked me. "Why does it mean so much to you? It's just a game, isn't it? I can see that it's a big thing for your father. That's why he plays so much and that's why he's so good at it. But why you?" She was half kidding, but I could see that it upset her. "This isn't a contest," she said. "We're not voting for Best Athlete in the County, are we?" I took her up on that and tried to explain the thing a little, but she wouldn't try to understand. "I just don't like a sorehead," she told me as she went out of the room.

I guess that brings me down to last summer and what happened. It was late in September, one of those wonderful weekends where it begins to get a little cool and the air is so bright. Father had played maybe six or seven sets of doubles Saturday, and then Sunday I came out with Janet, and he had his regular tennis gang there—Eddie Earnshaw and Mark O'Connor and that Mr. Lacy. I guess we men had played three sets of doubles, changing around, and we were sitting there catching our breath. I was waiting for Father to ask me for our singles. But he'd told me earlier that he hadn't been able to get much sleep the night before, so I'd decided that he was too tired for singles. Of course, I didn't even mention that out loud in front of the others—it would have embarrassed him. Then I looked around and noticed that my father

---

4. sloop: a sailing ship with a single mast and a single jib sail.

was sitting in one of those canvas chairs instead of standing up, the way he usually did between sets. He looked awfully pale, even under his tan, and while I was looking at him he suddenly leaned over and grabbed his stomach and was sick on the grass. We all knew it was pretty bad, and we laid him down and put his cap over his eyes, and I ran back to the house to tell Mother and phone up the doctor. Father didn't say a word when we carried him to the house in the chair and then Dr. Stockton came and said it was a heart attack and that Father had played his last game of tennis.

You would have thought after that and after all those months in bed that my father would just give up his tennis court—have it plowed over or let it go to grass. But Janet and I went out there for the weekend just last month and I was surprised to find that the court was in good shape, and Father said he had asked the gang to come over, just so I could have some good men's doubles. He'd even had a chair set up in the orchard, halfway out to the court, so he could walk out there by himself. He walked out slow, the way he has to, and then sat down in the chair and rested for a couple of minutes, and then made it the rest of the way.

I haven't been playing much tennis this year, but I was really on my game there that day at my father's. I don't think I've ever played better on that court. I hardly made an error and I was relaxed and I felt good about my game. The others even spoke about how well I played.

But somehow it wasn't much fun. It just didn't seem like a real contest to me, and I didn't really care that I was holding my serve right along and winning my sets no matter who my partner was. Maybe for the first time in my life, I guess, I found out that it was only a game we were playing—only that and no more. And I began to realize what my old man and I had done to that game. All that time, all those years, I had only been trying to grow up and he had been trying to keep young, and we'd both done it on the tennis court. And now our struggle was over. I found that out that day, and when I did I suddenly wanted to tell my father about it. But then I looked over at him, sitting in a chair with a straw hat on his head, and I decided not to. I noticed that he didn't seem to be watching us at all. I had the feeling, instead, that he was *listening* to us play tennis and perhaps imagining a game to himself or remembering how he would play the point—the big, high-bouncing serve and the rush to the net for the volley, and then going back for the lob and looking up at it and the wonderful feeling as you uncoil on the smash and put the ball away.

ABOUT THE AUTHOR•ABOUT THE AUTHOR•ABOUT THE AUTHOR•ABOUT THE AUTHOR

As the White House reporter for the New York Times, *Tom Wicker was in Dallas, Texas, on November 22, 1963, when President John F. Kennedy was assassinated. Wicker later wrote a book,* Kennedy Without Tears. *He retired as a political columnist for the* Times *in 1991, having been with the newspaper for a quarter of a century and having won numerous awards for his writing. He is the author of nine novels and five books of non-fiction, including, most recently,* Tragic Failure: Racial Integration in America.

Rough Passage: A Family's Voyage of Discovery

Any grandfather might be pleased to be invited to join his son's family on a sailing expedition. Any 62-year-old man contemplating mortality and Social Security might leap at the chance for a late-life adventure—three weeks on a 38-foot boat, crossing the Pacific Ocean from Hawaii to Tahiti.

But on May 20, seven days out of Honolulu, with nothing but ocean for hundreds of miles in any direction, I was no longer thinking of adventure or of grandfatherly acquaintance. After a hurried inspection below, my son Grey climbed into the cockpit of his sloop[1] *Vámonos* and gave us the bad news in a carefully restrained voice: "The sleeve's cracked and moving, and we're taking water below the waterline."

It was late afternoon, and the relentless Pacific sun was mercifully far down the western sky. My 3-year-old granddaughter, Stacey Kathleen, was playing quietly in her safety harness beside Sarah, her mother, who was at the wheel. I, more than half-seasick and a total newcomer to any but the most sedate forms of sailing, did not have to be told that a leak below the waterline was a serious matter, especially on a small boat alone in the middle of the ocean. I had no idea what "sleeve" Grey was talking about except that it had something to do with the steering gear and was causing the wheel on deck to feel "stiff."

---

1. sloop: a sailing ship with a single mast and a single jib sail.

Grey and Sarah stared at each other, and I looked at both of them in consternation.[2] Though my son had suffered nearly as much as I from seasickness—Sarah and Stacey seemed to have "iron stomachs"—Grey went immediately into action. First, by radio, he alerted a ham network[3] that keeps track of sailing traffic in that part of the Pacific, establishing our position, reporting our problem, seeking advice on emergency procedures, courses, and weather conditions.

Next, he and Sarah hauled into the cockpit the heavy bundle that, when opened and put overboard, would be our well-equipped life raft, together with a waterproof container of extra life-raft supplies. Then Grey took the wheel and sent Sarah below to tighten the cracked and leaking sleeve, through which, I later learned, ran the boat's vital steering post connecting the rudder to the wheel. (Grey is bulky; Sarah's small size made it easier for her to work below.)

Darkness came on and rain began to fall; *Vámonos* was tossing about in winds of more than 15 knots. There was nothing I could do but keep out of the way—not always easy on a small vessel—though I also tried, without much success, to ease things for little Stacey. Normally unintimidated[4] by life at sea, she had sensed the tension of the adults, as children will, and was upset and crying.

With more time to think than I wanted, and a crying child to goad me, I could not escape the incongruity of a sedentary grandfather and a frightened 3-year-old harnessed side-by-side to a tiny fiberglass platform at sea, a good bit closer to the Equator than to the assurances and comforts of everyday life. And as I watched my son moving about his boat, the darkening hours began to pose not only the seagoing emergency with which he was dealing, but a hard passage for me in my sense of myself as his father.

More than two years earlier, I had agreed to make the Hawaii-Tahiti trip with Grey and Sarah. After delaying it until 1988, while they built up their savings, we settled on May, the time of best sailing weather in that part of the Pacific. I scheduled a month's vacation, laid in outsize supplies of seasick medicine and suntan lotion, purchased a yachting cap, and arrived in Honolulu on April 30.

---

2. consternation: amazement and confusion.

3. ham network: a group of amateur radio operators.

4. unintimidated: not frightened by.

My son and his wife had been living in Hawaii for several years, after sailing on *Vámonos* from Catalina[5] in 1984. That year, Grey earned a history degree from the University of California at Berkeley, and Sarah—a paleontology student to whom he had been married for a year—dropped out to be with him. Using funds from Grey's substantial earnings as electronics expert and soundman for the Lemmings, a Berkeley rock group, they had bought at a fire-sale price an old sailboat that was tied up and deteriorating in a local marina.

Sarah Austin is a West Coast fishing captain's daughter who grew up on and knows a lot about boats. Grey had had summer sailing experience and had attended an advanced and demanding French sailing school on the English Channel. Together, over many months and mostly by their own labor, he and Sarah had redeemed that first boat, then sold it for enough to make a substantial down payment on the craft they first named *Sarah*, later *Vámonos*—a sleek Canadian-built ocean racer, 38-feet long, sloop-rigged, and light in the water.

After they sailed to Hawaii, the Berkeley history graduate first worked as an assistant in a diving shop on Maui, becoming a licensed diving instructor; then, moving to Honolulu, he worked in the boatyard at the Keehi Marine Center. The erstwhile paleontology student, meanwhile, brought my first grandchild into the world in 1985, and still managed to work most nights in various island restaurants.

I was uneasy at these deviations from the usual career paths. So I asked Grey once if he wasn't afraid that at perhaps age 40 he might regret not having used his postcollege years to get started as a professional or in business.

"A lot of people my age," he replied, "at about 40, are going to look back and regret they didn't do in their younger years the kind of thing I'm doing in mine. And it'll be too late for most of them."

I found no way or wish to argue with that. I knew that by living on *Vámonos*, they could live on Sarah's earnings and bank most of Grey's for their "grand design"—a round-the-world, three-year sail through the South Pacific to Australia, then through the Indian Ocean, the Red Sea, the Mediterranean, and the Atlantic. If all went well—and they were young enough to be sure that it would—they would return to the United States in time to put Stacey in first grade, not too far behind schedule.

---

5. **Catalina:** an island off the southwest coast of California.

It was on the first leg of this extravagant voyage—Honolulu to Tahiti, a trip of some 2,382 miles—that a dubious but flattered grandfather was invited to sail. I welcomed the chance to be with Grey and Sarah and Stacey; and I looked forward a little tentatively to something that I feared a reasonably full life had not quite afforded me—an adventure, an experience beyond the ordinary.

My only venture into ocean sailing had come a year earlier, when I had visited Hawaii briefly and cruised in *Vámonos* with Grey and family from Oahu around Diamond Head to the Hawaiian island of Lanai. That rough, 16-hour passage deluded[6] me into thinking that I had an "iron stomach," and that an ocean crossing might have regular way stations and moments of rest.

After arriving for the Tahiti run, I learned quickly that there's always at least one more thing to be done before you cast off. In our case, Grey said, among lesser problems, that a brand-new and expensive part was faulty, so that the depth-finder on *Vámonos* wouldn't work.

I was expressing so much impatience to leave—my vacation period was finite[7]—that Grey decided to sail without a functional depth-finder. Only if we wanted to explore certain ill-charted harbors—and he didn't, he assured me—would it really matter. We set our sailing date for Sunday, May 8.

That hot and sunny day, the weather service reported no problems in any direction within 1,000 miles of Honolulu. There were a few on board, but nothing to delay us, so we loaded up with ice blocks, fresh water, and gasoline. We sailed at 3:40 P.M.—three or four days late by my expectations, amazingly near schedule in Grey's and Sarah's more sophisticated opinion. . . .

Seven days later, with Tahiti more than a thousand miles still ahead, as Grey dashed over me the small allotment of fresh water that was supposed to rinse off the salt from my first bath in a week, I wanted only two things: to feel well again, and to be back on terra firma.[8] Neither seemed likely.

I had lost any sense of proportion when I learned that the horizon was closer than the sea floor. We had been out of ice for several days—try surviving for long without that, middle-class America—and I had been mostly eating plain bread for about a week. Nausea had made me unable to read so

---

6. deluded: fooled.

7. finite: limited.

8. terra firma: Lat., solid ground.

much as a page of the books I had brought along to occupy the pleasant seagoing days.

All the way from Honolulu, we had been sailing southeast (mostly south), making six knots or more on constant trade winds—"smoking along," as Sarah put it. (A knot is one nautical mile, or 2,000 yards, per hour.) But in her log for May 17, she had noted "monster seas," and the wind that night sometimes exceeded 30 knots; waves crashed over the open cockpit about every five minutes.

Monster seas, indeed; it does not encourage a seasick landsman, lashed into a constricted cockpit, to look up and see the ocean towering above him, or to feel the frail hull beneath him shooting up one side of a 12-to-15 foot wave and down the other side like a roller coaster without a track; or, worse, to have one of those monster seas break like a tidal wave on top of the bisected eggshell to which he is clinging.

By that seventh day, May 20, wind and sea had moderated enough for us to venture baths on deck and I could conceive, at least, of smooth sailing and a settled stomach. Tumbling sleekly in the water alongside, schools of porpoises had been chasing about the boat like children in a backyard pool. Even so, after a week at sea, I had acquired two more hard-learned maritime axioms.

First, life aboard a 38-footer at sea is, at best, crowded, cramped, smelly, wet, and free of even elemental privacy, not to mention comfort. Second, contrary to my illusions from the preparatory cruise to Lanai in 1987, ocean sailing does not cease at sundown, or when a motel is reached, or when one is tired of it. It goes on and on, day and night, hour after hour, seasickness and discomfort notwithstanding, hammering seas be damned.

Grey and Sarah were standing four-hour watches apiece during the dangerous nighttime hours—a tanker coming over the horizon can bear down on a sailing yacht in a few minutes. Despite my nearly paralyzing state of greenish illness, I shakily took over the watch at 6 A.M.

So when, in the cooling dusk of May 20, Grey first sensed the "stiffness" in the steering that alerted him to danger, I was not jolted out of utter euphoria. As *Vámonos* was then located, Grey and the helpful ham-radio operators had concluded, we could sail on course mostly south and a little east about 10 more days to Papeete on Tahiti, where there would be haul-out facilities for the repair of *Vámonos*'s steering gear, or perhaps a day or so less to one of the nearer French Polynesian islands. Alternatively, we could change course to westward and sail two or three days, about 350 miles—and downwind, which would make sailing more comfortable—to Christmas Island, a mere speck of land and lagoon 1,160 miles from Honolulu, and found just above the Equator on only the most detailed charts of the Pacific.

The second choice, drastically curtailing time at sea in a damaged boat, offered the best safeguard against further breakdown of the steering gear. But since on Christmas there were no haul-out facilities, and not much else, it might also mean the longest and most serious delay in the long-planned round-the-world cruise.

Grey and Sarah nevertheless altered course from 150 to about 240 degrees, and headed for Christmas Island. When informed of this decision, my first, ungenerous thought was not that the danger had been lessened, but that they had lopped seven or eight days off the hard time I was serving in *Vámonos.*

For unexplained reasons, following the change of course, the steering post slipped back into proper alignment and again turned easily within the cracked sleeve. This was a considerable relief—Grey let out a whoop when he felt the stiffness go out of the steering gear—but not a guarantee against new slippage, further damage to the sleeve or increasing leakage.

Grey and Sarah understood, as I did not at the time, that our relatively small leak threatened us only remotely with sinking; the more immediate and specific problem had been that we might lose the ability to steer *Vámonos.*

Precisely what such a loss might have meant to our safety, I did not then know to ask, and they never told me; but in those seas and at our distance from land and help, the threat clearly was enough to cause a real night of anxiety for these reasonably experienced sailors. Nor was the horrendous possibility of sinking totally out of their minds.

"You always keep a life raft on board, but you never think you'll really have to use it," Grey told me later. "When I went down and shined a light on that water coming in below the waterline, I suddenly could see all of us actually sitting out there in a raft in the middle of the ocean. My blood literally turned cold."

For me, the sense of helplessness while in ill-understood but palpable danger was the worst problem; it brought me, moreover, into a strange new relationship with my son.

Grey was 29 years old. Though he was married, a father, and long absent from my house, I still thought of him in some ways as a dependent, certainly as a junior (he is, in fact, Thomas Grey Wicker, Jr.), subject to my advice and consent, if not control. I had changed his diapers, dried his tears, taught him to catch a baseball, seen him through school and the pitfalls of adolescence; he was, as I had always known him, my child, to whom I had read "Winnie the Pooh" and lectured learnedly on life.

That night, rocked by those gusty winds, strapped in, rain-soaked, uselessly huddled near my granddaughter on the downwind side of the cockpit— *Vámonos* was heeled sharply to starboard—that version of my son slipped forever behind me. I had no choice but to put my life in his hands—just as, it came to me, the child he had been had often, if unknowingly, put his in mine. I saw that the father involuntarily had become the child; struggling with wheel, halyards, sails, compass, the child necessarily had become the man.

Such a passage, I suppose, sooner or later comes to most fathers and sons. It can never be easy for either; it was not for me, accustomed as I was to being in charge, being heard, taking responsibility. Perhaps the change actually had happened a week earlier when, in brilliant sunshine and high spirits, with Diamond Head rising on the beam, Grey had steered *Vámonos* for the open ocean. I had been no more able then than I was a week later to take care of that boat, or myself, at sea. But even far from familiar shores, it had taken a leak below the waterline to make me recognize that the time had come to give over.

Later that night, Grey told me to keep on my life jacket while I slept— much as I once had instructed a small boy at bedtime on a winter night to keep his blankets pulled up. I felt finally—even in the squally night and the unresolved emergency—a sense of relief, of real accomplishment. I had brought this man that far; I had done my part, after all, and it had not been a small one.

I knew a secret pride, because I had watched Grey handle his boat and our trouble, and seen that he knew what to do. Now that his time was here, the man my son had become would see us safely through. I slept soundly.

May 21 dawned gray drizzly, and as chilly as the South Pacific gets. We were sailing easily before the wind, more comfortably than at any time since leaving Honolulu. No further steering or leakage problems had developed overnight and by prearrangement the reassuring ham operators soon were on the air. They had comforting news: the United States Coast Guard in Hawaii had been alerted to our plight, with the result that what the hams described as a "commercial vessel"—otherwise unidentified and never seen—was standing by in our vicinity, ready to steam to the rescue if that became necessary.

In daylight and after reflection, however, Grey and Sarah took a more relaxed view of the steering problem; they decided, and convinced the ham network, that the help of the "commercial vessel" would not be needed. When its radio operator entered the far-flung conversation, they thanked him but urged his ship on its way. And *Vámonos*, in lighter but favorable winds, proceeded without further event, for nearly three days, toward landfall on Christmas Island shortly after noon May 23.

Christmas is some 30 miles long and surrounded by tricky waters, including something menacingly labeled on the charts the "Bay of Wrecks." Although we had approached the island's most favorable mooring area, we were still at sea long after dark and remained offshore all night. But shortly after dawn on Tuesday, May 24, with Sarah at the wheel—it had turned stiff again the day before—Grey dropped anchor just off the tiny village of London, near the unnavigably shallow entrance to the lagoon that occupies the center of the island (and offers, I later learned, some of the world's best bonefishing).

Christmas is so low-lying that it probably would be covered over by hurricane seas, if hurricanes struck so near the Equator. There's one telephone on the island, one airstrip, one flight in and one out every week, one hotel, and evidently no radiation left over from the atomic bomb tests the British conducted in the 1950s and the Americans in 1962.

Coconuts and fish are the main products, and about 2,000 native folk, unimpressed by visitors, live under the multi-island aegis[9] of the Kiribati Republic. Don't expect to find Sadie Thompson or Rita Hayworth[10] in the decidedly undecadent bar of the Captain Cook Hotel, where visiting fishermen can choose to pay 50 Australian dollars extra for an air-conditioned room.

But to me, the day we landed, the island looked as charming as the setting of an old Dorothy Lamour[11] movie. As we went ashore by dinghy[12]—a

----

9. aegis: protection.

10. Sadie Thompson or Rita Hayworth: heroine of short story by Somerset Maugham; actress who played the role in movie version.

11. Dorothy Lamour: actress of the 1940s who starred in several movies set on tropical islands.

12. dinghy: a small rowboat.

half-hour trip through choppy waters—that dauntless sailor, 3-year-old Stacey, fell sound asleep. I was not that worn out, but I had few regrets about leaving the canting[13] decks of *Vámonos*. Ocean sailing clearly was not my sport, although, in the last calm days and nights of cruising to Christmas, I finally had seen why going to sea held such attraction for Grey and Sarah and so many dedicated sailors.

Nothing matches sunrise or sunset over a vast and empty ocean. On a clear night, the display of stars in the vaulting heavens, moonlit paths across gently rolling waves, the occasional excitement of a shooting star or the literally unearthly passage of an orbiting satellite—such nights at sea can fill anyone with peaceful joy, and the humility of man returned to nature.

On our last easy day of sailing, as a strong current carried *Vámonos* in a light breeze, I lay on the foredeck in the shade of the mainsail, indolent and dozing, no longer sick, singularly free of care, with the water murmuring past the hull—the voice of the sea in a soothing mood. Across its limitless vista, as into a fire, I thought I could gaze forever; against its depths and power, the strains of life on shore seemed petty and false.

I had, besides, as I had wished, become better acquainted with Sarah and Stacey; in a 38-foot boat at sea, not much can be hidden. Whether I knew them better, or they me, is something else. I fear my granddaughter may remember mostly a queasy and querulous[14] old man with 10 days of grizzled beard. I will remember her not least for a certain acerbic[15] independence—a child, like her parents, not easily to be incorporated within the world's demanding routines.

Escape from those routines seems to me a prime reason why people are drawn to the sea. Not that ocean sailing doesn't make its demands and impose its rules, severe ones at that; but these are shaped from the fundamental need to survive in nature—a far different thing from the inculcated[16] desire to flourish in society. The sea's rules can be ignored only at real, physical peril, not at mere risk of social or financial penalty.

---

13. **canting:** tilting; leaning.
14. **querulous:** complaining.
15. **acerbic:** sour or harsh.
16. **inculcated:** instilled or taught.

For those who can meet the demands of sea and weather—elemental challenges long lost to modern technological societies—the boatman's life can be unhurried, footloose, rewarding in itself rather than as a passage to something else, whether affluence or power or both. Such a life can be content—the opposite of the rat race.

Having accidentally arrived, for example, at Christmas Island, Grey and Sarah—taking things as they came—determined to stay awhile. They would fish, snorkel, dive, enjoy life in the sun with Stacey; and one day, someday, they would get around to the rudder repairs that would have to be made before they could sail on.

The next day, however, a shaven, chastened grandfather gratefully caught the weekly three-hour flight from Christmas to Honolulu. I was eager to get back to my life, the kind of demands with which I had more or less learned to cope—back, as I had so often wished in the grimmest hours at sea, to terra firma.

But as I tried vainly, after takeoff, to catch a last glimpse of *Vámonos* anchored offshore, I still could hear Grey's exultant voice, as we finally departed Honolulu and he explained himself and his life better than he ever had:

"Now all I have to do is what I've got to do to sail my boat!"

Responding to What You Read

1. Why do you think that the narrator in "Tennis" took up golf and squash in college rather than tennis?

2. "I was uneasy at these deviations from the usual career paths," writes Tom Wicker in "Rough Passage..." about his son. What did he mean by this?

3. Each of the narrators in these two selections undergoes a change in attitude. Explain the change in both men.

Writer's Workshop

Write a short essay in which you compare and contrast the father-son relationships in these two selections. What tensions exist between each father and son? What bonds exist? What discovery does the son make in "Tennis"? What discovery does the father make in "Rough Passage . . ."? Share your conclusions with your classmates.

CHAPTER 5

Sports Classics

Just as there are classic books, classic movies, and classic cars, there are also sports classics—games, players, literature, even stadiums.

The poem "Casey at the Bat" and the Abbott and Costello radio routine "Who's on First?" have become classic pieces of American culture.

Being cut from a team, the last kid picked when sides are chosen, or the nonathletic kid in gym class are classic situations that have worried generations of Americans and, in some cases, left painful memories.

Joe DiMaggio, Tom Seaver, and Bill Bradley are classic ballplayers, one of whom married a classic movie star.

The debate over boxing as sport or bloodbath is a classic controversy in the world of sports.

To some people, the classic baseball stadium has real grass and no dome.

As you read the selections in this chapter, develop your own understanding of what makes someone or something a classic.

Who's on First?

Abbott and Costello

This routine is most effective if it's read aloud. As you read, think about how the authors created humor in this situation.

ABOUT THE AUTHOR•ABOUT THE AUTHOR•ABOUT THE AUTHOR•ABOUT THE AUTHOR

Bud Abbott and Lou Costello were a popular comedy team in America from the 1930s through the 1950s. They performed on stage, in movies, on radio, and on television. First performed on the Kate Smith Radio Hour *in the late 1930s, "Who's On First?" is probably their most famous comedy routine. Their classic films include* Buck Privates, Hold That Ghost, *and* Abbott and Costello Meet Frankenstein. *William "Bud" Abbott was born in 1895 and died in 1974. Lou Costello was born in 1908 and died in 1959.*

Who's on First?

Sebastian:	Peanuts!
Dexter:	Peanuts!
Sebastian:	Popcorn!
Dexter:	Popcorn!
Sebastian:	Crackerjack!
Dexter:	Crackerjack!
Sebastian:	Get your packages of Crackerjack here!
Dexter:	—Crackerjack—will you keep quiet? Sebastian! Sebastian, please! Don't interrupt my act!
Sebastian:	Ladies and gentlemen and also the children—will you excuse me for a minute, please? Thank you.
Dexter:	What do you want to do?

Sebastian:	Look, Mr. Broadhurst—
Dexter:	What are you doing?
Sebastian:	I love baseball!
Dexter:	Well, we all love baseball.
Sebastian:	When we get to St. Louis, will you tell me the guys' names on the team so when I go to see them in that St. Louis ballpark I'll be able to know those fellows?
Dexter:	Then you'll go and peddle your popcorn and don't interrupt the act anymore?
Sebastian:	Yes, sir.
Dexter:	All right. But you know, strange as it may seem, they give ballplayers very peculiar names.
Sebastian:	Funny names?
Dexter:	Nicknames. Nicknames.
Sebastian:	Not—not as funny as my name—Sebastian Dinwiddie.
Dexter:	Oh, yes, yes, yes!
Sebastian:	Funnier than that?
Dexter:	Oh, absolutely. Yes. Now on the St. Louis team we have Who's on first, What's on second, I Don't Know is on third—
Sebastian:	That's what I want to find out. I want you to tell me the names of the fellows on the St. Louis team.
Dexter:	I'm telling you. Who's on first, What's on second, I Don't Know is on third—
Sebastian:	You know the fellows' names?
Dexter:	Yes.
Sebastian:	Well, then, who's playin' first?
Dexter:	Yes.
Sebastian:	I mean the fellow's name on first base.
Dexter:	Who.
Sebastian:	The fellow playin' first base for St. Louis.
Dexter:	Who.
Sebastian:	The guy on first base.
Dexter:	Who is on first.
Sebastian:	Well, what are you askin' me for?
Dexter:	I'm not asking you—I'm telling you. *Who is on first.*
Sebastian:	I'm asking you—who's on first?

Dexter:	That's the man's name!
Sebastian:	That's whose name?
Dexter:	Yes.
Sebastian:	Well, go ahead and tell me!
Dexter:	Who.
Sebastian:	The guy on first.
Dexter:	Who.
Sebastian:	The first baseman.
Dexter:	Who is on first.
Sebastian:	Have you got a first baseman on first?
Dexter:	Certainly.
Sebastian:	Then who's playing first?
Dexter:	Absolutely.
Sebastian:	When you pay off the first baseman every month, who gets the money?
Dexter:	Every dollar of it. And why not, the man's entitled to it.
Sebastian:	Who is?
Dexter:	Yes.
Sebastian:	So who gets it?
Dexter:	Why shouldn't he? Sometimes his wife comes down and collects it.
Sebastian:	Whose wife?
Dexter:	Yes. After all, the man earns it.
Sebastian:	Who does?
Dexter:	Absolutely.
Sebastian:	Well, all I'm trying to find out is what's the guy's name on first base.
Dexter:	Oh, no, no. What is on second base.
Sebastian:	I'm not asking you who's on second.
Dexter:	Who's on first.
Sebastian:	That's what I'm trying to find out.
Dexter:	Well, don't change the players around.
Sebastian:	I'm not changing nobody.
Dexter:	Now, take it easy.
Sebastian:	What's the guy's name on first base?
Dexter:	What's the guy's name on second base.
Sebastian:	I'm not askin' ya who is on second.

Dexter:	Who's on first.
Sebastian:	I don't know.
Dexter:	He's on third. We're not talking about him.
Sebastian:	How could I get on third base?
Dexter:	You mentioned his name.
Sebastian:	If I mentioned the third baseman's name, who did I say is playing third?
Dexter:	No, Who's playing first.
Sebastian:	Stay offa first, will ya?
Dexter:	Well, what do you want me to do?
Sebastian:	Now what's the guy's name on first base?
Dexter:	What's on second.
Sebastian:	I'm not asking ya who's on second.
Dexter:	Who's on first.
Sebastian:	I don't know.
Dexter:	He's on third.
Sebastian:	There I go back on third again.
Dexter:	Well, I can't change their names.
Sebastian:	Say, will you please stay on third base, Mr. Broadhurst.
Dexter:	Please. Now, what is it you want to know?
Sebastian:	What is the fellow's name on third base?
Dexter:	What is the fellow's name on second base.
Sebastian:	I'm not askin' ya who's on second.
Dexter:	Who's on first.
Sebastian:	I don't know.
Dexter and Sebastian:	*Third base!*
Sebastian:	You got a pitcher on the team?
Dexter:	Wouldn't this be a fine team without a pitcher?
Sebastian:	I don't know. Tell me the pitcher's name.
Dexter:	Tomorrow.
Sebastian:	You don't want to tell me today?
Dexter:	I'm telling you, man.
Sebastian:	Then go ahead.
Dexter:	Tomorrow.
Sebastian:	What time?
Dexter:	What time what?
Sebastian:	What time tomorrow are you gonna tell me who's pitching?

Dexter:	Now listen, Who is not pitching. Who is on—
Sebastian:	I'll break your arm if you say who's on first.
Dexter:	Then why come up here and ask?
Sebastian:	I want to know what's the pitcher's name.
Dexter:	What's on second.
Sebastian:	I don't know.
Sebastian and Dexter:	*Third base!*
Sebastian:	Gotta catcher?
Dexter:	Yes.
Sebastian:	I'm a good catcher, too, you know.
Dexter:	I know that.
Sebastian:	I would like to play for the St. Louis team.
Dexter:	Well, I might arrange that.
Sebastian:	I would like to catch. Now, I'm being a good catcher, Tomorrow's pitching on the team, and I'm catching.
Dexter:	Yes.
Sebastian:	Tomorrow throws the ball and the guy up bunts the ball.
Dexter:	Yes.
Sebastian:	Now, when he bunts the ball—me being a good catcher—I want to throw the guy out at first base, so I pick up the ball and throw it to who?
Dexter:	Now that's the first thing you've said right.
Sebastian:	I DON'T EVEN KNOW WHAT I'M TALKING ABOUT.
Dexter:	Well, that's all you have to do.
Sebastian:	Is to throw it to first base.
Dexter:	Yes.
Sebastian:	Now who's got it?
Dexter:	Naturally.
Sebastian:	Who has it?
Dexter:	Naturally.
Sebastian:	Naturally.
Dexter:	Naturally.
Sebastian:	O.K.
Dexter:	Now you've got it.
Sebastian:	I pick up the ball and I throw it to Naturally.
Dexter:	No you don't, you throw the ball to first base.
Sebastian:	Then who gets it?

Dexter:	Naturally.
Sebastian:	O.K.
Dexter:	All right.
Sebastian:	I throw the ball to Naturally.
Dexter:	You don't. You throw it to Who.
Sebastian:	Naturally.
Dexter:	Well, naturally. Say it that way.
Sebastian:	That's what I said.
Dexter:	You did not.
Sebastian:	I said I'd throw the ball to Naturally.
Dexter:	You don't. You throw it to Who.
Sebastian:	Naturally.
Dexter:	Yes.
Sebastian:	So I throw the ball to first base and Naturally gets it.
Dexter:	No. You throw the ball to first base—
Sebastian:	Then who gets it?
Dexter:	Naturally.
Sebastian:	That's what I'm saying.
Dexter:	You're not saying that.
Sebastian:	Excuse me, folks.
Dexter:	Now, don't get excited. Now, don't get excited.
Sebastian:	I throw the ball to first base.
Dexter:	Then Who gets it.
Sebastian:	He better get it.
Dexter:	That's it. All right now, don't get excited. Take it easy.
Sebastian:	Now I throw the ball to first base, whoever it is grabs the ball, so the guy runs to second.
Dexter:	Uh-huh.
Sebastian:	Who picks up the ball and throws it to What. What throws it to I Don't Know. I Don't Know throws it back to Tomorrow—a triple play.
Dexter:	Yeah. It could be.
Sebastian:	And I don't care.
Dexter:	What was that?
Sebastian:	I said, *I don't care.*
Dexter:	Oh, that's our shortstop!

Responding to What You Read

The humor in "Who's on First?" is based on a total lack of communication between two people and the ensuing frustration. However, the two characters communicate to the audience very well. The hilarity of this comic dialogue has lasted over half a century. Consider how the effect of the dialogue might be different if it took place between the following two people:

- two people, one of whom knows very little about baseball
- an adult and a child
- an American and someone from another country who has a limited understanding of English

Explain your answers.

Writer's Workshop

The starting point of this routine is a little artificial—nicknames like "Who" and "What" aren't very common, even among baseball players. But notice how well the characters Dexter and Sebastian maintain their perspectives throughout the routine.

Try writing your own comic dialogue about sports. For example, you might try to explain baseball to a foreign student who is seeing the game for the first time. Once you choose a sport and a situation, brainstorm a list of the language exclusive to the sport, or vernacular, to use in your dialogue. Remember, "Who's on First?" works so well because of the honest misunderstanding on the part of the characters.

Casey at the Bat

Ernest Lawrence Thayer

Casey is probably the most famous batter in the history of baseball.

ABOUT THE AUTHOR•ABOUT THE AUTHOR•ABOUT THE AUTHOR•ABOUT THE AUTHOR

Ernest Lawrence Thayer was born in 1863. He was a philosophy major at Harvard University before he became a journalist. This classic poem was first published in the San Francisco Examiner *on June 3, 1888. A vaudeville actor named DeWolf Hopper recited "Casey at the Bat" on stages across the United States, thereby assuring it a place among the classics of American poetry. Ernest Lawrence Thayer died in 1940.*

Casey at the Bat

The outlook wasn't brilliant for the Mudville nine that day;
The score stood four to two with but one inning more to play.
And then, when Cooney died at first, and Barrows did the same,
A sickly silence fell upon the patrons of the game.

5   A straggling few got up to go in deep despair. The rest
Clung to that hope which springs eternal in the human breast;
They thought, If only Casey could get a whack at that
We'd put up even money now, with Casey at the bat.

But Flynn preceded Casey, as did also Jimmy Blake,
10 And the former was a lulu and the latter was a cake;
So upon that stricken multitude grim melancholy sat,
For there seemed but little chance of Casey's getting to the bat.

But Flynn let drive a single, to the wonderment of all,
And Blake, the much despised, tore the cover off the ball;
15 And when the dust had lifted, and men saw what had occurred,
There was Jimmy safe at second, and Flynn a-hugging third.

Then from five thousand throats and more there rose a lusty yell;
It rumbled through the valley, it rattled in the dell;
It knocked upon the mountain and recoiled upon the flat,
20 For Casey, mighty Casey, was advancing to the bat.

There was ease in Casey's manner as he stepped into his place;
There was pride in Casey's bearing and a smile on Casey's face.
And when, responding to the cheers, he lightly doffed¹ his hat,
No stranger in the crowd could doubt 'twas Casey at the bat.

25 Ten thousand eyes were on him as he rubbed his hands with dirt,
Five thousand tongues applauded when he wiped them on his shirt.
Then while the writhing pitcher ground the ball into his hip,
Defiance gleamed from Casey's eye, a sneer curled Casey's lip.

And now the leather-covered sphere came hurtling through the air,
30 And Casey stood a-watching it in haughty grandeur there.
Close by the sturdy batsman the ball unheeded sped;
"That ain't my style," said Casey. "Strike one," the umpire said.

From the benches, black with purple, there went up a muffled roar,
Like the beating of the storm waves on a stern and distant shore.
35 "Kill him! Kill the umpire!" shouted someone on the stand;
And it's likely they'd have killed him had not Casey raised his hand.

---

1. doffed: took off.

With a smile of Christian charity great Casey's visage[2] shone;
He stilled the rising tumult,[3] he bade the game go on;
He signaled to the pitcher, and once more the spheroid flew;
40   But Casey still ignored it, and the umpire said, "Strike two."

"Fraud!" cried the maddened thousands, and echo answered "Fraud!"
But one scornful look from Casey and the audience was awed;
They saw his face grow stern and cold, they saw his muscles strain,
And they knew that Casey wouldn't let that ball go by again.

45   The sneer is gone from Casey's lip, his teeth are clenched in hate,
He pounds with cruel violence his bat upon the plate.
And now the pitcher holds the ball, and now he lets it go.
And now the air is shattered by the force of Casey's blow.

Oh, somewhere in this favored land the sun is shining bright.
50   The band is playing somewhere, and somewhere hearts are light;
And somewhere men are laughing, and somewhere children shout,
But there is no joy in Mudville—mighty Casey has struck out.

---

2. visage: face.
3. tumult: commotion; din; uproar.

Responding to What You Read

1. How does the writer toy with the reader in the last two stanzas of the poem?

2. There's an old saying that "Pride goes before the fall." Explain what you think this expression means and how it might be applied to Casey.

3. A parody is a piece of writing that imitates and often makes fun of another work. Read the following two stanzas from "O'Toole's Touchdown," a parody of "Casey at the Bat." What elements of "Casey" does the writer of "O'Toole's" imitate?

> But look! It is a forward pass from quarter to O'Toole!
> The Mighty Mike has grabbed it; he has started for the goal!
> With ball clutched firmly to his breast, he speeds with bound on bound.
> He flies across the goal line, and then drops to the ground.

> 5 Oh, somewhere men are laughing, and children shout with glee;
> And somewhere bands are playing, and somewhere hearts are free.
> And somewhere in this favored land the glorious sun does shine.
> But there is no joy in Hokus, O'Toole crossed the wrong goal line!

Writer's Workshop

Try to write your own parody of "Casey at the Bat." It doesn't have to be thirteen stanzas—maybe just six or seven if you can tell your story in that space—but try to parallel Ernest Lawrence Thayer's rhythms, plot development, and technique for ending his piece. You can write about a sports event or another important event that happened at school or in your community.

Ace Teenage Sportscribe

by Donald Hall

Donald Hall recounts his high school days covering sports for a local newspaper during World War II.

ABOUT THE AUTHOR•ABOUT THE AUTHOR•ABOUT THE AUTHOR•ABOUT THE AUTHOR

See biography of Donald Hall on p. 215. "Ace Teenage Sportscribe" appeared in Hall's book Fathers Playing Catch With Sons.

Ace Teenage Sportscribe

When I was a freshman at Hamden High School—in a suburb of New Haven, Connecticut—back in 1942, I became aware of a rakish character, a senior who wore chic jackets and loafers, who talked fast, and who aroused interest in glamorous seventeen-year-old women clutching books to their sprouting bosoms. I *think* his name was Herbie, and I *know* that he wrote about high school sports for the *New Haven Register*. I looked on him with the envy that I usually reserved for athletes. Herbie was no more an athlete than I was; writing newspaper stories was compensation for this bitter accident of nature. Gradually I realized that next year Herbie would be gone to the war, and his employers would need a replacement. I dropped some hints—and Herbie tried me out by allowing me to cover a couple of baseball games. I was hired. I met the *Register's* sports editor—call him Ed McGuire—and signed on to cover Hamden High for ten cents a column inch. I was fifteen.

Autumn of my sophomore year was football and anguish. I rode the team bus to out-of-town games, the only ununiformed young male except for the manager who wore a leg brace from polio. I sat at the rear, behind already-shoulder-padded warriors like Batso Biscaglia the five-foot fullback, half-back Luigi Mertino, and Rafael Domartino, the center who weighed two hundred and eighty pounds. At this time, Hamden was a colony of Calabria.[1]

I sat at the rear in melancholy swooning isolation among cheerleaders in small green pleated skirts, little white socks, green sneakers—and great expanses of naked shimmering LEG. I sat in a lovesick impossible day-dream, so near and yet so far—and the girls (the prettiest in the school; by reputation the fastest) were pleasant and condescending. I heard them talk about dates after the game—each with her football player, one with a back-field—as they gossiped in front of me without taking account of me as *male*. Oh, I was male—and a hopeless shy devoted tongue-tied Oedipal nympholept,[2] haggard and woe-begone, palely loitering on a bus to Ansonia. . . . The cold ride back from the game, which we usually lost, the players sat silent and hurt; the girls were quiet as they looked ahead to pleasing the sullen boys.

At home I would write a brief game story and my father would drive me down to the *Register* with it. Soon I wrote for the *Journal-Courier* as well, poorer and slimmer of the city's two newspapers, published in the morning while the *Register* came out in the afternoon. The *Journal-Courier* could not afford to pay ten cents an inch. Scottie MacDonald was Assistant Sports Editor (the entire staff) and promised me *lots* of by-lines and an occasional couple of bucks. I remember those offices in a second- or third-floor build-ing in downtown New Haven. Scottie had a cubbyhole with a typewriter. He wore his hat all the time, set way back, above a brown suit and tie; he kept the tie pulled down and the top button of his shirt unbuttoned; pretty Bohemian[3] for 1942. Every two or three weeks he handed me a slip of paper with which I could extract two dollars petty cash from the cashier.

I wrote my *Register* story first, then worked it a second way for the *Courier*. For the *Register* I clipped my columns, measured them with a ruler, and presented my column-inches to Ed McGuire, who wore a perpetual

---

1. colony of Calabria: humorously meant, having many Italian residents; Calabria was a district of ancient Italy.

2. Oedipal nympholept: a young man full of sexual confusion, like the mythical hero Oedipus.

3. Bohemian: unconventional, radical.

green eyeshade, who always looked angry, who tucked a continual cigar in the corner of his mouth. (Everybody entered the *Front Page*[4] lookalike contest in those days.) He would re-measure my clips, take his cigar out of his mouth, spit, and write me a chit for the cashier. Eight dollars, maybe. . . .

I did not get rich as a sportswriter, but I observed an amelioration[5] of my social life. To my astonishment, people like Batso began to wave at me in the cafeteria; Pongi Piscatelli, the famous tackle *six-feet-tall* smiled at me in the corridor and said, "Hi, John." Maybe he thought all Protestants were named John. Well, I thought, "Don" *sounds* a lot like "John."

Baseball was always my favorite sport and I liked writing about it; but neither newspaper printed much about high school baseball. Basketball was virtually ignored at Hamden High. Sometimes I covered games at our gym and watched as our midget centers and forwards planted their feet and pushed up two-handed set shots, often in the direction of the basket. We always lost thirty-eight to nineteen. When the games were away, or when they coincided with hockey games, one of the athletes would feed me box scores over the telephone and I would fabricate a thirty-word story to go with it. The three-quarter-inch gamestory would appear in the *Journal-Courier* under a by-line. Glory.

The glory and the glamor accrued[6] to hockey. All over Hamden boys skated when they could toddle and played hockey as soon as they could lift a stick. Hamden was Ontario South. I do not know the etiology[7] of this obsession, but it was a tradition; hockey was already king when my father was a boy, before Hamden built its own high school. The best neighborhood athletes concentrated their powers on hockey—which was difficult in those days, when there were few indoor rinks and only two or three months of good ice. Hamden's teams were good, and although the school was much smaller than its archrival Hillhouse in New Haven—Hillhouse beat us easily in other sports—in hockey we often prevailed. Hamden High's hockey players went on to play for Yale, for Harvard, for Providence College, even out west for Big Ten schools.

---

4. Front Page: a reference to the popular play about fast-paced newspaper life, *The Front Page*, written by Ben Hecht and Charles MacArthur and first produced in 1928.

5. amelioration: improvement.

6. accrued: came as a result of.

7. etiology: cause, origin.

The biggest hockey occasions were Saturday night high school double-headers at the New Haven Arena, home of New Haven's minor league professional hockey team, site of Willie Pep's bouts as Featherweight Champion. West Haven, Hillhouse, Commercial, and Hamden gathered for hockey, and when the confrontation was between Hamden and Hillhouse, it was the Greeks and the Trojans. Often the crowd fights were as grand as fights on ice. Pongi Piscatelli, it was widely asserted, broke four noses one Saturday night alone.

The rule about no cheering from the press box was suspended for these games. There was a Hillhouse defense man I will call Bobby Adams who could not keep from smiling when his team was ahead. "Laughing-Boy Bobby Adams," I would write, "stopped giggling when Hamden's stalwarts forged three goals. . . ." Ed McGuire learned (from "Letters to the Editor," I suppose) that he had to keep an eye on my copy when Hamden played Hillhouse.

The Saturday night doubleheaders were my greatest challenge as infant-journalist because the *Register* turned into a morning paper on Sunday, and it was eleven at night before the games were over. I walked the few blocks from the Arena to the *Register* in wartime darkness and ascended to the deserted sports department, everybody gone home except an exasperated Ed McGuire. There he sat, cigar in mouth, eyes hidden under green celluloid,[8] telling me I was late and everything was late . . . stop standing around get to work. . . .

The typewriter was an enormous old manual standard. I put a sheet of paper into the machine, spread out my notes, and began to type—one-finger . . . *Rapidly*, but one-finger . . . Ed McGuire sat at this desk half the room away from me and pulled from a pint bottle that he kept in a drawer. If I paused in my typing to think of a word—or to consider variant orthography,[9] I could spell nothing in those days—his head snapped quickly up and he snarled something unintelligible except in import. Every now and then he stalked from his desk to mine, ripped out whatever I had typed, and disappeared to the Linotype room—presumably taking time to remove any "Laughing-Boy Bobby" editorials. I feathered another piece of paper into the steam-locomotive typewriter and continued midsentence.

---

8. celluloid: a reference to the green plastic eyeshade often worn by newspaper editors in the past.

9. orthography: the study of letters and spelling.

That year was my career, for after sophomore year I transferred from Hamden to Exeter, where I found it impossible to get A's by literacy alone. Symptoms of Journalist's Swelled Head disappeared when my Exeter teacher gave me C-minuses on my first English papers: "paragraphs too short"; "newspaper jargon . . ."

Earlier, the swelled head had been temporarily helpful in the struggle to grow up. I cherished the *adventure*; I daydreamed myself Ace Teenage Sportscribe, and I noticed faint signs of interest from certain young women—not, of course, the cheerleaders, but girls who wrote features for the Hamden High School *Dial*, girls who read books—girls I could *talk* to.

In the dark *Register* building I finished my last lines for Ed McGuire, who took them to the Linotype room muttering imprecations.[10] I put on my overcoat, mittens, and earmuffs; I stepped outside into the midnight air to wait a long time for the late-night bus that would take me four miles out Whitney Avenue and leave me at the corner of Ardmore to walk the dark block to my parents' house. I whistled white steam into the cold air of early morning, fifteen years old, thinking of *maybe* being brave enough to ask Patsy Luther to the movies—the proud author of a story right now multiplying itself into morning newsprint, ready to turn up on the doorstep in a few hours, large as life, BY DON HALL.

Responding to What You Read

1. Briefly describe Ed McGuire and Scottie MacDonald.

2. Pick one incident in this essay and describe what makes it funny. Is it Hall's use of big words where you don't expect them? Is it a contrast between the real and the ideal? Or is it something else?

Writer's Workshop

You may have a part-time job, either in or out of sports—delivering newspapers, babysitting, cutting lawns, working in a store. Write a brief character sketch of a person you met on your job. Show what the person looks like, how he or she speaks, and how the person acts.

---

10. imprecations: curses.

PERSPECTIVES

Offsides

Andrew Ward

Cut

Bob Greene

Sometimes you don't make the team, even when you're sitting on the bench. Maybe somebody else tells you or maybe you realize it on your own. How does it feel?

Andrew Ward was born in 1946. He has been a contributing editor for The Atlantic *magazine, a commentator on National Public Radio's* All Things Considered, *and an author of his own books. He received the Fund for Animals' 1989 Genesis Award for his commentaries on* All Things Considered. *The* Houston Chronicle *has written of Andrew Ward, "He just might be the best young humorist we have."*

Offsides

My height might have afforded a natural athlete some magnificent opportunities, but my growth rate always seemed to me ominous, like the overextension of a rubber band. In the mirror at night I would examine the stretch marks that crosshatched my middle like tribal tattoos, and I had a nightmare once in which I actually split apart and had to be patched together with special elastic substances. My bedroom was a half-refurbished cellar rec area in a home of penurious construction. The acoustical-tiled ceiling was six feet high, and I was always parting my hair on the halo-shaped fluorescent light fixtures in the dark.

I was nearing my present height of six feet four inches by the tenth grade, and had been plagued throughout my boyhood by middle-aged men who mistook me for basketball material. I managed to avoid actual team sign-up sheets all through junior high school, but during my first senior high school gym class Coach Odarizzi took me aside and said, "Ward, with that height you could go places. Why don't you take your glasses off and live a little?"

Somehow I found the coach's call to action irresistible. While I was not about to dispose of my glasses (which were crucial to any slim hope of athletic accomplishment I might have had), I did in fact show up for the first junior varsity practice that year.

After the usual setting-up exercises, we were informed of our first passing pattern. Three of us were to stand side by side at the starting line, the man in the middle holding the ball. When the whistle blew, each man was to weave in among the others, passing the ball to the man directly in front. I am still a little shaky on how it was supposed to work. I guess it was like braiding, or maybe square dancing. In any case, I was in one of the first trios, and when the whistle blew and I was passed the ball, I kind of zigzagged across the court in no particular pattern, throwing the ball at whoever was handy. I think at one point I threw the ball into the air and caught it myself, but I might have imagined that.

I never could chin myself. Still can't, without taking a little leap to start with, which is cheating. Chinning was part of our high school physical fitness test, and when my turn came (we were to chin ourselves as many times as we could in thirty seconds) I would jump up, grab hold of the bar, and just hang there, for all intents and purposes, until my time was up, or my hands slipped, or Coach Odarizzi told me to give it up.

"Work on that, Ward," he'd mutter, jotting something down on his clipboard. (Perhaps "jotting" is not the word for it; the coach was a laborious penman who tended to bite down on his tongue as he wrote.)

I suppose Richard Walters, who was more than a hundred pounds overweight, had a harder time of it than I did. He would spend his thirty seconds jumping up and down beneath the bar in a vain attempt to reach it, as the coach solemnly stood by with his stopwatch.

We usually kicked off gym class by climbing ropes to the gymnasium ceiling. I started on the smooth, knotless ropes, but after a few floor-bound, rope-burned days I was shown to the one knotted rope, before which I queued[1] up with the anemic, the obese, and the cowardly, who could not have made it up a ladder, let alone a rope.

I would grab hold of the rope and then try to get it tangled with my legs as I dangled. Within seconds, I would get this drained feeling in my arms and down I would slide to the floor, folding up like a spider. The coach sometimes said I wasn't trying, but he never noticed how the pits of my elbows hollowed during rope climbing—sure evidence of my exertion.

I don't think I was ever the very last to be chosen for gym class teams, but I was usually among the last four. This group also included Richard Walters,

---

1. queued: lined up.

who had about as much trouble getting around as he did chinning, a nearly blind boy named Merritt Hull who was always losing school days to urinary tract complications, and an eruptive menace named Merenski, who frequently fell into rages, kicking at groins when anyone tried to tell him what to do. By the time the choice was narrowed down to this foursome, one of the captains would say, "What the hell, at least he's tall," and I'd be chosen.

I still don't know what "offsides" means, and I avoid all games in which the term is used. I played soccer once in summer camp, but only because I had to, and every few days someone would shout that I was offsides. I would always apologize profusely,[2] and stomp around kicking at the turf, but I never knew what they were talking about.

Football huddles were a source of mystery and confusion for me. There would always be a short, feisty[3] character who called the plays. I rarely had a key role in these plays, and usually wound up somewhere on the line, halfheartedly shoving somebody around.

But I do remember a time when, in a desperation move, the captain selected me to go out for a long one. I guess the reasoning was that no one on the opposing team would ever suspect me of such a thing. I was told, in the redolent[4] hush of the huddle, that I was to break formation on 24, try a lateral cutback on 47, head forward on hike, and then plunket closed quarters in a weaving "T" down the straightaway. That may not have been the precise terminology, but it might as well have been.

I think I ran in place on 24, turned 360 degrees on 47, was totally ignored on hike, ran a little ways, and then turned in time to see everybody on both teams, it seemed, piling on top of the quarterback, who was shrieking, "Where are you? Where are you?" I suppose if I had gotten hold of the ball we might have managed a first down, but I don't know what that means, either.

The first gym teacher I remember was a soft-spoken and great-jawed man named Mr. Bobbins. Mr. Bobbins took me under his wing when I showed up in the middle of seventh grade, the new kid from India. My family had been living in India for four years, and most of us returned to find we were

---

2. **profusely:** abundantly.
3. **feisty:** spunky.
4. **redolent:** suggestive.

profoundly out of touch. It was basketball season when I arrived, and the class was already pounding up and down the court, shooting hoops. "The idea here, Andy," Mr. Bobbins said when I confessed my ignorance of the game, "is to put the ball through the basket."

I had known that much, but found Mr. Bobbins so reassuring that I asked, "From the top or from underneath?"

"Definitely from the top," Mr. Bobbins replied gravely. "You won't get anywhere the other way."

My gym suits fit me only in sports shop dressing rooms. By the time I got them to school they'd be several sizes too small. I don't think I ever passed a happy hour in a gym suit, and at no time was I unhappier than during the week we had coed gymnastics. All the equipment was set up in the girls' gym, and I guess the Phys. Ed. department figured it would be logistically too diffi-cult to have the boys and girls trade gyms for a couple of weeks.

Nowhere was I flatter of foot, spindlier and paler of leg, more equivocal[5] of shoulder, and heavier of acned brow than in the girls' gymnasium. We would have to line up boy-girl-boy-girl in front of the parallel bars, and it was no picnic when my turn came. I could never straighten my arms on the parallel bars, and spent a lot of time swinging from my armpits and making exertive noises.

We had to jump over horses in gymnastics class. We were supposed to run up to the things, grab them by their handles, and swing our legs over them. This seemed to me to be an unreasonable expectation, and I always balked on my approach. "You're always balking on your approach," the woman gym teacher would shout at me. "Don't balk on your approach." Thus lacking momentum, I would manage to grab the bars and kind of climb over the things with my knees. My only comfort was in watching Richard Walters try to clear the horse, which he never did, even by climbing.

The balance beam was probably the least threatening piece of equip-ment as far as I was concerned. I had a fair sense of balance and enormous, clutching feet, and I could make it across all right. But when the exercise called for straddling, and my flaring shorts endangered coed decorum,[6] I would pretend to slip from the balance beam and then hurry to the next piece of equipment. Coed gymnastics was in some ways a mixed bag, for

---

5. equivocal: of uncertain nature.
6. decorum: propriety, good taste.

while there was always the agony of failing miserably and almost nakedly before the fair sex (as it was known at the time), we were afforded chances to observe the girls exercising in their turbulent Danskins.[7] I hope I'll never forget how Janet Gibbs moved along the balance beam, how Denise Dyktor bounced upon the trampoline, how Carol Dower arched and somersaulted across the tumbling mats. Perhaps one of the true high points of my adolescence was spotting for Suzie Hawley, who had the most beautiful, academically disruptive calves in Greenwich High School, and who happened once to slip from the high bar into my startled and grateful clutches.

But that was a fleeting delight in a context of misery. Mostly I remember just standing around, or ducking from the end of one line to the end of another, evading the apparatus and mortification[8] of coed gymnastics as best I could.

Wrestling class was held in the cellar of the high school on gray, dusty plastic mats. Perhaps it was the cellar that made these classes seem clandestine, like cock fights.[9] We were all paired up according to weight. I think at one point I was six feet two inches and weighed 130 pounds, and I was usually paired up with five-feet-two-inch 130-pounders, rippling little dynamos who fought with savage intensity.

I would often start off a match by collapsing into my last-ditch defensive posture, spread-eagled on my belly, clutching at the mat. That way, no matter how much Napoleonic[10] might was brought to bear on flipping me over for a pin, one of my outstretched limbs would prevent it. I remember an opponent's actually bursting into tears, because every time he managed to fold one of my limbs into an operable bundle, out would flop another, too distant to reach without letting go of the first. I may never have won a match this way, but at least I lost on points, no pins.

By my senior year I had really stopped taking sports—even their mortifications—very seriously. I still hated to be among the last chosen, but no more for gym teams than for anything else. I took to making jokes when it seemed to me that my teammates were getting all worked up over nothing.

---

7. Danskins: a brand of leotards.

8. mortification: humiliation.

9. clandestine, like cock fights: held in secret, like the illegal sport of fighting gamecocks.

10. Napoleonic: like Napoleon, the ambitious French emperor who ruled in the 1800s.

I winked at opposing linemen, I limped around with tennis balls in my socks, I did Gillette commercials between plays, I stuffed the soccer ball under my T-shirt and accused my teammates of getting me into trouble.

None of this went over well with the athletes among us, nor with Coach Odarizzi. "Knock it off, Ward," he would bellow from the sidelines, "and grow up."

Playing games still comes up from time to time, and when it does, some of the old miseries return. I pass a couple of friends who are shooting baskets on an outdoor court. "Hey, Ward," one of them shouts. "Come on, Stretch. Let's see what you can do." I have mastered the weary shrug, the scornful wave, the hurried departure. But the ball is tossed my way—deftly,[11] by a man who comes to my shoulders—before I can escape.

I make a pawing motion to gather it toward me, try to trap it in the hollow of my stomach. It rolls down my clamped legs, bounces upon one of my size fourteens, rolls listlessly away. I reach for it with a clapping movement, capture it between my palms, straighten up, and sigh.

"Okay, Ace," someone shouts, "swish it in there."

"It's been a while," I say, giving the ball a tentative bounce. I squint over the top of the ball, regard the distant basket, hold my breath, and at last, with a hunching lunge, throw the damn thing.

It takes a direct route to the rim of the hoop, which makes a chattering noise on contact and sends the ball back in a high arc over my head. "Man," I say, lurching after it, "am I out of practice."

---

11. **deftly:** skillfully.

Born in 1947, Bob Greene is best known for the regular column he writes for the Chicago Tribune, *a column syndicated in over 200 newspapers. Referring to the breadth of Greene's topics, one writer said, "Water covers two-thirds of the earth, and Bob Greene covers the rest." Greene has written two biographies of basketball legend Michael Jordan as well as the novel* All Summer Long. *His columns have been collected into several books.*

Cut

I remember vividly the last time I cried. I was twelve years old, in the seventh grade, and I had tried out for the junior high school basketball team. I walked into the gymnasium; there was a piece of paper tacked to the bulletin board.

It was a cut list. The seventh-grade coach had put it up on the board. The boys whose names were on the list were still on the team; they were welcome to keep coming to practices. The boys whose names were not on the list had been cut; their presence was no longer desired. My name was not on the list.

I had not known the cut was coming that day. I stood and I stared at the list. The coach had not composed it with a great deal of subtlety; the names of the very best athletes were at the top of the sheet of paper, and the other members of the squad were listed in what appeared to be a descending order of talent. I kept looking at the bottom of the list, hoping against hope that my name would miraculously appear there if I looked hard enough.

I held myself together as I walked out of the gym and out of the school, but when I got home I began to sob. I couldn't stop. For the first time in my life, I had been told officially that I wasn't good enough. Athletics meant everything to boys that age; if you were on the team, even as a substitute, it put you in the desirable group. If you weren't on the team, you might as well not be alive.

I had tried desperately in practice, but the coach never seemed to notice. It didn't matter how hard I was willing to work; he didn't want me there. I knew that when I went to school the next morning I would have to face the boys who had not been cut—the boys whose names were on the list, who were still on the team, who had been judged worthy while I had been judged unworthy.

All these years later, I remember it as if I were still standing right there in the gym. And a curious thing has happened: in traveling around the country, I have found that an inordinately large proportion of successful men share that same memory—the memory of being cut from a sports team as a boy.

I don't know how the mind works in matters like this; I don't know what went on in my head following that day when I was cut. But I know that my ambition has been enormous ever since then; I know that for all of my life since that day, I have done more work than I had to be doing, taken more assignments than I had to be taking, put in more hours than I had to be spending. I don't know if all of that came from a determination never to allow myself to be cut again—never to allow someone to tell me that I'm not good enough again—but I know it's there. And apparently it's there in a lot of other men, too.

Bob Graham, thirty-six [at the time this essay was written], is a partner with the Jenner & Block law firm in Chicago. "When I was sixteen, baseball was my whole life," he said. "I had gone to a relatively small high school, and I had been on the team. But then my family moved, and I was going to a much bigger high school. All during the winter months I told everyone that I was a ballplayer. When spring came, of course I went out for the team.

"The cut list went up. I did not make the team. Reading that cut list is one of the clearest things I have in my memory. I wanted not to believe it, but there it was.

"I went home and told my father about it. He suggested that maybe I should talk to the coach. So I did. I pleaded to be put back on the team. He said there was nothing he could do; he said he didn't have enough room.

"I know for a fact that it altered my perception of myself. My view of myself was knocked down; my self-esteem was lowered. I felt so embarrassed; my whole life up to that point had revolved around sports, and particularly around playing baseball. That was the group I wanted to be in—the guys on the baseball team. And I was told that I wasn't good enough to be one of them.

"I know now that it changed me. I found out, even though I couldn't articulate it at the time, that there would be times in my life when certain people would be in a position to say 'You're not good enough' to me. I did not want that to happen ever again.

"It seems obvious to me now that being cut was what started me in determining that my success would always be based on my own abilities, and not on someone else's perceptions. Since then I've always been something of an overachiever; when I came to the law firm I was very aggressive in trying to run my own cases right away, to be the lead lawyer in the cases with which I was involved. I made partner at thirty-one; I never wanted to be left behind.

"Looking back, maybe it shouldn't have been that important. It was only baseball. You pass that by. Here I am. That coach is probably still there, still a high school baseball coach, still cutting boys off the baseball team every year. I wonder how many hundreds of boys he's cut in his life?"

Maurice McGrath is senior vice-president of Genstar Mortgage Corporation, a mortgage banking firm in Glendale, California. "I'm forty-seven years old, and I was fourteen when it happened to me, and I still feel something when I think about it," he said.

"I was in the eighth grade. I went to St. Philip's School in Pasadena. I went out for the baseball team, and one day at practice the coach came over to me. He was an Occidental College student who had been hired as the eighth-grade coach.

"He said, 'You're no good.' Those were his words. I asked him why he was saying that. He said, 'You can't hit the ball. I don't want you here.' I didn't know what to do, so I went over and sat off to the side, watching the others practice. The coach said I should leave the practice field. He said that I wasn't on the team, and that I didn't belong there anymore.

"I was outwardly stoic about it. I didn't want anyone to see how I felt. I didn't want to show that it hurt. But oh, did it hurt. All my friends played baseball after school every day. My best friend was the pitcher on the team. After I got whittled down by the coach, I would hear the other boys talking in class about what they were going to do at practice after school. I knew that I'd just have to go home.

"I guess you make your mind up never to allow yourself to be hurt like that again. In some way I must have been saying to myself, 'I'll play the game better.' Not the sports game, but anything I tried. I must have been saying, 'If I have to, I'll sit on the bench, but I'll be part of the team.'

"I try to make my own kids believe that, too. I try to tell them that they should show that they're a little bit better than the rest. I tell them to think of themselves as better. Who cares what anyone else thinks? You know, I can almost hear that coach saying the words. 'You're no good.'"

Author Malcolm MacPherson (*The Blood of His Servants*), forty, lives in New York. "It happened to me in the ninth grade, at the Yalesville School in Yalesville, Connecticut," he said. "Both of my parents had just been killed in a car crash, and as you can imagine, it was a very difficult time in my life. I went out for the baseball team, and I did pretty well in practice.

"But in the first game I clutched. I was playing second base; the batter hit a popup, and I moved back to catch it. I can see it now. I felt dizzy as I looked up at the ball. It was like I was moving in slow motion, but the ball was going at regular speed. I couldn't get out of the way of my own feet. The ball dropped to the ground. I didn't catch it.

"The next day at practice, the coach read off the lineup. I wasn't on it. I was off the squad.

"I remember what I did: I walked. It was a cold spring afternoon, and the ground was wet, and I just walked. I was living with an aunt and uncle, and I didn't want to go home. I just wanted to walk forever.

"It drove my opinion of myself right into a tunnel. Right into a cave. And when I came out of that cave, something inside of me wanted to make sure in one manner or another that I would never again be told I wasn't good enough.

"I will confess that my ambition, to this day, is out of control. It's like a fire. I think the fire would have pretty much stayed in control if I hadn't been cut from that team. But that got it going. You don't slice ambition two ways; it's either there or it isn't. Those of us who went through something like that always know that we have to catch the ball. We'd rather die than have the ball fall at our feet.

"Once that fire is started in us, it never gets extinguished, until we die or have a heart attack or something. Sometimes I wonder about the home-run hitters; the guys who never even had to worry about being cut. They may have gotten the applause and the attention back then, but I wonder if they ever got the fire. I doubt it. I think maybe you have to get kicked in the teeth to get the fire started.

"You can tell the effect of something like that by examining the trail you've left in your life, and tracing it backward. It's almost like being a junkie with a need for success. You get attention and applause and you like it, but you never quite trust it. Because you know that back then you were good enough if only they would have given you a chance. You don't trust what you achieve, because you're afraid that someone will take it away from you. You know that it can happen; it already did.

"So you try to show people how good you are. Maybe you don't go out and become Dan Rather; maybe you just end up owning the Pontiac dealership in your town. But it's your dealership, and you're the top man, and every day you're showing people that you're good enough."

Dan Rather, fifty-two, is anchor of the "CBS Evening News." "When I was thirteen, I had rheumatic fever," he said. "I became extremely skinny and extremely weak, but I still went out for the seventh-grade baseball team at Alexander Hamilton Junior High School in Houston.

"The school was small enough that there was no cut as such; you were supposed to figure out that you weren't good enough, and quit. Game after game I sat at the end of the bench, hoping that maybe this was the time I would get in. The coach never even looked at me; I might as well have been invisible.

"I told my mother about it. Her advice was not to quit. So I went to practice every day, and I tried to do well so that the coach would be impressed. He never even knew I was there. At home in my room I would fantasize that there was a big game, and the three guys in front of me would all get hurt, and the coach would turn to me and put me in, and I would make the winning hit. But then there'd be another game, and the late innings would come, and if we were way ahead I'd keep hoping that this was the game when the coach would put me in. He never did.

"When you're that age, you're looking for someone to tell you're okay. Your sense of self-esteem is just being formed. And what that experience that baseball season did was make me think that perhaps I wasn't okay.

"In the last game of the season something terrible happened. It was the last of the ninth inning, there were two outs, and there were two strikes on the batter. And the coach turned to me and told me to go out to right field.

"It was a totally humiliating thing for him to do. For him to put me in for one pitch, the last pitch of the season, in front of all the other guys on the team . . . I stood out there for that one pitch, and I just wanted to sink into the ground and disappear. Looking back on it, it was an extremely unkind thing for him to have done. That was nearly forty years ago, and I don't know why the memory should be so vivid now; I've never known if the coach was purposely making fun of me—and if he was, why a grown man would do that to a thirteen-year-old boy.

"I'm not a psychologist. I don't know if a man can point to one event in his life and say that that's the thing that made him the way he is. But when you're that age, and you're searching for your own identity, and all you want is to be told that you're all right . . . I wish I understood it better, but I know the feeling is still there."

Responding to the Selections

1. What is the difference between Andrew Ward's thoughts about himself as a student athlete and those of the individuals quoted in "Cut"?

2. Who was more affected in adult life by their youthful athletic experiences—Andrew Ward or the people quoted in "Cut"? Why?

Writer's Workshop

If you've been cut from a group and can identify with the people in the Bob Greene selection who had been "cut" from sports teams, tell your story. How do you think being cut affected you?

Alternate Media Response

Create a video in which you interview both males and females, including some adults, about their experiences being "cut" from an athletic team. If someone was "cut" from something else, such as a cast of a play, were his or her feelings similar to what athletes who were rejected felt?

Attitude

Garrison Keillor

Winning isn't everything, and sometimes it's not even how well you play the game that matters. What counts is how you look and act—how you knock the dirt out of your shoes.

ABOUT THE AUTHOR•ABOUT THE AUTHOR•ABOUT THE AUTHOR•ABOUT THE AUTHOR

Garrison Keiller was born in Anoka, Minnesota, in 1942 and began his career in radio while a student at the University of Minnesota. He has been in public radio since 1963 and is the host and writer of "A Prairie Home Companion." His books include Lake Wobegon Days *and* Wobegon Boy.

Attitude

Long ago I passed the point in life when major-league ballplayers begin to be younger than yourself. Now all of them are, except for a few aging trigenarians and a couple of quadros[1] who don't get around on the fastball as well as they used to and who sit out the second games of doubleheaders. However, despite my age (thirty-nine), I am still active and have a lot of interests. One of them is slow-pitch softball, a game that lets me go through the motions of baseball without getting beaned or having to run too hard. I play on a pretty casual team, one that drinks beer on the bench and substitutes freely. If a player's wife or girlfriend wants to play, we give her a glove and send her out to right field, no questions asked, and if she lets a pop fly drop in front of her, nobody agonizes over it.

---

1. **trigenarians...quadros:** made-up words to suggest people in their 30s and 40s.

Except me. This year. For the first time in my life, just as I am entering the dark twilight of my slow-pitch career, I find myself taking the game seriously. It isn't the bonehead play that bothers me especially—the pop fly that drops untouched, the slow roller juggled and the ball then heaved ten feet over the first baseman's head and into the next diamond, the routine singles that go through outfielders' legs for doubles and then triples with gloves flung after them. No, it isn't our stone-glove fielding or pussy-foot base-running or limp-wristed hitting that gives me fits, though these have put us on the short end of some mighty ridiculous scores this summer. It's our attitude.

Bottom of the ninth, down 18–3, two outs, a man on first and a woman on third, and our third baseman strikes out. *Strikes out!* In slow-pitch, not even your grandmother strikes out, but this guy does, and after his third strike—a wild swing at a ball that bounces on the plate—he topples over in the dirt and lies flat on his back, laughing. *Laughing!*

Same game, earlier. They have the bases loaded. A weak grounder is hit toward our second baseperson. The runners are running. She picks up the ball, and she looks at them. She looks at first, at second, at home. We yell, "Throw it! Throw it!" and she throws it, underhand, at the pitcher, who has turned and run to back up the catcher. The ball rolls across the third-base line and under the bench. Three runs score. The batter, a fatso, chugs into second. The other team hoots and hollers, and what does she do? She shrugs and smiles ("Oh, silly me"); after all, it's only a game. Like the aforementioned strikeout artist, she treats her error as a joke. They have forgiven themselves instantly, which is unforgivable. It is *we* who should forgive them, who can say, "It's all right, it's only a game." They are supposed to throw up their hands and kick the dirt and hang their heads, as if this boner, even if it is their sixteenth of the afternoon—*this* is the one that really and truly breaks their hearts.

That attitude sweetens the game for everyone. The sinner feels sweet remorse. The fatso feels some sense of accomplishment; this is not a bunch of rumdums he forced into an error but a team with some class. We, the sinner's teammates, feel momentary anger at her—dumb! dumb play!—but then, seeing her grief, we sympathize with her in our hearts (any one of us might have made that mistake or one worse), and we yell encouragement, including the shortstop, who, moments before, dropped an easy throw for a force at second. "That's all right! Come on! We got 'em!" we yell. "Shake it off! These turkeys can't hit!" That makes us feel good, even though the turkeys now lead us by ten runs. We're getting clobbered, but we have a winning attitude.

Let me say this about attitude: Each player is responsible for his or her own attitude, and to a considerable degree you can *create* a good attitude by doing certain little things on the field. These are certain little things that ballplayers do in the Bigs, and we ought to be doing them in the Slows.

1. When going up to bat, don't step right into the batter's box as if it were an elevator. The box is your turf, your stage. Take possession of it slowly and deliberately, starting with a lot of back-bending, knee-stretching, and torso-revolving in the on-deck circle. Then, approaching the box, stop outside it and tap the dirt off your spikes with your bat. You don't have spikes, you have sneakers, of course, but the significance of the tapping is the same. Then, upon entering the box, spit on the ground. It's a way of saying, "This here is mine. This is where I get my hits."

2. Spit frequently. Spit at all crucial moments. Spit correctly. Spit should be *blown*, not ptuied weakly with the lips, which often results in dribble. Spitting should convey forcefulness of purpose, concentration, pride. Spit down, not in the direction of others. Spit in the glove and on the fingers, especially after making a real knucklehead play; it's a way of saying, "I dropped the ball because my glove was dry."

3. At bat and in the field, pick up dirt. Rub dirt in the fingers (especially after spitting on them). Toss dirt, as if testing the wind for velocity and direction. Smooth the dirt. Be involved with dirt. If no dirt is available (e.g., in the outfield), pluck tufts of grass. Fielders should be grooming their areas constantly between plays, flicking away tiny sticks and bits of gravel.

4. Take your time. Tie your laces. Confer with your teammates about possible situations that may arise and conceivable options in dealing with them. Extend the game. Three errors on three consecutive plays can be humiliating if the plays occur within the space of a couple of minutes, but if each error is separated from the next by extensive conferences on the mound, lace-tying, glove adjustments, and arguing close calls (if any), the effect on morale is minimized.

5. Talk. Not just an occasional "Let's get a hit now" but continuous rhythmic chatter, a flow of syllables: "Hey babe hey baby c'mon babe good stick now hey babe long tater take him downtown babe . . . hey good eye good eye."

Infield chatter is harder to maintain. Since the slow-pitch is required to be a soft underhand lob, infielders hesitate to say, "Smoke him babe hey low heat hey throw it on the black babe chuck it in there back him up babe no hit no hit." Say it anyway.

6. One final rule, perhaps the most important of all: When your team is up and has made the third out, the batter and the players who were left on base do not come back to the bench for their gloves. *They remain on the field, and their teammates bring their gloves out to them.* This requires some organization and discipline, but it pays off big in morale. It says, "Although we're getting our pants knocked off, still we must conserve our energy."

Imagine that you have bobbled two fly balls in this rout[2] and now you have just tried to stretch a single into a double and have been easily thrown out sliding into second base, where the base runner ahead of you had stopped. It was the third out and a dumb play, and your opponents smirk at you as they run off the field. You are the goat, a lonely and tragic figure sitting in the dirt. You curse yourself, jerking your head sharply forward. You stand up and kick the base. How miserable! How degrading! Your utter shame, though brief, bears silent testimony to the worthiness of your teammates, whom you have let down, and they appreciate it. They call out to you now as they take the field, and as the second baseman runs to his position he says, "Let's get 'em now," and tosses you your glove. Lowering your head, you trot slowly out to right. There you do some deep knee bends. You pick grass. You find a pebble and fling it into foul territory. As the first batter comes to the plate, you check the sun. You get set in your stance, poised to fly. Feet spread, hands on hips, you bend slightly at the waist and spit the expert spit of a veteran ballplayer—a player who has known the agony of defeat but who always bounces back, a player who has lost a stride on the base paths but can still make the big play.

This is *ball*, ladies and gentleman. This is what it's all about.

---

2. **rout:** a decisive defeat.

Responding to What You Read

Garrison Keillor is having fun with baseball traditions in this short piece of prose. Name three conventions that baseball players observe that Keillor cites as being crucial to demonstrate if a player has the correct "attitude." Can you think of any that he missed?

Writer's Workshop

Pick a sport other than baseball or another activity with which you are familiar and write a few paragraphs about how to display the correct "attitude" in that sport. Try to come up with at least five or six essential things to do for individuals involved in this activity, as Garrison Keillor does in "Attitude." Remember, you are poking harmless fun at an activity whose mannerisms you know well.

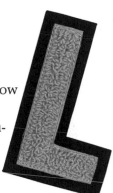

From *A Sense of Where You Are:*
A Profile of Bill Bradley at Princeton

John McPhee

Two highpoints in the college career of former senator and New York Knicks star Bill Bradley are recreated in this account of a memorable tournament.

ABOUT THE AUTHOR•ABOUT THE AUTHOR•ABOUT THE AUTHOR•ABOUT THE AUTHOR

John McPhee was born in 1931. He has worked as a TV scriptwriter and as a staffwriter for Time *magazine. In 1963 he realized his life's dream of writing for the* New Yorker *and has done that ever since. He is a prolific writer of nonfiction, writing on a variety of topics, from basketball to geology to Alaska. In 1999, he won the Pulitzer Prize for nonfiction.*

From *A Sense of Where You Are:*
A Profile of Bill Bradley at Princeton

From Chapter 2: Profile
This season,[1] in the course of a tournament held during the week after Christmas, [Bill]Bradley took part in a game that followed extraordinarily the pattern of his game against St. Joseph's. Because the stakes were higher, it was a sort of St. Joseph's game to the third power. Whereas St. Joseph's had been the best team in the East, Princeton's opponent this time was

---

1. **This season:** the 1964–1965 collegiate basketball season.

Michigan, the team that the Associated Press and the United Press International had rated as the best college team of all.

The chance to face Michigan represented to Bradley the supreme test of his capability as a basketball player. As he saw it, any outstanding player naturally hopes to be a member of the country's No. 1 team, but if that never happens, the next best thing is to be tested against the No. 1 team. And the Michigan situation seemed even more important to him because, tending as he sometimes does to question his own worth, he was uncomfortably conscious that a committee had picked him for the Olympic team, various committees had awarded him his status as an All-American, and, for that matter, committees had elected him a Rhodes Scholar. Michigan, he felt, would provide an exact measurement of him as an athlete.

The height of the Michigan players averages six feet five, and nearly every one of them weighs over two hundred pounds. Smoothly experienced, both as individuals and as a coordinated group, they have the appearance, the manner, and the assurance of a professional team. One of them, moreover, is Cazzie Russell, who, like Bradley, was a consensus All-American last year. For a couple of days before the game, the sports pages of the New York newspapers were crammed with headlines, articles, and even cartoons comparing Bradley and Russell, asking which was the better player, and looking toward what one paper called the most momentous individual confrontation in ten years of basketball.

One additional factor—something that meant relatively little to Bradley—was that the game was to be played in Madison Square Garden. Bradley had never played in the Garden, but, because he mistrusts metropolitan standards, he refused to concede that the mere location of the coming test meant anything at all. When a reporter asked him how he felt about appearing there, he replied, "It's just like any other place. The baskets are ten feet high."

Bradley now says that he prepared for the Michigan game as he had prepared for no other. He slept for twelve hours, getting up at noon. Then, deliberately, he read the New York newspapers and absorbed the excited prose which might have been announcing a prizefight: FESTIVAL DUEL: BILL BRADLEY VS. CAZZIE RUSSELL . . . CAZZIE–BRADLEY: KEY TEST . . . BRADLEY OR CAZZIE? SHOWDOWN AT HAND . . . BILL BRADLEY OF PRINCETON MEETS CAZZIE RUSSELL OF MICHIGAN TONIGHT AT THE GARDEN!! This exposure to the newspapers had the effect he wanted; he developed chills, signifying a growing stimulation within him. During most of the afternoon, when any other player in his situation would probably have been watching television, shooting pool, or playing ping-pong or poker—anything to divert the mind—Bradley sat alone and concentrated on the coming game, on the components of his own play, and on the importance to him and his team of what would occur. As much as anything, he wanted to prove that an Ivy League team could be as good as any other team. Although no newspaper gave Princeton even the slightest chance of winning, Bradley did not just hope to do well himself—he intended that Princeton should win.

Just before he went onto the court, Bradley scrubbed his hands with soap and water, as he always does before a game, to remove any accumulated skin oil and thus increase the friction between his fingers and the ball. When the game was forty-two seconds old, he hit a jump shot and instantly decided, with a rush of complete assurance of a kind that sometimes comes over an athlete in action, that a victory was not only possible but probable.

Michigan played him straight, and he played Michigan into the floor. The performance he delivered had all the depth and variation of theoretical basketball, each move being perfectly executed against able opposition. He stole the ball, he went back door, he threw unbelievable passes. He reversed away from the best defenders in the Big Ten. He held his own man to one point. He played in the backcourt, in the post, and in the corners. He made long set shots, and hit jump shots from points so far behind the basket that he had to start them from arm's length in order to clear the backboard. He tried a hook shot on the dead run and hit that, too. Once, he found himself in a corner of the court with two Michigan players, both taller than he, pressing in on him shoulder to shoulder. He parted them with two rapid fakes—a move of the ball and a move of his head—and leaped up between them to sink a twenty-two-foot jumper. The same two players soon cornered him again. The fakes were different the second time, but the result was the same. He took a long stride between them and went up into the air, drifting forward, as they collided behind him, and he hit a clean shot despite the drift.

Bradley, playing at the top of his game, drew his teammates up to the best performances they could give, too, and the Princeton team as a whole outplayed Michigan. The game, as it had developed, wasn't going to be just a close and miraculous Princeton victory, it was going to be a rout. But, with Princeton twelve points ahead, Bradley, in the exuberance of sensing victory, made the mistake of playing close when he did not need to, and when he was too tired to do it well. He committed his fifth personal foul with four minutes and thirty-seven seconds to go, and had to watch the end of the game from the bench. As he sat down, the twenty thousand spectators stood up and applauded him for some three minutes. It was, as the sportswriters and the Garden management subsequently agreed, the most clamorous ovation ever given a basketball player, amateur or professional, in Madison Square Garden. Bradley's duel with Russell had long since become incidental. Russell scored twenty-seven points and showed his All-American caliber, but during the long applause the announcer on the Garden loudspeakers impulsively turned up the volume and said, "Bill Bradley, one of the greatest players ever to play in Madison Square Garden, scored forty-one points."

Bradley had ratified[2] his reputation—not through his point total nearly so much as through his total play. After he left the court—joining two of his teammates who had also fouled out—Michigan overran Princeton, and won the game by one basket. Bradley ultimately was given the trophy awarded to the most valuable player in the tournament, but his individual recognition meant next to nothing to him at the time, because of Princeton's defeat.

It had become fully apparent, however, that Bradley would be remembered as one of basketball's preeminent stars. And like Hank Luisetti, of Stanford, who never played professional basketball, he will have the almost unique distinction of taking only the name of his college with him into the chronicles of the sport.[3]

From Chapter 5: National Championships

Having won a great victory over Providence and having lost to Michigan, there was nothing that Princeton could do in its final game that would either supersede the one or salvage anything from the other. Hence van Breda Kolff—who had been voted Coach of the Year only hours before the Michigan game—seemed to have a sizable problem in preparing his team for their playoff with Wichita, the midwestern regional champion. Princeton had a kind of responsibility in its final game not to move mechanically and dispiritedly around the court but to play as well as it could, to finish its season strongly, to prove to the remaining skeptic fringe that an Ivy League

---

2. ratified: validated, confirmed.
3. And like . . . of the sport: When John McPhee wrote this article, he did not know that Bradley would go on to play professional basketball.

team was not out of place in a national final, and, in doing so, to make itself the third-ranking team in the United States. All of that was true enough, but the Princeton players knew who belonged there and the effect of such exhortations was only enough to get them about halfway up for the game. In the end, the remark that set the fire came when van Breda Kolff said that no team, after three years, should let a player like Bill Bradley play his last game in anything but a win that would not be forgotten.

The Princeton-Wichita game ended, as a contest, when it had only been underway for about five minutes and the score was Princeton 16, Wichita 4. Princeton's team, as a unit, was shooting, dribbling, passing, and rebounding at the top of its form. Wichita tried to confuse Princeton and break its momentum by shifting rapidly back and forth from one kind of defense to another, but Princeton, hitting sixty-two percent from the floor, unconcernedly altered its attack to fit the requirements of each defense. The score at half time was Princeton 53, Wichita 39, and later, with nine minutes and some seconds to go, it was 84 to 58.

Princeton seemed to have proved what it needed to prove, and Bradley, who by then had scored thirty-two points, had been given the victory which van Breda Kolff had said he deserved. The thirteen thousand people in the coliseum, who had reacted to the previous games with a low hum and occasional polite clapping, had been more typical of a basketball crowd, apparently stirred by Princeton's ricochet passing and marvelously accurate shooting. Van Breda Kolff's team wasn't merely winning, it was winning with style.

But the game was over, and, one by one, van Breda Kolff began to take out his first team players, leaving Bradley in the game. Bradley hit a short one after taking the tap from a jump ball. He made two foul shots and a jumper from the top of the key. He put in two more foul shots, committed his own fourth personal foul, and looked toward van Breda Kolff in expectation of leaving the game; but van Breda Kolff ignored him. Getting the ball moments later, Bradley passed off to Don Roth. Smiling and shaking his head slightly, Roth returned the ball to Bradley.

There was a time-out and Bradley could hear people in the grandstands shouting at him that he ought to shoot when he got the ball. All of his teammates crowded around him and urged him to let it fly and not worry about anyone else on the floor. Van Breda Kolff, calmly enough, pointed out to him that his career was going to end in less than five minutes and this was his last chance just to have a gunner's go at the basket for the sheer fun of it. "So," remembers Bradley, "I figured that I might as well shoot."

In the next four minutes and forty-six seconds, Bradley changed almost all of the important records of national championship basketball. The most intense concentration of basketball people to collect anywhere in any given year is of course at the national championships, and as a group they stood not quite believing, and smiling with pleasure at what they were seeing. Bradley, having decided to do as everyone was urging him to do, went into the left-hand corner and set up a long, high, hook shot. "I'm out of my mind," he said to himself, but the shot dropped through the net. "O.K.," he thought moving back up the court, "I'm going to shoot until I miss."

A moment later, sprinting up the floor through the Wichita defense, he took a perfect pass, turned slightly in the air and tossed the ball over his shoulder and into the basket, with his left hand. The thirteen thousand people in the crowd, Wichita's huge mission of fans included, reacted with an almost unbelievable roar to each shot as it went into the basket. It was an individual performer's last and in some ways greatest moment. Everyone in the coliseum knew it, and, to Bradley, the atmosphere was tangible. "There would be a loud roar," he remembered. "Then it was as if everyone were gathering their breath." Taking a pass at the base line, he jumped above a defender, extended his arm so that the shot would clear the backboard, and sent a sixteen-foot jumper into the basket. Someone in the crowd started to chant, "I believe! I believe!" and others took it up, until, after each shot, within the overall clamor, the amusing chant could be heard.

From the left side, Bradley went up for a jump shot. A Wichita player was directly in front of him, in the air, too, ready to block it. Bradley had to change the position of the ball, and, all in a second, let it go. He was sure that it was not going to go in, but it did. Coming up the floor again, he stopped behind the key and hit another long jumper from there. Within the minute, he had the ball again and was driving upcourt with it, but a Wichita player stayed with him and forced him into the deep right-hand corner. Suddenly he saw he was about to go out of bounds, so he jumped in the air and—now really convinced that he was out of his mind—released a twenty-two-foot hook shot, which seemed to him to be longer and more haphazard than any hook shot he had ever taken and certain to miss. It dropped through the net. Thirty seconds later, he drove into the middle, stopped, faked, and hit a short, clean jumper. Twenty seconds after that, he had the ball again and went high into the air on the right side of the court to execute, perfectly, the last shot of his career. With thirty-three seconds left in the game, van Breda Kolff took him out.

Princeton had beaten Wichita 118 to 82 and had scored more points than any other team in any other game in the history of the national championships, a record which had previously been set and re-set in opening rounds of play. Bradley had scored fifty-eight points, breaking Oscar Robertson's individual scoring record, which had been set in a regional consolation game. Hitting twenty-two shots from the floor, he had also broken Robertson's field goal record. His one hundred and seventy-seven points made against Penn State, North Carolina State, Providence, Michigan, and Wichita were the most ever made by any player in the course of the national championships, breaking by seventeen points the record held by Jerry West, of West Virginia, and Hal Lear, of Temple. His sixty-five field goals in five games set a record, too. His team had also scored more points across the tournament than any other team ever had, breaking a record set six years earlier by West Virginia. It had made forty-eight field goals against Wichita, breaking a record set by U.C.L.A.; and it had made one hundred and seventy-three field goals in the tournament, twenty-one more than Loyola of Illinois made in 1963 while setting the previous record and winning the national championship. Where the names of three individuals and four universities once appeared in the records of the championships, only the names of Bradley and Princeton now appear, repeated and repeated again.

The team record for most field goals in five games was so overwhelming that it had already been set—at a lower level—before Bradley began his final sequence of scoring. But the other seven records had all been set during his remarkable display, and to establish them he had scored twenty-six points in nine minutes, missing once. After van Breda Kolff and the others had persuaded him to forget his usual standards and to shoot every time he got the ball, he had scored—in less than five minutes—sixteen points without missing a shot.

From Chapter 6: Points and Honors

When Bradley returned to Princeton, he stood on top of the bus which had brought the team from the airport and began to apologize to a crowd of undergraduates for letting them down. "We didn't produce," he said. "I don't know whether to say I'm sorry. . ."

"Say it fifty-eight times," someone shouted, and Bradley's apologies were destroyed by applause.

He had been voted the most valuable player in the national championships. His fifty-eight points, made in his last game, had been his career high—and, through the whole game, he had made three of every four shots he had taken. His .886 final free-throw average for the season was the highest in the United States. His season scoring average was over thirty points a game, and he had finished his career with 2,503 points, becoming, after Oscar Robertson, of Cincinnati, and Frank Selvy, of Furman, the third highest scorer in the history of college basketball.

Conquerors of this sort usually follow up their homecomings with a lingering parade through the streets of Rome, but Bradley disappeared less than twenty-four hours after his return, having arranged to live alone in a house whose owners were away. Far enough from the campus to be cut off from it completely, he stayed there for a month—while a couple of hundred reporters, photographers, ministers, missionaries, Elks, Lions, Rotarians, TV producers, mayors, ad men, and fashion editors tried unsuccessfully to find him. His roommates, who fought off the locusts that actually came to the campus, began to feel a little jaundiced about the invasions of society. Bradley, meanwhile, had gone into seclusion in order to write his senior thesis, and, working about fifteen hours a day for thirty days, he completed it. The thesis was thirty-three thousand words long, and he finished it one month to the day after the game with Wichita. It received a straight 1— grades at Princeton begin with 1 and end with 7—and Bradley was graduated with honors.

Meanwhile, a group of people in Princeton started the procedures necessary to change the name of their street to Bradley Court. The New York Knickerbockers, in order to protect themselves against any possibility that Bradley might change his mind about professional basketball and eventually play for another N.B.A. team, made him their first choice selection in the annual player draft. According to the guesses of newspapers, they offered him over fifty thousand dollars to sign. He heard from Oxford that, after his arrival there, he would be *in statu pupillari*[3] at Worcester College.

---

4. ***in statu pupillari:*** Lat., granted a scholarship.

And finally, his classmates at Princeton, not long before their graduation, summed him up in their "1965 Senior Class Poll," a rambling, partly
serious and partly comical list of superlatives, ranging through eighty-one
categories including "Biggest Socialite," "Biggest Swindler," "Most Brilliant,"
"Most Impeccably Dressed," "Most Ambitious," "Roughest," "Smoothest,"
"Laziest," "Hairiest," and "Most Likely to Retire at Thirty." Bradley was
elected to none of these distinctions. He was named as "Most Popular," and
"Most Likely to Succeed." As "Princeton's Greatest Asset," the Class of 1965
selected Bradley and a deceased woman who had just left the university
twenty-seven million dollars. One category read: "Biggest Grind: Niemann,
Lampkin; Thinks He Is: Bradley." His classmates also designated Bradley as
the person they most respected. And, as a kind of afterthought, they named
him best athlete.

Responding to What You Read

1. Describe how Bill Bradley prepared for the Madison Square Garden game
   against Michigan and its All-American, Cazzie Russell.

2. Why does the account of Bradley's performance in the last four minutes
   and forty-six seconds of the Wichita game read like a work of fiction?

Writer's Workshop

Since John McPhee first wrote about Bill Bradley in 1965, Bradley has gone
on to become a Rhodes Scholar, an outstanding profes-
sional basketball player, a United States senator, and a
candidate for president of the United States. Research
an aspect of Bradley's life since 1965 and narrate one
part of it in the kind of detail that McPhee uses to
describe the moments in basketball. You might want
to go to past newspaper accounts of Bradley's playing days or to newspaper or magazine accounts of
his political career. Your goal is to write a vivid,
detailed narrative of some aspect of Bill Bradley's
life, as John McPhee did.

PERSPECTIVES

Stop the Fight!

Norman Katkov

Who Killed Benny Paret?

Norman Cousins

Where does the sport end and the brutality begin?

ABOUT THE AUTHOR•ABOUT THE AUTHOR•ABOUT THE AUTHOR•ABOUT THE AUTHOR

Norman Katkov was born in Russia and grew up in St. Paul, Minnesota. He was a New York newspaper reporter then moved to Los Angeles and won Emmy awards for his work as a television writer. His seven novels include Millionaire's Row, The Judas Kiss, and Blood and Orchids, which was a national bestseller.

Stop the Fight!

She had been at him since early morning, and now, during supper, Gino Genovese played with the spaghetti on his plate as he sat at the kitchen table, facing his wife.

"I had enough prize fighters in my family," she said. "My husband was a prize fighter. Not my son. Not while I live; you hear me, Gino?"

"Anna, I told you a thousand times." He spoke quietly and he was very patient. "Young Gino won't fight after tonight. Take my word."

"He's a baby," she said, and Gino realized she hadn't heard him at all.

"He's eighteen, Anna; finished with high school. Young Gino is a man."

"No!" she shouted. She brought her hand down flat on the oilcloth covering the table. "He's not a man." Her voice rose. "He's not a man to me!"

Gino looked at the open window and grimaced. "Anna, please. The neighbors."

"The neighbors," she repeated dully, and pushed her hair back from her forehead. "Is there someone on Water Street who doesn't know my baby is a fighter?"

Some fighter, Gino thought. The kid had won the Golden Gloves and had six pro matches, so that made him a fighter already. He leaned over to close the window, and when he had settled back in his chair, he saw that his wife was staring at nothing, her elbow on the table and her hand to her cheek; her head moving back and forth, back and forth, as though she were in mourning.

"Anna," he said gently, and reached out to touch her. "The spaghetti will get cold, sweetheart," Gino said, but she didn't see him and at last he bent over his plate.

I should have gone to work today instead of taking off, he said to himself, thinking of Marinkov and Stein and Annalora, and the rest of the Park Department crew of which he was foreman. *What good did I do her by staying home?* he thought, as he wound the spaghetti around his fork. *She's like the old women with the kerchiefs over their heads who sit in the sun on Clara Street. She's forty years old and she acts eighty years.*

"Why couldn't he sleep home?" Anna demanded. "Answer me that? My own son. What's the matter with his bed?" she asked, pointing toward Young Gino's room.

Gino sat motionless, the spaghetti trailing from his fork to the plate. "I told you, Anna, his manager wants him to rest. His manager says we would make him excited."

"His manager says," Anna replied. "Who is his manager—chief of police?"

"Anna, what do you want, sweetheart?" He dropped the fork and raised his hands over the plate. "Did I tell Young Gino to fight? Did I go see him fight in the Golden Gloves or since the Golden Gloves? When he came to me and wanted to turn pro, did I tell him yes? When he asked me to be his manager, did I say yes?" Gino reached for a glass of water. "So he went and got Len Farrell for a manager, what should I do then? Should I throw Young Gino out of the house, or turn him over and paddle him because he got my old manager?" He bent forward. "Listen to me, Anna, baby, Young Gino won't fight after tonight. It's the last time tonight."

"He didn't need the boxing gloves," Anna said.

Gino closed his eyes for a moment, and shook his head slowly. "That's five years ago, sweetheart."

"He didn't need them," she said.

Gino sucked in breath and bit his lip. He set the glass down on the table. "Your brother bought him the gloves, Anna."

"My brother, you, Len Farrell, you're all the same." She held the table with both hands, her hair now loose from the pins and falling in disarray about her neck and over her ears and down her cheeks. "You won't be satisfied until they make him a cripple. Then you'll be satisfied. True, Gino?"

And he got up from his chair and walked out of the kitchen. He went through the hall into the living room, and stood with his hands in his pockets, his knees against the cold radiator, looking out onto Water Street.

I did the right thing, he thought, as he felt the soft curtain brush against his face. *That Pete Wojick will give Young Gino a good licking, and then finish— the kid won't have a stomach for fighting after tonight, that's all.*

Gino had seen it happen enough times: a lad starting out; being over-matched; getting a beating that took the heart out of him for always. You had to bring a kid along very careful when he started, building up his confidence.

All right, Gino thought, and he grimaced again, *it's done with. At least I won't have to listen to her any more after tonight.* He remembered how Len Farrell had protested the match; he remembered pleading with his old man-ager, agreeing that Wojick was too seasoned for Young Gino, too tricky and wise, with a right hand that could strike like a poleax.

"I've got to stop him fighting, Len," Gino had said. "My wife—she's mak-ing me crazy. Let Wojick give him the deep six once and the kid will quit." Gino had gone one afternoon a month ago to the Rose Room Gym downtown to watch his son work out, standing far back among the spectators, so the boy wouldn't see him. "Young Gino's a boxer, a cutie. He won't like getting hurt, Len." He had gone on, talking and talking, until at last Farrell had agreed to make the match—eight rounds in the semifinal at the ball park tonight.

Gino heard Anna moving around in the kitchen, and suddenly, for no reason that he knew, turned away from the window, crossed the living room and went into his son's bedroom.

Gino touched the bed and smoothed the spread, and on the wall above the headboard saw the farm scene Young Gino had painted when he was seven. Anna had taken it to be framed. She had framed the Palmer Method penman-ship certificate, and three months ago, in June, she had framed her son's high-school diploma, hanging it there on the wall behind Young Gino's bed.

He turned away and took a step toward the chest of drawers standing at an angle beyond the windows, and knew then why he had come into Young Gino's room. There was the big, double frame that Anna had not bought, which Young Gino had brought home, and in it, the two glossy pictures: the boy on the right and the father on the left.

The boy had dug out Gino's black silk trunks and boxing shoes, and gone to the same photographer across the street from the Rose Room who, twenty years earlier, had taken the father's picture. He had posed the same: right hand high on the bare chest, and left extended; head cocked and shoulders forward.

Standing before the chest of drawers, Gino could see no difference between them, and then noticed the boy's shoulders, sloping more than his father's, and the really enormously big arms for a welterweight.

"I never weighed more than one forty-three," Gino said aloud, and remembered when he had quit. He had finished with fighting one night two blocks from here on the porch of Anna's father's house. She had said she would never see him if he fought again. He'd had thirty fights then, and Len Farrell was ready to take him to Chicago. First to Chicago, and then New York, if he was good enough. That night Gino had asked Anna to marry him.

He remembered, all right, because he had gone into Anna's house and telephoned Len Farrell to tell the manager he was finished.

"No big loss," Gino said aloud. "I wouldn't have been much; I had no punch," and heard Anna behind him; heard her breathing heavy.

"You're proud, Gino, aren't you? Your son is a fighter; you lived to see it," she said, but he would not turn. He didn't turn as he heard her cross the room, but held fast to the chest of drawers.

"You fooled me good, Gino," she said. "Used me for a real dummy, making him a fighter behind my back, lying behind my back," and she reached for the double frame and held it high over her head and flung it to the floor.

He heard the glass smash as he turned. He felt the frame hit his shoe, but didn't look down. He looked at her until her hands went to her cheeks, her lips trembling, the color leaving her face white, and her eyes wide, watching him.

But he said nothing. He went past her, out to the small back porch, taking his jacket off the hook as he pushed open the door and came down the steps. He got into the jacket as he stood beside the car parked in the driveway, and then slid in behind the wheel, turning the key, starting the motor, shifting gears in the old coupé and backing out into the street, his mind blank, not letting himself think as he turned up toward the boulevard leading to the downtown section.

He was driving into the sun, which hung low beyond the green dome of the cathedral on Dayton Avenue, and he squinted as he came into sight of the office buildings. Once he went through a red light, listening to the horns on either side of him. Once he stopped for a semaphore, waiting until long after the light had changed to green and a trailer truck behind him blasted its horn.

Gino came into Kellogg Circle and turned, driving down Washington Street to the bus depot and around it to the alley behind the Rose Room.

He parked behind a supermarket and got out of the car, slamming the door behind him and walking out to Exchange Place. He never smoked, but now he went into a drugstore, bought a pack of cigarettes and lit one, inhaling too deeply and coughing as the unfamiliar smoke seared his throat and mouth. He held the cigarette awkwardly and walked toward the newsstand on Seventh Street, but saw Tots Todora, and Bubbling-Over Norris, and Joey Richards, all of them fight fans, and he didn't want to talk with them. He didn't want to see them. He had a feeling to see Young Gino.

He had a feeling to talk to his son or touch him. He remembered, as he walked faster, the years when Young Gino was growing up, sleeping in his own bedroom.

Gino would wake in the night and know—really know—that his son was not sleeping. Gino would get out of bed real slow and careful, not to disturb Anna. Walking in his bare feet, he would turn on the light in the hall, tiptoe into his son's room and stand beside his son's bed and watch him sleep. He would stand there for he never knew how long, looking down at his son, and always, before he left, he would move the covers around his son, and move the hair from his son's forehead, and bend forward to kiss Young Gino.

He never told Anna and he never told his son, and now, turning into the hotel lobby, he had the same feeling he had to see Young Gino. He walked past the room clerk to the house phones and asked for Len Farrell's room.

"Five-o-two, I'm ring...ging," the operator said, and in a moment Gino heard Farrell say hello.

"Len?" Gino said. "Gino. I'm downstairs."

"Hello, lieutenant," Farrell said.

"I want to come up, Len."

"Sure, lieutenant; I held out two tickets for you," Farrell said.

"Len, it's Gino. Where's the kid? I want to see the kid."

"I'll bring them down myself, lieutenant. A pleasure. For the police department, any time," Farrell said.

"Len. Len!"

"I'll be down right away," Farrell said, and hung up.

After a moment, Gino dropped the receiver on the cradle. He saw the room clerk watching him, and moved away from the row of telephones, out into the lobby.

He walked to the newsstand near the doors and bought a paper and was looking at the front page when Len Farrell appeared.

"You must be crazy," Len said.

"I'm crazy?" Gino folded the paper and pushed it under his arm. "What's the matter with you? Lieutenant. Police force."

Farrell shook his head. He was a tall thin man with slick black hair, combed straight back. "What if the kid had answered the phone?" he asked. "I've had him quiet all day, and all he'd need would be to talk to you. A good thing I can still think, which is more than you can do."

"How is he, Len?"

"He's fine."

"How does he feel?" Gino asked.

"Like a tiger. How do you expect him to feel? He thinks he can lick the world."

"Yeah."

"I must have been out of my mind to make this match," Farrell said.

"He'll get over it," Gino said.

"Sure," Farrell said. "You just keep telling yourself that."

"What else could I have done?" Gino asked.

Farrell shook his head and carefully buttoned his jacket. "Don't ask me. Don't bring me in this. You're the mastermind," Farrell said. "Wojick. If it was my way, I wouldn't let Young Gino near Wojick for a year."

"You told me that already. Give me a ticket, Len."

"Oh, no," Farrell said, and stepped back, but Gino took the manager's arm. He held the arm, his fingers bunching the coat sleeve, looking at Farrell until the older man reached into his pocket. "Let go of my arm," Farrell said.

"I want a ticket. If I don't get it from you, I buy one," Gino said. "I want to see that fight, Len."

Farrell took a long white envelope from his pocket. "You're not sitting ringside," he said. "The kid might see you. I'll have enough trouble with him as it is."

"Fifteen rows back," Gino said. "I can't see good any more if I'm any farther away from the ring."

He took the ticket from Farrell and shoved it into his rear pants pocket. "Take care of him, Len," Gino said.

"Yes. Yes, I'll take care of him." Farrell slipped the flap into the envelope. He held the envelope to his lips like a child with a blade of grass, and he whistled softly. "He could have been a real good fighter, Gino. A real classy fighter."

"He'll live without it," Gino said, and didn't want to talk about the kid any more.

He said goodbye to Farrell and left the lobby, walking out into the early evening. The street lights were glowing, the sun was gone from the heavens and the sky was a dull orange, turning black. He went into a diner and ordered a sandwich and a glass of milk and ate it. That took twenty minutes. In the basement of the bus depot he had his shoes shined. That took ten minutes. He watched a Chicago-bound bus load and leave, and afterward found an empty bench and sat down in a corner of it. He squirmed around on the bench, sitting in one position for a moment and then changing to another, and a third, and a fourth, until at last he was bent forward, his legs uncrossed, his elbows on his knees and one hand massaging the other.

Gino heard the dispatcher announce the arrival of a Kansas City bus and got off the bench. "Get it over with," he said aloud, and left the depot, crossing the deserted Federal Building Plaza to the alley where he had left his car.

It was completely night now. Driving out to the ball park, Gino remembered the hours before his own fights. He had been very nervous always, and in the afternoon, when Farrell had put him to bed, Gino had never been able to sleep, but lay motionless, his eyes closed, trying not to think of the fight.

"I wasn't yellow," he said aloud as he came into Lexington Avenue, a mile from the ball park. It was his chief worry always—that the referee, or Farrell, or the sports writers, or those at ringside and those beyond, would think him without courage. Often he would fight with complete abandon, standing toe to toe with an opponent who could hit much harder, in a desperate need to convince everyone of his fearlessness.

He saw the lights of the ball park and drove slowly until a youth standing beside a crudely lettered sign gestured at him. Gino turned into the lad's back yard, converted into a parking lot for the night. He paid the boy and walked along the road until he was across the street from the dark walls of the ball park.

He wasn't going in at the main gate, so that he would have to pass the long refreshment counter behind home plate; he'd made up his mind to that. Gino could see them standing there now: Ernie Fliegel and a few of the Gibbons family; maybe My Sullivan and Billy Light, whom Gino had boxed once in Milwaukee. They would be on him about Young Gino, teasing and baiting him, and he didn't want any of it tonight. He'd had all he could take for one day.

Gino saw the open doors near right field and crossed Lexington Avenue, handing his ticket to the gateman and walking ahead quickly, turning away from the foul line as he neared the stands, crossing out onto the playing field.

The ring was set up on the pitcher's mound. As he crossed second base, Gino could see the permanent stands, spreading in a huge V from home plate. There were twenty rows of chairs around the ring. Gino stood well back from the last row, looking at a couple of inept heavyweights, moving awkwardly through four dull rounds.

Once, during the second four-rounder, an usher asked him if he wanted to sit down, but Gino shook his head. Once, during the six-round bout that followed, Gino saw Frankie Battaglia, who had boxed as a middleweight when he was fighting. Gino turned his back, waiting until he'd heard the bell sound for the end of a round before he looked back at the ring.

It came too soon. One second the ring was clear and Gino could see the cigarette smoke drifting toward the lights, and the next instant Pete Wojick was in the ring, manager and trainers around him.

"He's big. He's too big," Gino said, as Wojick's manager took the robe from the fighter's shoulders and the welterweight began moving about in the corner, punching short lefts and rights, hooks and jabs and uppercuts, into the night air.

The referee stood in a neutral corner, arms resting on the ropes. Across the ring, the announcer looked toward the visiting-team dugout from which the boxers entered the ball field. Gino saw the heads turning, the men standing up in front of their seats, and remembered it was a practice of Farrell's to keep the opponent waiting. He heard the murmurs of the impatient crowd, and saw his son come out of the dugout. Young Gino was wearing his father's old robe, which he had found in the trunk in the front closet. He came down the aisle toward the ring, his gloves pushed against each other and resting on his chest.

Gino lit a cigarette and held it in his hand. He saw Farrell step on the bottom rope and pull up on the middle one for Young Gino. He saw the boy come into the ring and stand absolutely still, arms at his sides, looking across at Wojick. He saw Farrell put his hand in under the robe and massage

Young Gino's back, and then he heard the announcer who had come to the center of the ring:

". . . the fighting son of a fighting father, Young Gino Genovese!" as Gino moved to the aisle and bent almost double, hurrying to his seat in the fourteenth row, the cigarette dropping from his hand. He said, "Pardon me," and started moving down the row, holding the backs of the seats in front of him, saying, "Excuse," and "Sorry," until he dropped into the empty folding chair, hearing the bell and raising his head in the darkness to see the two fighters come toward the middle of the ring.

Just let it be quick, Gino said to himself, sitting with his hands in his lap, his legs tucked under the chair and his ankles crossed, as he watched the kid jab Wojick's ear with his left hand.

He fights like the picture he took, Gino thought as he watched his son, boxing straight up and down in the classic manner, the left arm out, the right carried high on the chest, the head cocked just a little to one side and the feet far apart.

Wojick took two more lefts and came forward, hooking to the stomach and then to the kidneys as he closed with Young Gino, holding until the referee separated them. Wojick was shorter, carrying absolutely no weight in his legs, with the body of a middleweight.

Young Gino moved around him, jabbing all the time, holding the right on his chest and waiting. They regarded each other carefully for maybe forty-five seconds, circling each other, and then Wojick hooked hard to the stomach.

And again to the stomach, so that Young Gino went back a step and Wojick was on top of him. He came forward all in a rush, his head low, moving in and mauling with both hands, driving Young Gino into the ropes and holding him there. Wojick was in close now, so the kid couldn't punch at all, pushing his head in under Young Gino's chin. He used Young Gino's body as leverage, punching with both hands to the stomach and the kidneys and the stomach again, until at last the kid's arms came down for an instant and Wojick brought the right up and over.

But Young Gino had slipped out, taken a step to his left and moved clear and away from Wojick, out toward the middle of the ring, his stomach pink now from the pounding he'd taken.

Wojick came out to meet him, moving his arms as he shuffled forward, and Young Gino jabbed him. He hit Wojick six times running, long jabs that held the older fighter off balance, moving very carefully, keeping to the center of the ring.

He boxed beautifully, and as Wojick started to hook with his left, Young Gino came in, jabbing short and hard in a perfectly executed counterpunch and bringing the right hand over flush to Wojick's chin.

And Wojick went down as the entire ball park went up on its feet. Young Gino moved to a corner and Wojick took a six count. The referee wiped Wojick's gloves on his shirt, and Young Gino was in there swinging. Wojick was in trouble, the legs still wobbly and his eyes glassy, but he had his arms up.

"Wait!" Gino yelled at his son. "Find him!" he yelled, but they were screaming in the ball park, wanting the knockout, and the kid was swinging and punching wildly, as Wojick kept his head down and his forearms covering his face and waited for the bell.

And lasted until the bell, as the crowd settled down slowly, almost one by one, and all around him Gino could hear them shouting at one another and grinning and talking about the kid and how great he was, except they hadn't seen what Gino had seen—that Wojick had not taken another punch, but had caught all the kid's blows on his arms and shoulders and gloves.

Near Gino somebody said, "How do you like that kid, Louie? A champ, isn't he?"

Somebody said, "The best since McLarnin."

And somebody said, "I seen the old man. The kid's better. The kid got the punch the old man never had," and in the darkness Gino rubbed one hand with the other and heard the bell and looked up at the ring.

Young Gino came out very fast, the water from the sponge glistening on his hair and shoulders. He went almost across the ring and jabbed twice and tried the right, missing with the right, as Gino cursed Farrell.

That Farrell must be nuts, he thought, *not telling the kid to wait.* He looked over at Young Gino's corner for Farrell, and heard the crowd suck in breath and turned quickly to the ring to see his son against the ropes.

"What happened?" Gino asked. He had the arm of the man next to him. "What happened?" he asked, watching Wojick follow his son around the ring.

"Wojick belted him a right hand," the man next to him said, and Gino saw his son staggering.

He saw Wojick following Young Gino, fighting cautiously now, out of
the crouch, the left arm no more than six inches from his chest and the
right pulled back next to the stomach.

Young Gino tried to clinch, but Wojick stepped away and hooked. He
hooked twice to the body and then to the head. In the fourteenth row
Gino watched Wojick very carefully and saw him push his left foot forward.
He saw him weave and he saw Wojick's left glove drop just a couple of
inches as the right started down at the stomach and whistled in and caught
Young Gino high in the face.

"Down," Gino whispered. "Go down, kid," he said. "Go down!" he said, as
he felt the pain in his heart, and saw Wojick jab twice more and get set and
drop his left glove again and bring the right hand in along Young Gino's jaw.

"It's over," Gino whispered. "At least, it's finished fast," but his son
clinched. Held on and hooked his arms in Wojick's gaining ten seconds'
rest before the referee separated them.

Clinched again immediately, and Gino saw his son straighten up when
they were split once more and saw him keep the left out, staying away from
Wojick until just before the bell, when he took another right to the chin
that spun him clear around so that he fell against the ropes, hanging there
until the gong sounded and Farrell was in the ring to lead him to the corner.

The doctor came then. He went into the ring, and Gino whispered,
"Stop it. Just stop it."

But the crowd yelled "No!" at the doctor. They yelled, "Let the kid alone!"
and "He's okay, doc!" and, "That kid's tough!" until at last the doctor nodded
at the referee and left the ring, while Farrell worked over Young Gino.

The kid got up at the ten-second buzzer. He pulled his arm free of
Farrell and rose, standing away from the stool in the corner, his arms hanging, looking across at Wojick.

The crowd loved it. They loved it that Young Gino went across the ring
to carry the fight to Wojick. They loved it when Young Gino landed a right
to Wojick's heart that stopped the older fighter for a few seconds. They
loved it that the kid was anxious, and all the time Gino watched Wojick
and Wojick's left glove, waiting for it to drop until, after a minute of the
round was gone, Young Gino missed with his right and was open.

Gino saw the left glove drop. He saw Wojick get set, the shoulders
drooping, and he felt the right when it landed on his son's chin.

Gino waited for the kid to fall. He watched Young Gino helpless. He saw his son get hit with a second right and a third, and while the boy staggered around the ring, refusing to fall, taking whatever Wojick could deliver, Gino said, "That's enough." He said, "That's all," and got out of his chair.

He heard them yelling "Sit down!" but he started pushing his way toward the aisle, bent forward, felling the hands against him, as he was shoved from one man to the next until he was in the aisle at last, running toward the ring.

An usher reached for Gino, but missed him. A cop grabbed him, holding his arm, as Gino watched the ring and prayed for the bell, hearing the cop's voice, but not what the cop said, while the kid held on to Wojick, beaten and out on his feet, and nothing holding him up except heart.

"Let me alone," Gino said. "That's my kid," he said to the cop. "Ask Farrell," he said, pointing with his free arm. He turned toward the cop. "My kid," Gino said to the cop. "Let me in my kid's corner," he said, as the bell sounded and the cop released him.

Gino pulled at his jacket as he ran. He got the jacket off and dropped it there at the foot of the three steps leading to the ring, and then he was in the ring, kneeling before his son as Farrell worked on Young Gino.

"Don't talk," Gino warned. "Breathe deep and let it out slow. Wojick's left. It drops when he's going to use the right. The left drops maybe an inch when he shoots the right! You got that? Nod if you got that," and watched his son nod as he rubbed the boy's legs. "Stay away this round. It's only the fourth. Stay away and box him and watch the left. You're a winner, kid; you got that knockdown thing going for you. Watch the left and bring your right in over it. Remember," as the warning buzzer sounded, and Gino rose, putting his hand flat against his son's chest. "Now you rest, big shot. Rest and watch the left," and Young Gino smiled at him.

Gino felt the smile warming him. He felt the smile all through him, and reached out to brush the kid's hair away from the forehead, and then he had the stool as the bell sounded and Young Gino went out to the center of the ring.

Gino held the stool as he came down the steps. *Let him fight*, Gino decided. *If he wants it that much, let him do what he wants. She'll have to take it, that's all. I'll do what I can, be good and listen to her, but she'll have to get used to it.*

Me, I'm her husband; she had a right to tell me to quit. Not the kid, she can't tell the kid what to do with his life; and he turned to look at his son in the ring.

Norman *Cousins (1915–1990) was a long-time editor of the* Saturday Review. *Cousins, among other accomplishments, represented Pope John XXIII and successfully negotiated the release of two cardinals from eastern European prisons; helped found public television in the United States; and was an adjunct professsor in the Program of Medicine, Law, and Human Values at the School of Medicine at U.C.L.A. One of Cousins's most famous books is* Anatomy of an Illness, *about his own struggles with disease and his belief that the mind can greatly help heal an ailing body. The following selection is a classic essay decrying boxing.*

Who Killed Benny Paret?

Sometime about 1935 or 1936 I had an interview with Mike Jacobs, the prizefight promoter. I was a fledgling[1] reporter at that time; my beat was education but during the vacation season I found myself on varied assignments, all the way from ship news to sports reporting. In this way I found myself sitting opposite the most powerful figure in the boxing world.

There was nothing spectacular in Mr. Jacobs' manner or appearance; but when he spoke about prizefights, he was no longer a bland little man but a colossus who sounded the way Napoleon must have sounded when he reviewed a battle. You knew you were listening to Number One. His saying something made it true.

We discussed what to him was the only important element in successful promoting—how to please the crowd. So far as he was concerned, there was no mystery to it. You put killers in the ring and the people filled your arena. You hire boxing artists—men who are adroit at feinting, parrying, weaving, jabbing, and dancing, but who don't pack dynamite in their

---

1. **fledgling:** beginner.

fists—and you wind up counting your empty seats. So you searched for the killers and sluggers and maulers—fellows who could hit with the force of a baseball bat.

I asked Mr. Jacobs if he was speaking literally when he said people came out to see the killer.

"They don't come out to see a tea party," he said evenly. "They come out to see the knockout. They come out to see a man hurt. If they think anything else, they're kidding themselves."

Recently, a young man by the name of Benny Paret was killed in the ring. The killing was seen by millions; it was on television. In the twelfth round, he was hit hard in the head several times, went down, was counted out, and never came out of the coma.

The Paret fight produced a flurry of investigations. Governor Rockefeller was shocked by what happened and appointed a committee to assess the responsibility. The New York State Boxing Commission decided to find out what was wrong. The District Attorney's office expressed its concern. One question that was solemnly studied in all three probes concerned the action of the referee. Did he act in time to stop the fight? Another question had to do with the role of the examining doctors who certified the physical fitness of the fighters before the bout. Still another question involved Mr. Paret's manager; did he rush his boy into the fight without adequate time to recuperate from the previous one?

In short, the investigators looked into every possible cause except the real one. Benny Paret was killed because the human fist delivers enough impact, when directed against the head, to produce a massive hemorrhage in the brain. The human brain is the most delicate and complex mechanism in all creation. It has a lacework of millions of highly fragile nerve connections. Nature attempts to protect this exquisitely intricate machinery by encasing it in a hard shell. Fortunately, the shell is thick enough to withstand a great deal of pounding. Nature, however, can protect man against everything except man himself. Not every blow to the head will kill a man—but there is always the risk of concussion and damage to the brain. A prizefighter may be able to survive even repeated brain concussions and go on fighting, but the damage to his brain may be permanent.

In any event, it is futile to investigate the referee's role and seek to determine whether he should have intervened to stop the fight earlier. That is not where the primary responsibility lies. The primary responsibility lies with the people who pay to see a man hurt. The referee who stops a fight too soon from the crowd's viewpoint can expect to be booed. The crowd wants the knockout; it wants to see a man stretched out on the canvas. This is the supreme moment in boxing. It is nonsense to talk about prizefighting as a test of boxing skills. No crowd was ever brought to its feet screaming and cheering at the sight of two men beautifully dodging and weaving out of each other's jabs. The time the crowd comes alive is when a man is hit hard over the heart or the head, when his mouthpiece flies out, when the blood squirts out of his nose or eyes, when he wobbles under the attack and his pursuer continues to smash at him with poleax[2] impact.

Don't blame it on the referee. Don't even blame it on the fight managers. Put the blame where it belongs, on the prevailing mores[3] that regard prizefighting as a perfectly proper enterprise and vehicle of entertainment. No one doubts that many people enjoy prizefighting and will miss it if it should be thrown out. And that is precisely the point.

---

2. poleax: medieval weapon combining blade, ax, hammer, and spike.
3. mores: customs or moral attitudes.

Responding to What You Read

1. In literature, a symbol is an object that represents something more than just itself. Frequently a symbol represents an abstract idea or concept. How does the double picture frame with photos of Gino and his son serve as a symbol in this short story?

2. Why do you think the author ended "Stop the Fight!" where he did, without the reader finding out who won the fight?

3. In a sentence, what is Norman Cousins' view of boxing? Knowing something about Cousins' background—read the brief biographical statement before the selection—why do you think Cousins takes this view?

4. Imagine that Norman Cousins and Gino Genovese meet for coffee and talk about boxing. Write a short conversation between the two men that explores how they feel about this sport.

Writer's Workshop

Norman Cousins uses a subtle method to try to sway the reader's opinion on an issue he feels strongly about. He begins with a personal anecdote. Then he offers an example—the death of Benny Paret. Next, Cousins considers who is responsible for Paret's death and rejects several alternatives. Finally, he states his own opinion.

Where do you stand on the effect of sports on society? Is it positive or negative? Write an essay in which you explain your point of view and try to persuade others to agree with you. For example, you might argue that the aggressive nature of a sport helps release tension among the participants or the spectators. Be sure to have examples in your essay that support your argument— or use one effective extended example as Norman Cousins does.

PERSPECTIVES

Tom Seaver's Farewell

A. Bartlett Giamatti

DiMaggio, Failing, Is 84 Today

Ira Berkow

Some players become legends on and off the field.

A. *Bartlett Giamatti had a distinguished, though too brief, life. Born in 1938, he received degrees in English and comparative literature from Yale University. He taught Italian and comparative literature at Princeton and Yale, and was president of Yale from 1978 until 1986, when he was appointed president of baseball's National League. For five months until his death in 1989 he served as commissioner of baseball. "Tom Seaver's Farewell" was originally published in* Harper's Magazine *in 1977 and won a prize as one of the best sports pieces of that year. The essay is included in the collection* A Great and Glorious Game: Baseball Writings of A. Bartlett Giamatti. *Kenneth Robson, editor of the collection, says of "Tom Seaver's Farewell," "As in most of his work, Giamatti creates a moral fable out of what many of us consider ordinary events."*

Tom Seaver's Farewell

Shea Stadium is not Eden, and the picture of Tom and Nancy Seaver leaving its graceless precincts in tears did not immediately remind me of the *Expulsion of Adam and Eve*[1] in the Brancacci Chapel. And yet, absorbing the feelings generated by Seaver's departure from New York led me to the kind of inflated cogitation that links Masaccio and the Mets, if only because the feelings were so outsized and anguished and intense. After all, Brad Park had gone to Boston, and Namath to Los Angeles, and Julius Erving to, if you will, Philadelphia. Clearly evil had entered the world, and mortality had fixed us with its sting. If Seaver is different, and evidently he is, the reasons must be sought somewhere other than in the columns of the daily press. In fact, the reasons for Seaver's effect on us have to do with the nature of baseball, a sport that touches on what is most important in

---

1. Expulsion of Adam and Eve: This famous 15th-century fresco (a painting done on a moist plaster surface) is part of a series painted by Masaccio on the walls of the Brancacci Chapel in the Santa Maria del Carmine church in Florence, Italy.

American life. Where Park, Namath, and Erving are only superb at playing their sports, Seaver seems to embody his.

George Thomas Seaver almost did not become a Met. In February of 1966, the Atlanta Braves signed the University of Southern California undergraduate to a contract and assigned him to Richmond. At that point, Commissioner William Eckert stated that the signing violated the college rule. The contract was scrapped. USC, however, declared Seaver ineligible. The commissioner announced that any team, except Atlanta, matching the Richmond contract could enter a drawing for rights to negotiate. The Indians, the Phillies, and the Mets submitted to the wheel of fortune, the Mets were favored, and Seaver, signed in early April, went to Jacksonville of the International League. He was twenty-one and would spend one year in the minor leagues.

Seaver pitched .500 ball for Jacksonville, 12–12, with an earned run average of 3.13. He would not have as weak a season again until 1974, when he would go 11–11, with an ERA of 3.20. Yet even at Jacksonville he struck out 188 batters, thus foreshadowing his extraordinary performance with the Mets, with whom, from 1968 to 1976, he would never strike out fewer than 200 batters a season—a major-league record. And from the beginning Seaver pitched as much with his head as with his legs and right arm, a remarkably compact, *concentrated* pitcher, brilliantly blending control and speed, those twin capacities for restraint and release that are the indispensable possessions of the great artist. There is no need to rehearse the achievements of Seaver with the Mets: three Cy Young awards; Rookie of the Year with a last-place ball club in 1967; the leading pitcher in the league at 25–7 (ERA 2.21) in 1969, the same year he took the Mets to their first World Series (and, in the process, reelected John Lindsay as Mayor of New York—a cause for the trade no one has yet explored). In 1970 and 1971, he led the league in strikeouts (283; 289—a league season record for right-handers) and in ERA (2.81; 1.76—which is like having an IQ of 175, though the ERA is easier to document and vastly more useful). On one April day in 1970, Seaver struck out ten Padres, in a row, nineteen in all—an auto-da-fé[2] that has never been bettered. One could go on.

---

2. **auto-da-fé:** originally, the sentencing and burning of heretics during the Spanish Inquisition. Here it is used loosely to mean the inflicting of punishment.

The late sixties and early seventies were celebrated or execrated for many things besides someone being able to throw a baseball consistently at ninety-five miles per hour. These were the days of the Movement, the Counterculture, the Student Revolution; of civil-rights activism, antiwar battles, student "unrest." Yippies yipped, flower children blossomed and withered, America was being greened, by grass and by rock and by people who peddled them. This was a pastoral time, and it would, like all pastorals, turn sere,[3] but for three or four years, while Seaver was gaining control over a block of space approximately three feet high, eighteen inches wide, and sixty feet six inches long, many other of America's "young" were breaking loose. That great wave against structure and restraint—whatever its legitimacy—begun publicly by people like Mario Savio at Berkeley in 1964, was now rolling East, catching up in its powerful eddies and its froth everyone in the country. In 1964 Tom Seaver, Californian, was moving on from Fresno City College to USC, his move East to come two years later. Here are, I think, the origins of the Seaver mystique in New York, in the young Californian who brought control, in the "youth" who came East bearing—indeed, embodying—tradition.

Most Americans do not distinguish among Californians at all, and if they do, it is certainly not with the passionate self-absorption of the natives. Yet we should, for there are real differences among them, differences far more interesting than those implied by the contrast most favored by Californians themselves, the one between the self-conscious sophisticates of San Francisco and the self-conscious zanies of Los Angeles. There are, for instance, all those Californians, north and south, who are not self-conscious at all. Such is Seaver, who is from Fresno.

Fresno—the name means "ash tree," that is, something tangible, durable; not the name of a difficult saint, with all its implications about egotism and insecurity, nor a mass of heavenly spirits, with its notions of indistinct sprawl, but "ash tree"—Fresno is inland, about the middle of the state, the dominant city in the San Joaquin Valley, that fertile scar that runs parallel to the ocean between the Coastal Ranges and the Sierra Nevada. Fresno is the kingdom sung by Saroyan[4]—flat, green, hot, and fertile; the land of hardworking Armenians, Chicanos, Germans; the cradle of cotton, alfalfa, raisin grapes, melons, peaches, figs, wine. Fresno is not chic, but it is secure. You do not

---

3. sere: withered, dried.
4. Saroyan: William Saroyan (1908–1981), American writer of short stories, plays, and novels.

work that hard and reap so many of the earth's goods without knowing who you are and how you got that way. This is the California Seaver came from, and in many ways it accounts for his balance as a man as well as a pitcher, for his sense of self-worth and for his conviction that you work by the rules, and that you are rewarded, therefore, according to the rules of merit.

All this Seaver brought East, along with his fastball and his luminous wife, Nancy. They were perceived as a couple long before this became a journalistic convenience or public-relations necessity. They were Golden West, but not Gilded, nor long-haired, nor "political," nor opinionated. They were attractive, articulate, photogenic. He was Tom Terrific, the nickname a tribute to his all-American quality, a recognition, ironic but affectionate, that only in comic strips and myth did characters like Seaver exist. I have no idea what opinions Seaver held then on race, politics, war, marijuana, and the other ERA,[5] but whatever they were, or are, they are beside the point. The point is the way Seaver was perceived—as clean-cut, larger than life, a fastballer, "straight," all at a time when many young people, getting lots of newspaper coverage, were none of the above. And then there was something else, a quality he exuded.

I encountered this quality the only time I ever met Seaver. One evening in the winter of 1971 I spent several hours with the Seavers and their friends and neighbors the Schaaps (he is the NBC-TV broadcaster) in the apartment of Erich Segal, then at the height of his fame as the author of *Love Story*. The talk was light, easy and bright, and was produced almost entirely by the Schaaps, Nancy Seaver, and Segal. Because I was about the only member of the gathering who was a household name only in my household, I was content to listen, and to watch Tom Seaver. He sat somewhat apart, not, I thought, by design, not, surely, because he was aloof, but because it seemed natural to him. He was watchful, though in no sense wary, and had that attitude I have seen in the finest athletes and actors (similar breeds), of being relaxed but not in repose, the body being completely at ease but, because of thousands of hours of practice, always poised, ready at any instant to gather itself together and move. Candid in his gaze, there was a formality in his manner, a gravity, something autumnal in the man who played hard all summer. He sat as other men who work with their hands sit, the hands clasped chest high or folded in front of him, often in

---

5. ERA: Equal Rights Amendment.

motion, omnipresent hands that, like favored children, are the objects of constant if unconscious attention and repositories of complete confidence.

Seaver had, to be brief, *dignitas*, all the more for never thinking for a moment that he had it at all. A dignity that manifested itself in an air of utter self-possession without any self-regard, it was a quality born of a radical equilibrium. Seaver could never be off balance because he knew what he was doing and why it was valuable. He contrasted completely with the part of the country he was known to come from and with the larger society that he was seen as surrounded by. With consummate effortlessness, his was the talent that summed up baseball tradition; his was the respect for the rules that embodied baseball's craving for law; his was the personality, intensely competitive, basically decent, with the artisan's dignity, that amidst the brave but feckless[6] Mets, in a boom time of leisure soured by divisions and drugs, seemed to recall a cluster of virtues seemingly no longer valued.

And Seaver held up. His character proved as durable and strong as his arm. He was authentic; neither a goody two-shoes nor a flash in the pan, he matured into the best pitcher in baseball. Character and talent on this scale equaled a unique charisma. He was a national symbol, nowhere more honored than in New York, and in New York never more loved than by the guy who seemed in every other respect Seaver's antithesis, the guy who would never give a sucker an even break, who knew how corrupt they all were, who knew it was who you knew that counted, who knew how rotten it all really was—this guy loved Seaver because Seaver was a beautiful pitcher, a working guy who got rewarded; Seaver was someone who went by the rules and made it; Seaver carried the whole lousy team, God love 'em, on his back, and never shot his mouth off, and never gave in, and did it right. The guy loved Seaver because Seaver did not have to be street-wise.

In bars in Queens, in clubs in the Bronx, in living rooms in front of channel 9 in Suffolk and Nassau, out on Staten Island, everywhere, but particularly in the tattered reaches of Shea Stadium, they loved him for many things, but above all because he never thought he had to throw at anybody's head. From the Columbia riots to the brink of fiscal disaster, there was someone in New York who did not throw at anybody. They loved it in him, and in that act sought for it in themselves.

---

6. feckless: weak, ineffective.

None of this reasoning, if such it is, would appeal to the dominant New York baseball writers, who have used the Seaver trade as a *casus belli;*[7] nor the M. (for, I think, Moralistic) Donald Grant, chairman of the board of the Mets, who would quickly tell us that Seaver wanted too much money, meaning by that something he would never say aloud but would certainly formulate within himself—Tom wanted *too much*. Tom wanted, somehow, to cross the line between employee and equal, hired hand and golf partner, "boy" and man. What M. Donald Grant could not abide—after all, could he, Grant, ever become a Payson? Of course not. Everything is ordered. Doesn't anyone understand anything anymore?—Tom Seaver thought was his due. He believed in the rules, in this game governed by law; if you were the best pitcher in baseball, you ought to get the best salary of any pitcher in baseball; and money—yes, money—ought to be spent so baseball's best pitcher would not have to work on baseball's worst-hitting team.

Of course Tom Seaver wanted money, and wanted money spent; he wanted it for itself, but he wanted it because, finally, Tom Seaver felt about the Mets the way the guy from Astoria felt about Seaver—he loved them for what they stood for and he wanted merit rewarded and quality improved. The irony is that Tom Seaver had in abundance precisely the quality that M. Donald Grant thinks he values most—institutional loyalty, the capacity to be faithful to an idea as well as to individuals. Grant ought to have seen that in Seaver; after all, the man worked for the Mets for eleven years. Grant ought to have had the wit to see a more spacious, generous version of what he prizes so highly in himself. Certainly the guy who had watched Seaver all those years knew it, knew Seaver was holding out for something, a principle that made sense in one who played baseball but that grew from somewhere within him untouched by baseball, from a conviction about what a man has earned and what is due him and what is right. The fan understood this and was devastated when his understanding, and Seaver's principle, were not honored. The anguish surrounding Seaver's departure stemmed from the realization that the chairman of the board and certain newspaper columnists thought money was more important than loyalty, and the fury stemmed from the realization that the chairman and certain writers thought everybody else agreed with them, or ought to agree with them.

---

7. casus belli: (Latin) an event that allegedly justifies declaring war.

On June 16, the day after Seaver was exiled to Cincinnati by way of Montreal, a sheet was hung from a railing at Shea bearing the following legend:

> I WAS A
> BELIEVER
> BUT NOW WE'VE
> LOST
> SEAVER

I construe that text, and particularly its telling rhyme, to mean not that the author has lost faith in Seaver but that the author has lost faith in the Mets' ability to understand a simple, crucial fact: that among all the men who play baseball there is, very occasionally, a man of such qualities of heart and mind and body that he transcends even the great and glorious game, and that such a man is to be cherished, not sold.

ABOUT THE AUTHOR•ABOUT THE AUTHOR•ABOUT THE AUTHOR•ABOUT THE AUTHOR

See the biography of Ira Berkow on p. 126. In connection with this piece of writing Berkow says, "I knew DiMaggio and I was able to make this piece my own, I believe."

DiMaggio, Failing, Is 84 Today

In the press room of Yankee Stadium not long ago I saw Joe DiMaggio sitting at a table with a few friends. Even in repose he looked elegant, still trim in his dark suit, hair graying and thin but neatly coiffed. I was reminded of a remark by Henry Kissinger when he sat near DiMaggio in the owner's box in Yankee Stadium. The Yankees had lost a play-off game and Kissinger, on the way out, had said, "Joe, put on a uniform—they can use you." In the mind's eye, Joe still could lope after a fly ball.

When I saw DiMaggio now I related to him an unfortunate incident that happened to him some 45 years ago and which he didn't know about.

I was a small boy growing up in Chicago in the 1950s, I told him, and aware of the DiMaggio legend, as was anyone else who followed baseball in America. I had written to the Yankees for a photograph of him, was sent a glossy head shot with him in his baseball cap, and nailed the picture to my bedroom wall. The unfortunate part, I told DiMaggio, was that I hammered the nail right through his forehead.

"You did?" he said, wincing.

"Looks like it's O.K. now," I said.

"Oh yeah," he said. "I heal fast."

Today, which marks DiMaggio's 84th birthday, one wonders if he can heal as he lies in a hospital in Hollywood, Fla., amid reports that he has been battling lung cancer as well as pneumonia. He is fighting for his life. One wonders whether the man who once hit in 56 straight big-league games, a record that has stood for 57 years, can summon the energy and, perhaps, the requisite miracle to regain health.

Even before his admission to the hospital on Oct. 12, DiMaggio's name was in the news, in an indirect fashion. The Yankees' sterling center fielder, Bernie Williams, the American League's leading hitter and Gold Glove fly-chaser, heir to DiMaggio and Mickey Mantle, and a free agent, has been in controversial negotiations with the Yankees. Williams is as distinguished a ballplayer, if not as iconic,[1] as his famous predecessors.

It is difficult for fans to imagine that their athletic heroes are vulnerable to everything human. The youth of the ballplayer, or, sometimes, even the coach, is eternal, if only in photographs and film—DiMaggio in his baggy pinstripes is still rapping out hits in his familiar long stride and sweeping stroke of the bat—and in our memory.

Red Holzman can still be seen in that fashion in the huddle, instructing Bradley and Frazier, and Weeb Ewbank may be forever visualized discussing strategy with a mud-splattered Joe Namath on the sidelines. In that sense, Coach Holzman of the Knicks and Coach Ewbank of the Jets, who died recently, remain vital to us.

And Catfish Hunter, because of the Lou Gehrig's disease he has, may soon lose such control in his muscles that he will be unable to even grip a baseball. Such thoughts seem to fall off the radar screen of our comprehension.

And so it is with Joe D., that intensely proud man, that sometimes impatient and unforgiving man, who, the Yankee management knew, would be insulted if, at Old-Timers' Day, he should not be the last announced.

On the day I apologized for pounding that nail into his head, I gave DiMaggio a photograph of him and Marilyn Monroe taken by Richard Sanborn, who is now a judicial magistrate living in Maryland. Sanborn had been a sergeant in the Army stationed in Tokyo in 1954 when DiMaggio and Monroe went on their honeymoon to Japan. I had done a column on DiMaggio, and Sanborn sent it to me to give to DiMaggio, saying he had always wanted Joe to have it and didn't know how to get it to him. Would I do it? I did.

As most people know, bringing up his former wife to DiMaggio would end any conversation with him. It was too personal. But I handed DiMaggio the photograph. He thought it was great. "And this guy was just

---

1. iconic: emblematic; symbolic; like an object of uncritical devotion.

an amateur photographer?" DiMaggio said. "I've got to send him a note and thank him."

Shortly after, alone with DiMaggio, I said, "Marilyn looked beautiful in the picture." "She *was* beautiful," DiMaggio said, as though relating an insight.

I said, "Joe, there's a question I've always wanted to ask you, if you don't mind." He nodded, knitting his brow. "There's that great anecdote first written by Gay Talese," I went on, "about when you were in Japan and Marilyn was asked by the brass to entertain the troops in Korea. When she returned to your hotel room, you asked how it went and she said, 'Oh, Joe, you never heard such cheering!' And you said quietly, 'Yes I have.'

"Did it happen?"

"Yes," DiMaggio said, "it did."

Responding to What You Read

1. In a paragraph explain what it is about Tom Seaver that Giamatti praises most.

2. What is the point of the anecdote about Marilyn Monroe and Joe DiMaggio in Japan? Why do you think the author ends with this anecdote?

Writer's Workshop

Is there someone in the world of sports whom you admire as much as Giamatti admires Tom Seaver or Berkow admires Joe DiMaggio? Write a tribute to that person, using specific examples and references to capture exactly what it is that you admire.

The Thrill of the Grass

W. P. Kinsella

An extended baseball strike affords a fan the chance to realize a dream and perhaps make the game a little better for the players. Wishful thinking?

ABOUT THE AUTHOR•ABOUT THE AUTHOR•ABOUT THE AUTHOR•ABOUT THE AUTHOR

Canadian author W. P. Kinsella has written two novels and eleven short story collections. His novel Shoeless Joe *was adapted into the popular film* Field of Dreams *starring Kevin Costner. His publisher says that Kinsella "lives in the Pacific Northwest where he and his wife are card-carrying scouts for the Atlanta Braves."*

The Thrill of the Grass

1981: the summer the baseball players went on strike. The dull weeks drag by, the summer deepens, the strike is nearly a month old. Outside the city the corn rustles and ripens in the sun. Summer without baseball: a disruption to the psyche. An unexplainable aimlessness engulfs me. I stay later and later each evening in the small office at the rear of my shop. Now, driving home after work, the worst of the rush hour traffic over, it is the time of evening I would normally be heading for the stadium.

I enjoy arriving an hour early, parking in a far corner of the lot, walking slowly toward the stadium, rays of sun dropping softly over my shoulders like tangerine ropes, my shadow gliding with me, black as an umbrella. I like to watch young families beside their campers, the mothers in shorts, grilling hamburgers, their men drinking beer. I enjoy seeing little boys dressed in the home team uniform, barely toddling, clutching hotdogs in upraised hands.

I am a failed shortstop. As a young man, I saw myself diving to my left, graceful as a toppling tree, fielding high grounders like a cat leaping for butterflies, bracing my right foot and tossing to first, the throw true as if a steel ribbon connected my hand and the first baseman's glove. I dreamed of leading the American League in hitting—being inducted into the Hall of Fame. I batted .217 in my senior year of high school and averaged 1.3 errors per nine innings.

I know the stadium will be deserted; nevertheless I wheel my car down off the freeway, park, and walk across the silent lot, my footsteps rasping and mournful. Strangle-grass and creeping charlie are already inching up through the gravel, surreptitious, surprised at their own ease. Faded bottle caps, rusted bits of chrome, an occasional paper clip, recede into the earth. I circle a ticket booth, sun-faded, empty, the door closed by an oversized padlock. I walk beside the tall, machinery-green, board fence. A half mile away a few cars hiss along the freeway; overhead a single-engine plane fizzes lazily. The whole place is silent as an empty classroom, like a house suddenly without children.

It is then that I spot the door-shape. I have to check twice to be sure it is there: a door cut in the deep green boards of the fence, more the promise of a door than the real thing, the kind of door, as children, we cut in the sides of cardboard boxes with our mother's paring knives. As I move closer, a golden circle of lock, like an acrimonious[1] eye, establishes its certainty.

I stand, my nose so close to the door I can smell the faint odor of paint, the golden eye of a lock inches from my own eyes. My desire to be inside the ballpark is so great that for the first time in my life I commit a criminal act. I have been a locksmith for over forty years. I take the small tools from the pocket of my jacket, and in less time than it would take a speedy runner to circle the bases I am inside the stadium. Though the ballpark is open-air, it smells of abandonment; the walkways and seating areas are cold as basements. I breathe the odors of rancid popcorn and wilted cardboard.

The maintenance staff were laid off when the strike began. Synthetic grass does not need to be cut or watered. I stare down at the ball diamond, where just to the right of the pitcher's mound, a single weed, perhaps two inches high, stands defiant in the rain-pocked dirt.

---

1. acrimonious: bitter; harsh.

The field sits breathless in the orangy glow of the evening sun. I stare at the potato-colored earth of the infield, that wide, dun[2] arc, surrounded by plastic grass. As I contemplate the prickly turf, which scorches the thighs and buttocks of a sliding player as if he were being seared by hot steel, it stares back in its uniform ugliness. The seams that send routinely hit ground balls veering at tortuous angles, are vivid, grey as scars.

I remember the ballfields of my childhood, the outfields full of soft hummocks and brown-eyed gopher holes.

I stride down from the stands and walk out to the middle of the field. I touch the stubble that is called grass, take off my shoes, but find it is like walking on a row of toothbrushes. It was an evil day when they stripped the sod from this ballpark, cut it into yard-wide swathes, rolled it, memories and all, into great green-and-black cinnamonroll shapes, trucked it away. Nature temporarily defeated. But Nature is patient.

Over the next few days an idea forms within me, ripening, swelling, pushing everything else into a corner. It is like knowing a new, wonderful joke and not being able to share. I need an accomplice.[3]

I go to see a man I don't know personally, though I have seen his face peering at me from the financial pages of the local newspaper, and the *Wall Street Journal*, and I have been watching his profile at the baseball stadium, two boxes to the right of me, for several years. He is a fan. Really a fan. When the weather is intemperate, or the game not close, the people around us disappear like flowers closing at sunset, but we are always there until the last pitch. I know he is a man who attends because of the beauty and mystery of the game, a man who can sit during the last of the ninth with the game decided innings ago, and draw joy from watching the first baseman adjust the angle of his glove as the pitcher goes into his windup.

He, like me, is a first-base-side fan. I've always watched baseball from behind first base. The positions fans choose at sporting events are like politics, religion, or philosophy: a view of the world, a way of seeing the universe. They make no sense to anyone, have no basis in anything but stubbornness.

I brought up my daughters to watch baseball from the first-base side. One lives in Japan and sends me box scores from Japanese newspapers, and

---

2. **dun:** dull, grayish brown.
3. **accomplice:** a person who knowingly helps another person in a crime.

Japanese baseball magazines with pictures of superstars politely bowing to one another. She has a season ticket in Yokohama; on the first-base side.

"Tell him a baseball fan is here to see him," is all I will say to his secretary. His office is in a skyscraper, from which he can look out over the city to where the prairie rolls green as mountain water to the limits of the eye. I wait all afternoon in the artificially cool, glassy reception area with its yellow and mauve chairs, chrome and glass coffee tables. Finally, in the late afternoon, my message is passed along.

"I've seen you at the baseball stadium," I say, not introducing myself.

"Yes," he says. "I recognize you. Three rows back, about eight seats to my left. You have a red scorebook and you often bring your daughter . . ."

"Granddaughter. Yes, she goes to sleep in my lap in the late innings, but she knows how to calculate an ERA and she's only in Grade 2."

"One of my greatest regrets," says this tall man, whose moustache and carefully styled hair are polar-bear white, "is that my grandchildren all live over a thousand miles away. You're very lucky. Now, what can I do for you?"

"I have an idea," I say. "One that's been creeping toward me like a first baseman when the bunt sign is on. What do you think about artificial turf?"

"Hmmmf," he snorts, "that's what the strike should be about. Baseball is meant to be played on summer evenings and Sunday afternoons, on grass just cut by a horse-drawn mower," and we smile as our eyes meet.

"I've discovered the ballpark is open, to me anyway," I go on. "There's no one there while the strike is on. The wind blows through the high top of the grandstand, whining until the pigeons in the rafters flutter. It's lonely as a ghost town."

"And what is it you do there, alone with the pigeons?"

"I dream."

"And where do I come in?"

"You've always struck me as a man who dreams. I think we have things in common. I think you might like to come with me. I could show you what I dream, paint you pictures, suggest what might happen . . ."

He studies me carefully for a moment, like a pitcher trying to decide if he can trust the sign his catcher has just given him.

"Tonight?" he says. "Would tonight be too soon?"

"Park in the northwest corner of the lot about 1:00 A.M. There is a door about fifty yards to the right of the main gate. I'll open it when I hear you."

He nods.
I turn and leave.

The night is clear and cotton warm when he arrives. "Oh, my," he says, staring at the stadium turned chrome-blue by a full moon. "Oh, my," he says again, breathing in the faint odors of baseball, the reminder of fans and players not long gone.

"Let's go down to the field," I say. I am carrying a cardboard pizza box, holding it on the upturned palms of my hands, like an offering.

When we reach the field, he first stands on the mound, makes an awkward attempt at a windup, then does a little sprint from first to about halfway to second. "I think I know what you've brought," he says, gesturing toward the box, "but let me see anyway."

I open the box in which rests a square foot of sod, the grass smooth and pure, cool as a swatch of satin, fragile as baby's hair.

"Ohhh," the man says, reaching out a finger to test the moistness of it. "Oh, I see."

We walk across the field, the harsh, prickly turn making the bottoms of my feet tingle, to the left-field corner where, in the angle formed by the foul line and the warning track, I lay down the square foot of sod. "That's beautiful," my friend says, kneeling beside me, placing his hand, fingers spread wide, on the verdant square, leaving a print faint as a veronica.[4]

I take from my belt a sickle-shaped blade, the kind used for cutting carpet. I measure along the edge of the sod, dig the point in and pull carefully toward me. There is a ripping sound, like tearing an old bed sheet. I hold up the square of artificial turf like something freshly killed, while all the time digging the sharp point into the packed earth I have exposed. I replace the sod lovingly, covering the newly bared surface.

"A protest," I say.

"But it could be more," the man replies.

"I hoped you'd say that. It could be. If you'd like to come back . . ."

"Tomorrow night?"

"Tomorrow night would be fine. But there will be an admission charge . . ."

"A square of sod?"

---

4. veronica: any handkerchief or veil bearing the faint image of Christ.

"A square of sod two inches thick..."

"Of the same grass?"

"Of the same grass. But there's more."

"I suspected as much."

"You must have a friend..."

"Who would join us?"

"Yes."

"I have two. Would that be all right?"

"I trust your judgment."

"My father. He's over eighty," my friend says. "You might have seen him with me once or twice. He lives over fifty miles from here, but if I call him he'll come. And my friend . . ."

"If they pay their admission they'll be welcome . . ."

"And *they* may have friends . . ."

"Indeed they may. But what will we do with this?" I say, holding up the sticky-backed square of turf, which smells of glue and fabric.

"We could mail them anonymously to baseball executives, politicians, clergymen."

"Gentle reminders not to tamper with Nature."

We dance toward the exit, rampant with excitement.

"You will come back? You'll bring others?"

"Count on it," says my friend.

They do come, those trusted friends, and friends of friends, each making a live, green deposit. At first, a tiny row of sod squares begins to inch along toward left-center field. The next night even more people arrive, the following night more again, and the night after there is positively a crowd. Those who come once seem always to return accompanied by friends, occasionally a son or young brother, but mostly men my age or older, for we are the ones who remember the grass.

Night after night the pilgrimage continues. The first night I stand inside the deep green door, listening. I hear a vehicle stop; hear a car door close with a snug thud. I open the door when the sound of soft-soled shoes on gravel tells me it's time. The door swings silent as a snake. We nod curt greetings to each other. Two men pass me, each carrying a grasshopper-legged sprinkler. Later, each sprinkler will sizzle like frying onions as it wheels, a silver sparkler in the moonlight.

During the nights that follow, I stand sentinel-like at the top of the grandstand, watching as my cohorts arrive. Old men walking across a parking lot in a row, in the dark, carrying coiled hoses, looking like the many wheels of a locomotive, old men who have slipped away from their homes, skulked down their sturdy sidewalks, breathing the cool, grassy, after-midnight air. They have left behind their sleeping, grey-haired women, their immaculate bungalows, their manicured lawns. They continue to walk across the parking lot, while occasionally a soft wheeze, a nibbling, breathy sound like an old horse might make, divulges their humanity. They move methodically toward the baseball stadium which hulks against the moon-blue sky like a small mountain. Beneath the tint of starlight, the tall light standards which rise above the fences and grandstand glow purple, necks bent forward, like sunflowers heavy with seed.

My other daughter lives in this city, is married to a fan, but one who watches baseball from behind third base. And like marrying outside the faith, she has been converted to the third-base side. They have their own season tickets, twelve rows up just to the outfield side of third base. I love her, but I don't trust her enough to let her in on my secret.

I could trust my granddaughter, but she is too young. At her age she shouldn't have to face such responsibility. I remember my own daughter, the one who lives in Japan, remember her at nine, all knees, elbows and missing teeth—remember peering in her room, seeing her asleep, a shower of well-thumbed baseball cards scattered over her chest and pillow.

I haven't been able to tell my wife—it is like my compatriots[5] and I are involved in a ritual for true believers only. Maggie, who knew me when I still dreamed of playing professionally myself—Maggie, after over half a lifetime together, comes and sits in my lap in the comfortable easy chair which has adjusted through the years to my thickening shape, just as she has. I love to hold the lightness of her, her tongue exploring my mouth, gently as a baby's finger.

"Where do you go?" she asks sleepily when I crawl into bed at dawn.

I mumble a reply. I know she doesn't sleep well when I'm gone. I can feel her body rhythms change as I slip out of bed after midnight.

---

5. compatriots: colleagues; companions.

"Aren't you too old to be having a change of life," she says, placing her toast-warm hand on my cold thigh.

I am not the only one with this problem.

"I'm developing a reputation," whispers an affable[6] man at the ballpark. "I imagine any number of private investigators following any number of cars across the city. I imagine them creeping about the parking lot, shining pen-lights on license plates, trying to guess what we're up to. Think of the reports they must prepare. I wonder if our wives are disappointed that we're not out discoing with frizzy-haired teenagers?"

Night after night, virtually no words are spoken. Each man seems to know his assignment. Not all bring sod. Some carry rakes, some hoes, some hoses, which, when joined together, snake across the infield and outfield, dispensing the blessing of water. Others cradle in their arms bags of earth for building up the infield to meet the thick, living sod.

I often remain high in the stadium, looking down on the men moving over the earth, dark as ants, each sodding, cutting, watering, shaping. Occasionally the moon finds a knife blade as it trims the sod or slices away a chunk of artificial turf, and tosses the reflection skyward like a bright ball. My body tingles. There should be symphony music playing. Everyone should be humming "America The Beautiful."

Toward dawn, I watch the men walking away in groups, like small patrols of soldiers, carrying instead of arms, the tools and utensils which breathe life back into the arid ballfield.

Row by row, night by night, we lay the little squares of sod, moist as chocolate cake with green icing. Where did all the sod come from? I picture many men, in many parts of the city, surreptitiously[7] cutting chunks out of their own lawns in the leafy midnight darkness, listening to the uncomprehending protests of their wives the next day—pretending to know nothing of it—pretending to have called the police to investigate.

When the strike is over I know we will all be here to watch the workouts, to hear the recalcitrant[8] joints crackling like twigs after the forced inactivity. We will sit in our regular seats, scattered like popcorn throughout

---

6. **affable:** friendly.

7. **surreptitiously:** secretly.

8. **recalcitrant:** not obedient; resistant.

the stadium, and we'll nod as we pass on the way to the exits, exchange secret smiles, proud as new fathers.

For me, the best part of all will be the surprise. I feel like a magician who has gestured hypnotically and produced an elephant from thin air. I know I am not alone in my wonder. I know that rockets shoot off in half-a-hundred chests, the excitement of birthday mornings, Christmas eves, and home-town doubleheaders, boils within each of my conspirators. Our secret rites have been performed with love, like delivering a valentine to a sweetheart's door in that blue-steel span of morning just before dawn.

Players and management are meeting round the clock. A settlement is imminent. I have watched the stadium covered square foot by square foot until it looks like green graph paper. I have stood and felt the cool odors of the grass rise up and touch my face. I have studied the lines between each small square, watched those lines fade until they were visible to my eyes alone, then not even to them.

What will the players think, as they straggle into the stadium and find the miracle we have created? The old-timers will raise their heads like ponies, as far away as the parking lot, when the thrill of the grass reaches their nostrils. And, as they dress, they'll recall sprawling in the lush outfields of childhood, the grass as cool as a mother's hand on a forehead.

"Goodbye, goodbye," we say at the gate, the smell of water, of sod, of sweat, small perfumes in the air. Our secrets are safe with each other. We go our separate ways.

Alone in the stadium in the last chill darkness before dawn, I drop to my hands and knees in the center of the outfield. My palms are sodden. Water touches the skin between my spread fingers. I lower my face to the silvered grass, which, wonder of wonders, already has the ephemeral[9] odors of baseball about it.

---

9. ephemeral: short-lived.

Responding to What You Read

1. Describe in one or two paragraphs what the narrator of this story is like, what makes him "tick."

2. "The Thrill of the Grass" is one man's fantasy about how he'd like to change his local ball park. While it's an entertaining story, it's not likely that it could ever occur. What events in the story border on the impossible?

Writer's Workshop

Create a sports fantasy of your own. If you could change anything you wanted about a sport that you love, as this narrator loves baseball, what would you change? You can be a player, coach, or fan, but tell your story in the first person, as W. P. Kinsella does in "The Thrill of the Grass."

Alternate Media Response

Imagine yourself as the Hollywood producer who decides that "The Thrill of the Grass" is the perfect material for a movie. Do some preliminary work to encourage investors to back your production. Whom will you get to direct the film? Who will write the screenplay? Which ballpark will you use for location shooting? Which famous movie stars will you cast in the different roles? Work alone or with others to brainstorm your "wish list" for "The Thrill of the Grass—the Movie."

ACKNOWLEDGMENTS

Acknowledgment is gratefully made to the following publishers, authors, and agents for permission to reprint these works. Every effort has been made to determine the copyright owners. In the case of any omissions, the Publisher will be pleased to make suitable acknowledgment in future editions.

The following acknowledgments are arranged sequentially in the order in which selections appear in this anthology. The number at the beginning of each entry identifies the page on which that selection starts.

Preface

xiii Quotation from *A Great and Glorious Game: Baseball Writings of A. Bartlett Giamatti*, edited by Kenneth S. Robson. Copyright © 1998 by Kenneth S. Robson. Reprinted by permission of Algonquin Books of Chapel Hill, a division of Workman Publishing.

xiii Quotation from "Making Art of Sport" by Michiko Kakutani, the *New York Times Magazine*, December 15, 1996. Copyright © 1996 by The New York Times. Reprinted by permission.

Chapter 1

1 Quotations from "Down the Stretch, Michael Decides He'll Do It Himself" by Kevin Kernan, the *New York Post*, June 15, 1998.

3 "In Beijing Students' Worldview, Jordan Rules" by Elizabeth Rosenthal, the *New York Times*, June 16, 1998. Copyright © 1998 by The New York Times. Reprinted by permission.

6 "The Back Page: You Don't Imitate Michael Jordan" by David Remnick, *The New Yorker*, January 25, 1999. Reprinted by permission; © 1999 David Remnick. Originally in *The New Yorker*. All rights reserved.

8 Quotation from "A Tangled Web" by Phil Taylor, *Sports Illustrated,* June 15, 1998, p. 56.

11 "Finding Myself: On the Field, In the Gym" by Jeannie Krauter Ryan. Reprinted by permission of the author.

19 "Pitcher" from *The Orb Weaver* by Robert Francis. © 1960 by Robert Francis, Wesleyan University Press by permission of University Press of New England.

22 "The Passer" from *Collected Poems, 1932-1961* by George Abbe. Reprinted by permission of William L. Bauhan, Publisher, Dublin, New Hampshire.

23 Quotation from "Appreciation: A Prophetic Delver," by Lance Morrow, *Time*, February 3, 1997, p. 75.

24 "In the Pocket" from *The Eye-Beaters, Blood, Victory, Madness, Buckhead* by James Dickey. Copyright © 1968, 1969, 1970 by James Dickey. Used by permission of Doubleday, a division of Random House, Inc.

26 "Eight-Oared Crew" by Harry Sylvester.

38 From *The Four-Minute Mile* by Roger Bannister. Reprinted by permission of The Lyons Press.

46 "Running the New York City Marathon" by Caroline Wood Richards. Adapted by permission of the author.

50 "Jump Shot" by Richard Peck. Copyright © 1971 by Richard Peck. Reprinted by permission.

53 Quotation from the *New York Times Book Review* in *Looking for Luck* by Maxine Kumin, 1992, book jacket.

53 Quotation from the *San Francisco Examiner and Chronicle* in *Looking for Luck* by Maxine Kumin, 1992, book jacket.

54 "400-Meter Freestyle," copyright © 1959 and renewed 1987 by Maxine Kumin, from *Selected Poems 1960-1990* by Maxine Kumin. Reprinted by permission of W. W. Norton & Company, Inc.

56 "In the Swim" by Alexis Collins. Reprinted by permission of the author.

61 "Fishing." Excerpt from "The Prelude." William Wordsworth, *The Prelude*. London: E. Moxon, 1850.

62 Quotation from *Pairs: New Poems* by Philip Booth, book jacket.

62 "Instruction in the Art," from *Letter From a Distant Land* by Philip Booth. Copyright © 1957 by Philip Booth. Used by permission of Viking Penguin, a division of Penguin Putnam Inc.

Chapter 2

66 From *Baseball's Great Experiment: Jackie Robinson and His Legacy, 2nd Edition* by Jules Tygiel. Copyright © 1997 by Jules Tygiel. Used by permission of Oxford University Press, Inc.

73 "Take the Plunge" by Gloria Emerson. Reprinted by permission of International Creative Management, Inc. Copyright © 1976 by Gloria Emerson.

76 "Sky Diving" from *Poems from Three Decades* by Richmond Lattimore. Reprinted by permission of Alice Lattimore.

78 "Why I Play the Game" by Morgan McCarthy. Reprinted by permission of the author.

82 "Lou Gehrig—An American Hero" by Paul Gallico. Reprinted by permission of Harold Ober Associates Incorporated. Copyright 1941 by Paul Gallico. Copyright renewed 1969 by Paul Gallico.

93 "Great Day For Baseball In the 90s" by Harvey Araton, the *New York Times*, September 6, 1995. Copyright © 1995 by The New York Times. Reprinted by permission.

96 Quotation from "Hand It to Cal" by Richard Hoffer, *Sports Illustrated,* December 1995, p. 75.

97 "Johnson Is Everywhere, Leaving His Critics to Gape" by William C. Rhoden, the *New York Times*, January 11, 1999. Copyright © 1999 by The New York Times. Reprinted by permission.

101 "In These Girls, Hope Is a Muscle: A Season in the Life of the Amherst Hurricanes" by Madeleine H. Blais, the *New York Times*, April 18, 1993. Copyright © 1993 by The New York Times. Reprinted by permission.

115 From *Rabbit, Run* by John Updike. Copyright © 1960 and renewed 1988 by John Updike. Reprinted by permission of Alfred A. Knopf, Inc.

118 "Ex-Basketball Player." From *The Carpentered Hen and Other Tame Creatures* by John Updike. Copyright © 1957, 1982 by John Updike. Reprinted by permission of Alfred A. Knopf, Inc.

121 "The Sprinters" from *The Sidewalk Racer and Other Poems of Sports and Motion* by Lillian Morrison. Copyright © 1965, 1967, 1968, 1977 by Lillian Morrison. Reprinted by permission of Marian Reiner for the author.

122 Quotation from *Complete Poems* by A. E. Housman, Henry Holt and Company, 1959, p. 1.

122 "To An Athlete Dying Young." A. E. Housman, from *The Collected Poems of A. E. Housman.* New York: Henry Holt and Company, Inc., 1940.

Chapter 3

126 From Columbia, an Athletes' Romance, in Sickness and in Laughter" by Ira Berkow, the *New York Times*, January 3, 1999. Copyright © 1999 by The New York Times. Reprinted by permission.

136   Quotation from *Clemente!* by Kal Wagenheim, book jacket.

136   From *Clemente!* by Kal Wagenheim. Reprinted by permission of the author.

139   "Clemente to Sosa, and Beyond" by Harvey Araton, the *New York Times*, November 13, 1998. Copyright © 1998 by The New York Times. Reprinted by permission.

142   "The 7–10 Split." From *The Anarchist's Convention* by John Sayles. Copyright © 1975, 1976, 1977, 1978 by John Sayles. By permission of Little, Brown and Company (Inc.).

152   "A Rare Bird Sighted Again" by Vic Ziegel, *New York Daily News*. © New York Daily News, L.P. Reprinted with permission.

155   "Mark Fidrych" by Tom Clark. Copyright © 1983 by Tom Clark. Reprinted by permission.

157   Quotation from *Life* magazine in *The Gift of Asher Lev* by Chaim Potok, book jacket.

157   Quotation from Elie Wiesel in *The Gift of Asher Lev* by Chaim Potok, book jacket.

157   From *The Chosen* by Chaim Potok. Copyright © 1967 by Chaim Potok. Reprinted by permission of Alfred A. Knopf, Inc.

183   "Van Arsdale's Pond." From *Hockey Sur Glace*, copyright 1996 by Peter La Salle. Reprinted by permission of Breakaway Books.

191   From liner notes in *From Fresh Water* CD. Used by permission of Ariel Rogers & Fogarty's Cove Music © ℗ 1984.

191   "Flying" © ℗ 1984 Stan Rogers. Used by permission of Fogarty's Cove Music and Ariel Rogers.

195   "Ballad of a Ballgame." Words and Music by Christine Lavin. Copyright © 1992 CL2 (ASCAP)/DreamWorks Songs (ASCAP)/Rounder Music (ASCAP). Worldwide rights for CL2 and DreamWorks Songs are administered by Cherry Lane Music Publishing Company, Inc. (ASCAP). All Rights Reserved. Used by permission.

199   "Baseball" by Bill Zavatsky. Copyright © 1985 by Bill Zavatsky. Used by permission of the author.

Chapter 4

204   "Raymond's Run." From *Gorilla, My Love* by Toni Cade Bambara. Copyright © 1971 by Toni Cade Bambara. Reprinted by permission of Random House, Inc.

215   Excerpt from "Fathers Playing Catch with Sons" from *Fathers Playing Catch with Sons* by Donald Hall. Copyright © 1985 by Donald Hall. Reprinted by permission of North Point Press, a division of Farrar, Straus & Giroux, LLC.

218   "That Dark Other Mountain" from *Robert Francis' Collected Poems: 1936-1976*. (Amherst: University of Massachusetts Press, 1976. Copyright © 1976 by the University of Massachusetts Press). Reprinted by permission.

220   "Playing to Win" by Margaret A. Whitney, the *New York Times*, July 3, 1998. Copyright © 1998 by The New York Times. Reprinted by permission.

224   "Letter To The Editor" by Malvine Cole from the *New York Times Magazine*. Reprinted by permission of Jeremy Cole.

226   "Basketball Season" by Donna Tartt. Reprinted by permission of International Creative Management, Inc. Copyright by Donna Tartt.

232   "Three Cheers for My Daughter" by Kathleen Cushman, the *New York Times Magazine*, October 23, 1998. Copyright © 1998 by The New York Times. Reprinted by permission.

237   "Tracee" from *Assignment: Sports* by Robert Lipsyte. Copyright © 1984 Robert M. Lipsyte. Reprinted by permission of the author.

244   "This Skater Chooses to Come Home, of All Things" by George Vecsey, the *New York Times*, December 2, 1998. Copyright © 1998 by The New York Times. Reprinted by permission.

249   "Tennis." From *The Stone Arbor and Other Stories* by Roger Angell. Copyright © 1961 by Roger Angell; first appeared in *The New Yorker*. By permission of Little, Brown and Company (Inc.).

256 "Rough Passage: A Family's Voyage of Discovery" by Tom Wicker, the *New York Times* Magazine, July 24, 1988. Copyright © 1988 by The New York Times. Reprinted by permission.

Chapter 5

268 "Who's On First?" by Bud Abbott and Lou Costello. © 1999 TCA Television Corp., Diana K. Abbott Colton and Hi Neighbor. Abbott & Costello courtesy of TCA Television Corp., Diana K. Abbott Colton, and Hi Neighbor.

275 "Casey at the Bat." Ernest Lawrence Thayer, *Casey at the Bat*. Kansas City: H.G. Pert, 1905.

278 From "O'Toole's Touchdown." Martin Gardner, *The Annotated Casey at the Bat*. Chicago: The University of Chicago Press, 1984, pp. 168–169.

279 "Ace Teenage Sportscribe" from *Fathers Playing Catch with Sons* by Donald Hall. Copyright © 1985 by Donald Hall. Reprinted by permission of North Point Press, a division of Farrar, Straus & Giroux, LLC.

285 "Offsides" by Andrew Ward. Copyright © 1976 by Andrew Ward. Originally appeared in the April, 1976 issue of the *Atlantic Monthly*. Reprinted by permission.

291 "Cut" from *Cheeseburgers: The Best of Bob Greene* by Bob Greene. Reprinted by permission of Sterling Lord Literistic, Inc. Copyright by Bob Greene.

297 "Attitude" by Garrison Keillor. Reprinted with the permission of Scribner, a Division of Simon & Schuster Inc. from *Happy To Be Here* by Garrison Keillor. Copyright © 1979, 1982 Garrison Keillor.

302 Excerpts from "Profile," "National Championships," and "Points and Honors" from *A Sense of Where You Are: A Profile of Bill Bradley at Princeton* by John McPhee. Copyright © 1978 by John McPhee. Reprinted by permission of Farrar, Straus and Giroux, LLC. Published in Canada by Macfarlane Walter & Ross, Toronto. Reprinted by permission.

312 "Stop the Fight!" by Norman Katkov. Copyright 1952, renewed 1980; used by permission of the author's agent, Harold Matson Co., Inc.

324 "Who Killed Benny Paret?" by Norman Cousins, *The Saturday Review*, 1979. Reprinted by permission of *The Saturday Review*, © 1979, General Media International, Inc.

329 "Tom Seaver's Farewell" from *A Great and Glorious Game: Baseball Writings of A. Bartlett Giamatti*, edited by Kenneth S. Robson. Copyright © 1998 by Kenneth S. Robson. Reprinted by permission of Algonquin Books of Chapel Hill, a division of Workman Publishing.

336 "DiMaggio, Failing, Is 84 Today" by Ira Berkow, the *New York Times*, November 25, 1998. Copyright © 1998 by The New York Times. Reprinted by permission.

339 "The Thrill of the Grass," from *The Thrill of the Grass* by W. P. Kinsella. Copyright © 1984 by W. P. Kinsella. Used by permission of Viking Penguin, a division of Penguin Putnam Inc. and Penguin Books Canada Ltd.

INDEX OF AUTHORS AND TITLES